RELIGION IN ACTION

How America's Faiths Are Meeting New Challenges

By Lee E. Dirks

NEWSBOOK

The National Observer

Silver Spring, Md.

Published by The National Observer
11501 Columbia Pike, Silver Spring, Md.

Library of Congress Catalog Number: 65-15132

Printed in the United States of America
By Danner Press of Canton, Inc., Canton, Ohio

Contents

Faith at the Frontier

RELIGION is at a turning point. From many sides, traditional values—Protestant, Catholic, Jewish—are being challenged. Materialism . . . Racial violence . . . Communism . . . Indifference . . . Moral decay . . . Slums. . . . All of these forces pose questions that churchmen believe they must answer now.

To keep its readers on top of this dramatic story, The National Observer inaugurated an unprecedented policy of covering religious news in depth, on the scene. This coverage has taken National Observer newsmen to scores of cities in the United States and abroad—to Rome and San Diego; to Des Moines and Montreal; to Coventry, England, and Fargo, North Dakota.

Now, in our fourth Newsbook, *Religion in Action,* we present the fruits of our efforts in book form. We bring you in touch with events that affect your life directly or indirectly—that affect the lives of others, whether they are devout or agnostic.

A council in Rome extinguishes the last flickerings of the Counter Reformation and ignites the flame of an Age of Unity. A religious lobby in Washington dramatizes the churches' deepest involvement in political affairs since the days of Prohibition. "Back to the Bible!" cries America's best-known evangelist; a strife-sick world listens. From fire-bombed ruins, an English cathedral rises again to proclaim the meaning of Christ's resurrection in a world threatened by nuclear holocaust.

There is yet more: Events shaping themselves that involve religion and your life in ways you may never have considered. Every day, like scientists in a laboratory, churchmen are experimenting with new ways of ministering to people. In Detroit, religious pioneers labor in factories at lunchtime; in Las Vegas, they work quietly in the gambling casinos and plush showrooms at 2 a.m. On a Florida beach, pro football stars and jazz musicians remind carousing collegians that their spring vacation week is a week of religious significance too.

Behind all of these stories is fresh, first-hand reporting. Behind them are conversations with bishops and parish priests, with Martin Luther King and with persons who speak in strange tongues, with sources at the Vatican Council in Rome who prefer to remain unidentified and with similar sources at the National Council of Churches in New York.

Behind them, too, is Lee E. Dirks, The National Observer's prize-winning reporter. Mr. Dirks was selected as the "Religion Writer of 1964" by the Religious Newswriters Association "for excellence in reporting the news of religion in the secular press."

Assisting Mr. Dirks in gathering material for *Religion in Action* were Mark R. Arnold, August Gribbin, and Wesley Pruden, Jr. Douglas M. Davis provided editorial guidance. The cover design is by Edwin A. Roberts, Sr.; the illustrations and page layouts are by Kathryn Henkel. Photographs are from the Associated Press, United Press International, Religious News Service, Magnum Photos, Inc., and Pictorial Parade, Inc., unless otherwise credited. ♦

The Vatican Council

The Vatican: The Ecumenical Council: An event of world-wide significance. In the foreground, the twelve cardinal presidents of the Vatican Council.

A Few Men Decide For Millions

Fresh Winds Flow Through the Roman Catholic Church, And a Breeze Is Felt in Many Faiths and Many Lands

ROME.

RAYS FROM the late afternoon sun danced on the red-tile roofs atop the hill called Aventino in Rome, the Eternal City. In the Piazza Cavalieri di Malta an adventurer from the New World waited for a taxi, alone in the quiet square except for a deliveryman slumbering in a gray three-wheeler and a couple making love in a Fiat.

Then the pilgrims began to arrive. First a lonely cyclist, next a handsome carriage with a guide and two matronly tourists, then a happy Italian threesome. One by one they approached the dust-brown wall around a courtyard, looked through a tiny hole in the huge green door, turned in awe, and left.

Intrigued, the adventurer stepped to the door himself. Suddenly he saw the splendid dome of St. Peter's Basilica—the dome alone, in the distance, framed by a courtyard arbor of green and a walkway of white crushed stone. The view was at once startling and refreshing.

Startling and refreshing, too, is the dramatic new vision of Christianity inspired by the Council that since 1962 has been making history beneath the dome of St. Peter's. In this Vatican Ecumenical Council many Christians, Catholics and non-Catholics alike, see the most significant religious event of the past four centuries.

True, Pope Paul VI and a minority of Catholic bishops blocked a Council affirmation of the principle of religious liberty in the 1964 session. The action temporarily frustrated the hopes of more than half of the Council fathers and fueled Protestant suspicions that the pope still possesses absolute power in the church. Declared one Protestant observer at the Council who is more enthusiastic than most Protestants about the Christian unity movement: "We have seen the naked face of what we have always feared in Rome."

But the ages pass quickly here in the Eternal City. Not long ago, in the sweep of history, Charlemagne was crowned emperor of the Holy Roman Empire in St. Peter's. Only yesterday, Michelangelo painted the ceiling of the Sistine Chapel in Vatican City and Bernini fashioned the semicircular colonnade that welcomes the faithful to St. Peter's Square.

Thus, in the perspective of the ages, the disillusionment so much in evidence at the closing of the third session will evaporate. The ages will affirm what mortals today find hard to perceive—that the Vatican Council is producing vast changes both inside the Roman Catholic Church and outside it.

The idea for a council came to the late Pope John XXIII in 1959, not "as the slowly ripening fruit of long deliberation," as he once said, but as "the sudden flowering of an unexpected spring." With the instinct of a peasant but the faith in God of a pope, he decided to "open the windows of the church and let in some fresh air."

Despite temporary obstructions, fresh air has been filtering through the church ever since. It has softened the image of the church as a monolith, unchanging and unchangeable. Freedom of debate, freely engaged in, has produced new ideas and structures by which the Catholic Church will apply its teachings to contemporary conditions.

The fresh winds have stirred air currents

far beyond the Roman Catholic Church. They have instilled hope among Protestants and Eastern Orthodox, however tenuous this hope may be, that Christ's prayer "that they all may be one" may some day be fulfilled. They have strengthened the conviction of some that a Christian community, united in mission if not in structure, may prove the cultural cement that ultimately will destroy communism.

No one here in Vatican City pretends that the work of Christian renewal and reunion has been finished. It has just begun. But the achievements to date are impressive.

In a document called *De Ecclesia,* promulgated in 1964, the Vatican Council has produced the most comprehensive definition of the Catholic Church by the church in the nearly 2,000 years since Christ. *De Ecclesia* erects the theological superstructure on which the entire renewal of the Catholic Church is built.

New Era Begins

In a document called *De Oecumenismo,* also promulgated in 1964, the pope and the church's bishops have written the charter for a new era of Christian unity. The document gives priests not merely freedom to discuss theology and engage in cooperative projects with Protestant ministers, but positive encouragement to do so. It goes further, granting Catholics permission under "special circumstances" to worship with Protestants in non-Catholic services.

In late 1963, the voices of pessimism were belittling the labors of the Vatican Council. "What went wrong?" asked a weekly newsmagazine as it reported gloomily on delays on the documents on religious liberty and the Jews in the second session. It called Pope Paul VI a "Hamlet" who "failed to intervene when intervention was called for" and the Council itself "a parliament of stalemate, compromise, and delay."

Now this "Hamlet" and his "parliament of stalemate" have laid the theological foundations for Catholic renewal and Christian reunion in unmistakable terms. The documents affirming the principle of religions liberty commands such strong support among the bishops that delaying tactics cannot ultimately prevent its adoption. And the document absolving the Jews of specific blame for the crucifixion of Christ was approved in a vote that assures its promulgation at the final Council session.

Catholic renewal is taking many forms.

The dome of St. Peter's.

Some of the forms, such as the revision of the liturgy, are instantly recognizable; others, such as the deeper sense of mission among clergymen and laymen, are subtle and thus more difficult to detect.

The renewal is organizational in part. The First Vatican Council, convened in 1869 and cut short in 1870 by the Franco-Prussian War, defined the pope as infallible in questions of faith and morals but failed to delineate the functions and authority of the bishops of the church—the cardinals, archbishops, and bishops. The First Vatican Council, which never resumed, has thus fostered the idea among both Catholics and non-Catholics that the pope is all-powerful.

Vatican II alters this idea. In *De Ecclesia,* the Council declares that the pope and the bishops share the supreme authority to govern the church and expound its teachings. "Collegiality," a word unused a decade ago but on the lips of everyone now at the Vatican Council, does not diminish the primacy of the pope or affect his infallibility on faith and morals; what it does do is make the bishops co-responsible for the church with the pope.

In two actions at the close of the 1964 Council session, Pope Paul demonstrated that authority still lies heavily in the hands of the pope. Within hours of the final vote on Christian unity, he submitted 19 "suggestions" for changes; rather than reject the entire document, the bishops approved the changes wholesale. Later Pope Paul issued a statement declaring the Virgin Mary the "mother of the church," placating a minority of bishops dissatisfied with what they consider insufficient Council emphasis on Jesus' mother.

Still, institutional evidence of the bishops' new authority unquestionably will emerge from Vatican II. Perhaps the evidence will be a "senate" of representatives from national conferences of bishops that would meet at the Vatican for three months or so each year; perhaps it will be periodic meetings of all of the church's bishops. Whatever the form, the new institution will take precedence over the Curia, the Vatican bureaucracy.

Renewal penetrates deeper than the merely organizational. Simply by drawing the bishops together, and especially by revising the liturgy of the church, the Vatican Council has quickened the feeling among many Catholics of the church as the family of God. The Mass is now said in living English, and hymns seem to be sung with greater enthusiasm and understanding. Many mourn the demise of much of the Latin in the Mass, but many more report their spiritual life enriched through understanding.

Cajole an American bishop into specifying the single most important result of the Council. Most likely he will reply "the awareness of other cultures—and their awareness of us." The answer may be unexpectedly trite coming from a bishop, but it is also enlightening.

How else define the interest among worshipers in a November 1964 Council Mass, from the

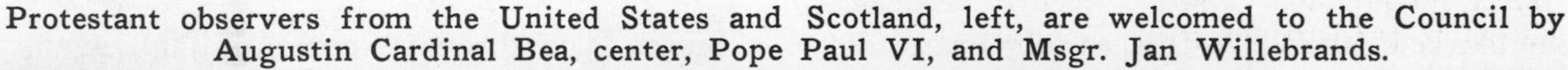

Protestant observers from the United States and Scotland, left, are welcomed to the Council by Augustin Cardinal Bea, center, Pope Paul VI, and Msgr. Jan Willebrands.

The day begins: An early arrival at the Council.

pope to a few humble visitors, as they heard the beating of tom-toms and the clashing of cymbals in the Ethiopian Rite? From the visitors' gallery next to the black-and-gold Bernini canopy beneath the dome in St. Peter's, the visitor could see bishops from England and India, from Japan and Tanganyika, worshiping beneath the magnificent gold ceiling of the nave.

For an hour and 15 minutes the Mass went on, the bishops dressed in their usual purple that Americans would call red and the cardinals in their red that Americans would call orange. Some bishops grew restless, and some thought again about the delicious comment of a Brazilian bishop the previous time the Ethiopian Rite had been celebrated during the Council: "What are they doing? Getting ready to boil a cardinal?" But the rich diversity of the church, and the awareness that the family of God embraces such diversity, came through again to the bishops.

Renewal also promises a deeper sense of mission in the church. The Vatican Council has fired up enthusiasm among bishops mired in administration. It has instilled new zeal into theologians whose ideas were once held suspect and into laymen whose ideas were once held inconsequential.

Enthuses one bishop: "Not only the bishops but the cancer patients, not only the theologians but the soldiers, not only the priests but the factory workers with 'five kids too many,' have a part to play in the consecration of the world."

The idea of the layman as an apostle of Christ, long preached by Protestantism, still bounces off many American Catholic bishops with little effect. In earlier days many Catholic laymen were ill-educated immigrants—little

Nuns in St. Peter's Square catch a glimpse of the pope.

equipped for a responsible role in the church. Some bishops, failing to understand that the layman as well as the priest can display a consuming fervor in religious work, still think of the lay worker as an adviser in secular matters rather than a partner in a religious cause.

Yet the Vatican Council has spoken of the "priesthood of the laity" in the same way the Protestants speak of the "priesthood of all believers." The Council bases its doctrine regarding laymen on the same scriptural passages that Protestants cite: "Ye are . . . a royal priesthood," for example, and "Go ye into all the world." To drive home the point that the "new" emphasis on laymen is grounded in ancient doctrine, the Council quoted nothing written or said since the Fourth Century.

The doctrine on laymen illustrates how doctrine can "change," though the church teaches that its doctrine does not err.

Bishop John J. Wright of Pittsburgh, one of the theological giants of the Council, compares church doctrine to a tree. "New Testament verses are the seeds of doctrine," he says. "With each popping out of a branch, with each flowering of a leaf, you have a new branch and a new leaf. But each branch and each leaf is in the pattern of the original seed." The Catholic definition of Christ as the "deposit of faith" implies never-ending growth—a development of doctrine—despite an unchanging identity.

The development of doctrine is most apparent in the new Catholic attitudes the Council is shaping as a result of scientific discoveries and new political and social conditions.

Of the many facets of the *aggiornamento,* the modernization of the church, none is so compelling as new doctrines for new world problems. Not that the church intends to conform to the world. But it is examining world problems—peace, poverty, population growth, family relations, and others—and trying to formulate church doctrine on them.

These are the issues the public watches most closely, for they touch on such controversial topics as birth control, mixed marriage pledges, and nuclear disarmament. The Council did not begin debating them until the 1964 session, and it will not redefine doctrine on them until the final session, if then.

Soundings in Vatican City indicate that the Council will set forth theological guidelines on these issues, but that it may refrain from giving the specific answers for which many Catholics are clamoring. "Why doesn't the Council approve the pill right now?" mocks a bishop, acting the part of the anxious mother. "Why doesn't it tell me right away when I should go on a diet?"

What the Council must provide, this bishop says, is not a series of glib solutions on sexual morality, political ethics, or race relations, but the hard theological foundation on which solutions can be based. Thus the Council itself may never decide whether to preserve or abolish premarital pledges by non-Catholics to raise their children as Catholics, often criticized for encouraging hypocrisy and deceit; it may never examine in detail the medical and scientific aspects of birth control pills, which many bishops feel incompetent to assess anyway. Instead, it may leave detailed answers in these areas to special commissions such as the commission appointed by Pope Paul VI in mid-1964 on the birth control question.

The Dramatic Side

In no area have the effects of the Vatican Council been more dramatic than in the area of Christian unity.

The price of Christianity's divisions is growing. Christians in the emerging nations warn that Asians and Africans will reject Christianity unless it practices within its ranks the love it professes. "Comfortable" Christians in the United States may be able to afford the luxury of bickering, they say, but Christianity worldwide cannot.

Catholics freely credit Protestants with having pioneered in the current unity movement. The Twentieth Century interest in Christian unity traces back to a world missionary conference in Edinburgh, Scotland, in 1910 that led eventually to the World Council of Churches, in which many Protestant and Eastern Orthodox churches participate.

Protestant-Catholic unity can develop, however, only if both sides are receptive. Catholics at the Council joke that not too many years ago the definition of a liberal priest was a priest seen with a Protestant minister. Today a priest attracts attention if he fails to be seen frequently with a Protestant minister.

The men behind the Christian unity movement hold no utopian vision that paradise lies just ahead. Christian unity, they believe, will prove a painstakingly slow process. In the view of Methodist Bishop F. Gerald Ensley, the unity movement resembles agriculture more than architecture, for it must develop from within. The process, he believes, moves from acquaintance to acceptance to affiliation and finally to assimilation; the dialogue among Catholics, Eastern Orthodox, and Protestants is still in the first stage, acquaintance.

Effects Show

In both Catholic renewal and Christian reunion, the change inspired by Vatican II has only begun. Laymen's organizations are starting to shed their old preoccupation with getting their members to attend communion once a month in favor of a new emphasis on training their members to translate their Christian commitment into action. Seminaries, aware that priests who are taught old concepts perpetuate old concepts, know they must drastically revise their curricula. The bishops of the United States are starting to remold the National Catholic Welfare Conference into a true national conference of bishops.

In all of this there is resistance. Well after the opening of the Vatican Council one bishop wrote a friend that he thanked God none of the new movements and new ideas had gotten into his diocese.

But in all of this there is hope too. "I came over to the Council thinking the church in the United States was the last word," says Bishop Robert J. Dwyer of Reno in his genial, candid manner. "Now I'm not so sure we are."

A Midwestern bishop who had always prided himself on running a tight diocese from above found himself, to his surprise, consulting laymen for advice. "I said to myself, Bishop, what happened to you?" he recalls. Then he gives his answer simply, forcefully. "Pope John happened to me. He cracked me wide open."

Pope John happened to millions. The vision came swiftly, suddenly, like the startling glimpse of St. Peter's from a placid piazza. But this vision, like the memory of the view from the hill called Aventino, will not soon go away. ♦

Evening: Churchmen discuss the day's work in the Council.

Catholic-Protestant Differences

MONTREAL.

ENTHUSIASM for Christian unity, so infectious since the late Pope John XXIII convened the historic Second Vatican Council, has tended to obscure a hard fact: Serious differences obstruct the road to ultimate reunion between Protestants and Roman Catholics.

Both faiths remain adamant on matters of substance. Augustin Cardinal Bea, the genial head of the Vatican's Secretariat for Promoting Christian Unity, has stressed repeatedly that the Catholic Church will not yield on theological issues: "There can be no question of seeking a compromise on . . . divinely revealed doctrine."

Protestant apostles of unity have spoken just as firmly. "We also are not interested in compromises," declared the Rev. Hans H. Harms, of the Evangelical Church in Germany at a World Council of Churches conference on Christian unity at McGill University here in July 1963. The Rev. Dr. Harms, like Cardinal Bea, is one of most ardent advocates of unity within his faith; he was opening channels between the World Council and the Vatican even before the reign of Pope John began.

Long conversations with some of the Protestant theologians and Catholic "observers" at the conference here illuminated the chief issues in dispute between the two faiths. The conversations also answered a puzzling question: Why, in the face of these differences, did theologians even bother to assemble here from all over the world for what one divinity school professor termed a mid-summer "chat under a hit tin roof"?

Perhaps the thorniest theological problem at issue between the faiths is papal infallibility. Catholics consider the pope infallible "when teaching officially and solemnly on matters of faith and morals." Protestants reject the idea that God speaks through only one man on the most crucial issues. The declaration of the Vatican Council that the pope shares the governing powers of the church with its bishops does not diminish the doctrine of papal infallibility.

Mary, the mother of Jesus, presents a second theological barrier to unity. By papal decree and popular veneration, Catholics assign to Mary a place all her own; they teach that Mary was born free of sin and ascended bodily into heaven, and that the mother of Jesus is the "mother of the church." Some Protestants believe that Protestantism too long has neglected the maternal dimension of Christianity in deference to its paternal and fraternal dimensions, but almost every Protestant thinker believes that the Catholic emphasis on Mary detracts from the unique position of Christ.

A wide gulf exists, too, on the validity of existing churches. Catholics believe that theirs is the "one true church"—that its teachings as expressed by pope or council cannot err and that salvation can be found only within the church. Pope John clearly stated that unity can be achieved only by a Protestant and Eastern Orthodox return to Rome after an internal reform of the Roman Catholic Church.

Catholic declarations at the Vatican Council that persons born into non-Catholic Christian churches cannot be blamed for the "sin" of the original separation in the days of the Reformation have helped assuage Protestant resentment over this position. So has the Council's assertion that salvation can exist outside the "visible limits" of the Catholic Church, which implies a mystical bond among Christians within broader "invisible" limits of the church. But many Protestants believe that the

Obstacles to Unity

The Age-Old Fences Between Faiths Remain, Despite Dramatic Efforts on Both Sides—And Some Progress

—Robert de Gast

revised wording still makes them "second-class Christians" in Catholic eyes. Insists one Protestant: "God's family is composed of all—not part of—His children."

The validity issue creates problems in practical areas—mixed marriages, for example, and missionary work. Bishop Joachim Beckmann of the Evangelical Church in the Rhineland insists that it is inconsistent for Catholics to accord the polite term of "separated brethren" to Protestants as long as Protestants are "treated in canonical marriage law . . . like pagans." The Rev. Dr. Harms makes a similar complaint in the missionary field. On the remote island of Nias in Indonesia, he says, German Protestant missionaries converted about 80 per cent of the heathen inhabitants to Christianity, only to have a Catholic missionary society begin proselyting there—not among the non-Christians but among the converts, "tearing the 'live' people out of the church we set up."

Missionary poaching and ill feeling over mixed marriages can be reduced by changes in policy, or at least changes in emphasis, from above. More difficult to erase are differences over issues of public policy that vitally affect Catholics and Protestants.

Disputes in the United States over public aid to parochial schools, birth control laws in various states, and tax exemptions for church-owned business properties—merely three of the many public issues on which the faiths differ—arise more from the hard facts of social and economic power than from differences in religious doctrine. But arise they do. And they raise emotions that are formidable roadblocks to Christian unity.

Misunderstanding adds to the difficulty of achieving Christian unity. Many Catholics still believe that Martin Luther, an ordained priest,

The signs of potential unity show up now and again. Here are the presidents of the World Council of Churches, convened in India: Sir Francis Ibiam of Nigeria; Dr. Martin Niemoeller of Germany; Archbishop Iakovos of North and South America; Dr. Ramsey, archbishop of Canterbury, England; Dr. David Moses of India; and Mr. Charles Parlin of the U.S.A.

started the Reformation because he had fallen in love with a woman. Many Protestants still believe that the Catholic Church is a monolithic, totalitarian structure that tolerates no freedom of thought, despite repeated evidence to the contrary from the Vatican Council. Pope John stressed that "authority, if not rooted in charity, is tyranny." Declared the Rev. Godfrey Diekmann, editor of the Catholic magazine Worship and an observer here: "Christ had the highest authority, but He exercised it by giving His life for His flock."

Finally, there is pure prejudice. And prejudice dies hard.

"When Protestant parents return home and find their children crying because their Catholic baby sitter has told them that Catholics go to heaven and Protestants go to hell," says one Episcopalian clergyman in whose parish this happened, "they never forget it." The fact that the Roman Catholic Church has specifically repudiated this doctrine—Richard Cardinal Cushing of Boston excommunicated a priest several years ago for preaching it—makes little difference to the parents in whom prejudice has been implanted.

With these obstacles, will Christian unity ever be achieved?

The unity of which ecumenical leaders speak is not so much organic unity as it is unity of purpose—not so much an organizational merger as it is a merger of the will to fulfill a common mission. This may ultimately lead to organic unity, but ecumenical leaders almost to a man discount this as a possibility in their lifetimes.

"The true meaning of the ecumenical movement lies in a spiritual discovery," says the Rev. W. A. Visser 't Hooft, general secretary of the World Council of Churches. "No serious participant in our movement wants to give up his spiritual integrity and his real convictions. But we all hear the prayer: 'That all may be one.' "

By this standard, progress has indeed been made toward Christian unity.

The climate of interfaith relationships has changed dramatically. No longer can a Christian thinker write of "scandalous" and "acrimonious" relations between Catholics and Protestants in the United States, as the prestigious Reinhold Niebuhr wrote less than a decade ago in *Essays in Applied Christianity*.

When Catholics can sing the "battle hymn" of the Protestant Reformation—Martin Luther's *A Mighty Fortress Is Our God*—as they now do from a new Catholic hymnal, the Age of the Counter Reformation must surely be declared dead. When Protestants can discuss the possibility of an ultimate reunion with Rome, as many now do, a new Age of Unity must surely have begun.

Sudden Arrival

"We seem suddenly to have arrived," exulted the Rt. Rev. Oliver S. Tomkins, bishop of Bristol in the Church of England and a 25-year veteran of the Christian unity movement, as he strolled coatless across the McGill University campus here. "Millions of people around the world realize now, as they didn't a few years ago, that Christian unity is something worth talking about. It's no longer considered the hobby of a few cranks."

A few days later Paul-Emile Cardinal Leger of Montreal demonstrated his belief that Christian unity is something worth not only talking about but praying about—with Protestants. When Cardinal Leger worshiped with the theologians meeting here in search of Christian unity, he became the first Roman Catholic of his stature to join other Christians in confessing the "sin" of Christian divisions, in his words, and in asking God to "break our heart of stone and give us a heart able to repent."

The following year, under the leadership of men such as Cardinal Leger, the Vatican Council indicated it will relax the church's stance on the sensitive issue of common worship. Catholics no longer will be prohibited from participating in non-Catholic worship services; under "special circumstances" defined by local bishops or national councils of bishops, they could engage in common worship with non-Catholics.

How can further unity be achieved?

By each faith sharpening and explaining its own positions, say ecumenical-minded Protestants and Catholics. By each faith making a genuine effort to understand the arguments of the other. By adapting old doctrines to modern conditions. By seeking new insights into old truths together.

Consider the progress on two theological issues. Traditionally, Catholics have stressed the importance of the sacraments, Protestants the importance of the direct Word of God. In the past two or three decades Protestants have moved toward more reliance on the sacraments, while Catholics now recognize the importance of the words that precede and accompany them.

Scripture vs. Tradition

A second illustration: Protestants had long insisted that their faith rests on scripture alone while Catholics had noted that the scriptures were written only after early church forms had arisen and thus had stressed the importance of church tradition as the "living faith." Here, too, Protestants and Catholics both have showed signs of modifying their stands; Protestants see increasingly that the expression of their faith has been influenced by the course of history, while Catholics have undertaken extensive studies in Biblical scholarship.

Each of these developments—the more charitable view of the other faith, the combined search for truth in scholarship and common worship, each faith's richer understanding of its own theological heritage—has given the Christian world new hope that it can some day overcome its divisions.

But the obstacles to ultimate reunion remain. Each faith may define its positions in different and more acceptable words from time to time. But Protestants plan no quick return to the Catholic Church. And Catholics will not yield on the substance of their faith. ♦

Protestant Mergers

The Protestants Find Unity Difficult, Even Among Themselves: Hosanna to the Vision, Not the Costs

OBERLIN, OHIO.

THE REV. Eugene Carson Blake, the highest executive officer of the United Presbyterian Church, hunched his huge frame forward in an easy chair here and argued the cause of Protestant unity.

A united Protestant church, he said, could carry the Christian message more effectively to city slums. It could expand missionary efforts overseas. It could "make the word and the sacrament available to every person in every acre of the land."

Union, he conceded, "wouldn't guarantee that we would succeed. But it would give us the

Slow Progress

Wood relief in Protestantism's Interchurch Center, New York City.

resources—the finances, the leadership, the imagination—to accomplish the job."

Eugene Carson Blake spoke with a vision of hope that chilly Wednesday evening in March 1963. He spoke as leaders of six Protestant denominations chatted warmly after a worship service at the Oberlin College chapel about their common search for Protestant unity.

A year later, in the stately Princeton Inn in Princeton, New Jersey, Eugene Carson Blake leaned wearily over a tiny writing table to scribble out a "progress" statement that spoke of "difficulties, setbacks, and disappointments" in the Protestant unity movement. This time his voice conveyed dismay as he interrupted his thoughts of the disenchanted delegates to the 1964 talks a floor below. "We're just trying to pick up the pieces," he told an acquaintance.

The Rev. Dr. Blake had reason to feel disheartened. It was he who had first proposed that unity talks be held among leaders of the United Presbyterian Church, the Protestant Episcopal Church, the Methodist Church, and the United Church of Christ. He had made his proposal in a sermon in San Francisco in December 1960; Episcopal Bishop James A. Pike of California endorsed the proposal, and it became known as the Blake-Pike Plan.

The four denominations formed a Consultation on Church Union in an initial meeting in Washington, D.C., in April 1962. Later that year the Disciples of Christ and the Evangelical United Brethren (EUB) joined the original four in the consultation.

If a merger should go through—and its advocates have always admitted it would take years, probably decades—the impact upon religion in America would be enormous. The six denominations alone have more than 21,000,000 members, making this by far the broadest attempt at union in American Protestant history. Whereas previous mergers simply have formed larger denominations, a bond of these six bodies would go a long way toward replacing the loose federation that now binds two-thirds of the nation's Protestants, the National Council of Churches.

The Mysterious Report

But mergers don't come easily. No better evidence can be offered than the four days of deliberations in the Princeton Inn.

When the pioneers in the current search for Protestant unity assembled on a Monday in Princeton, many expected to clear the way for the actual drafting of a merger plan. Before they drifted away three days later, they were struggling to salvage what progress they had made over the previous three years.

A reminder by an Episcopal delegate on Monday that his delegation was required to insist on its views of the ministry sent a minor tremor through the consultation. But the earthquake erupted when news broke of a Methodist report that, strangely, was never intended for or submitted to the consultation.

The report, prepared by the Methodist delegation for the Methodists' quadrennial convention later in April 1964, declared that it was premature to ask the nation's Methodists for their blessing to proceed with a unity plan. It identified five "areas of concern" about the unity talks: (1) An apparent Episcopalian conviction that communion should be restricted rather than open to everyone, (2) the United Church of Christ and Disciples of Christ tradition of placing great authority in local congregations as distinguished from the Methodists' strong "connectional" form of government, (3) the Disciples' baptismal practices, which differ from the Methodists', (4) the effect a merger would have upon future relationships with other Methodist bodies outside the United States, and (5) the lack of enthusiasm in some other denominations for strong Methodist stands on such social issues as drinking and gambling.

"How far," the report asked, "are Methodists warranted in compromising their convictions, long held, to achieve . . . union?"

The report infuriated many of the delegates. To begin with, they found several elementary inaccuracies in the report. The report referred repeatedly to the "Disciples Church" but never used the full name of this body or the accepted "Disciples of Christ." Three times it misspelled "immersion" as "emersion" in referring to baptismal practices.

More important, the Disciples and the Episcopalians fumed that the Methodists had misinterpreted their doctrinal beliefs—the Disciples' beliefs on baptism, the Episcopalians' on the ministry.

The Methodists' failure to discuss their reservations openly—partly, no doubt, because two of their most eloquent spokesmen on Protestant unity could not attend—also incensed a number of delegates. Muttered one: "You get the feeling the Methodists are saying one thing above the table and doing something else beneath it."

Episcopalians Object

Within hours after word of the Methodist report first spread in the corridors, the Episcopal delegates decided they would not ask their triennial convention in the fall of 1964 to authorize them to draft a plan of union. Though seven of the nine Episcopal delegates argued that "serious debate" could be held only if they had the planks of a positive plan in front of them, the delegation decided its sentiment needed to be unanimous if it were to seek action by its parent body.

The next morning the Rev. James I. McCord, president of Princeton Theological Seminary and retiring chairman of the unity talks, assessed the effect of the Episcopal and Methodist moves. "This means a clear delay of at least four years in getting down to the hard work of drafting a plan of union," he said. "Until we get to that stage, we have no idea where we are going."

If the backstage bickering did nothing else, it brought a touch of reality to the talks that had been absent in previous sessions. It also pointed up some of the real roadblocks to Protestant unity.

Church structure is one of these roadblocks. Protestant mergers in the past generally have united denominations not only of similar theological heritage, but also with the same form of church government; the Lutherans, for example, have reduced the number of their separate denominations in the United States from nearly 300 in the mid-1800s to about 10 now. More recently, the success of the Congregational-Christian Churches and the Evangelical and Reformed Church—the one with a congregational structure and the other with a modified presbyterian structure—in uniting into the United Church of Christ in 1957 has proved that churches with different forms of government can merge.

Never before, however, have merger discussions been held among American denominations that include each of the three basic forms of church organization: Episcopal (imposing a central authority), presbyterian (placing authority in groups of churches), and congregational (insuring autonomy of the local church). Many delegates believe that the structure of the united Protestant church, if such a church is ever established, would be presbyterian.

A second major roadblock is the nature and authority of ministers. Episcopalians insist that the only valid ministry is one that has been ordained through an unbroken line of bishops back to the earliest church. The other denominations, which have not maintained this unbroken line, refuse to take any step that would

Episcopal Bishop Richard S. Emrich: "We must pool our riches."

Presbyterian Rev. James I. McCord: "This means a clear delay. . . . "

Presbyterian Rev. Eugene Carson Blake: A grand design.

imply that their heritage is not legitimate. Reordaining their ministers, a solution adopted by a committee in Great Britain working on a union of Anglicans and Methodists there, would imply this in their view.

"If it's a matter of admitting we've been illegitimate for 200 years," declares one Methodist, "our success shows that we need more illegitimacy." He regrets the sidestepping of the problem so far, contending that "if we can't work this out, there's no sense in talking any further."

Episcopal Bishop Richard S. Emrich of Detroit stresses just as firmly that if union comes, apostolic succession (the unbroken line) will be preserved. "Only a jaundiced Puritan can fail to see the beauty of the apostolic succession, of the chain of hands down through the ages," he says. The united church must take the outer forms and the inner spirit and weld them together. "We must pool our riches," he asserts, "and one of the riches we in the Episcopal Church have to offer is the apostolic succession."

With these staggering problems to overcome, why do so many Protestant leaders labor in pursuit of a goal neither they, nor their sons or their grandsons, may ever achieve?

Tragic Disunity

In Bishop Emrich's words, it is because they deplore "the tragedy of the disunity of the church, our inability to meet together, pray together, and be one at the local level." Inevitably, competing local churches consume energies they could better spend in a united effort. Sometimes this fosters destructive suspicions that clearly contradict Christ's admonition in John 17:21 "That they all may be one."

In the Rev. Dr. Blake's grand design, the united Protestant church would be "truly catholic, truly reformed, and truly evangelical." Few of the participants in the unity talks quibble with this goal, but some wonder whether working now with such diverse denominations is the way to achieve it.

"The way to move in the ecumenical movement," declared Charles C. Parlin, a Methodist layman and one of the six presidents of the World Council of Churches, as he looked out onto the golf course at the Princeton Inn, "is for family groups to move as fast as they can without waiting to settle knotty theological problems with remote denominations."

Martin Luther. His Sixteenth Century opposition to a "mighty, monolithic" church still influences Protestantism, makes merger talks difficult.

This attitude helps explain why Methodist hearts seemed strangely chilled at Princeton. With a merger pending with the Evangelical United Brethren, they wanted to avoid any chance of jeopardizing action within their own family group. Theological differences between the Methodists and the EUB are not nearly as wide as between the Methodists and the Episcopalians, for example, or between the Methodists and the Presbyterians.

Some of the most pungent criticism of the Blake proposal centers on the motives behind the movement. Many Protestants—particularly clergymen in the more conservative denominations—say they detect aspirations of personal power among the leaders of the unity forces; they liken the "administrative pooh-bahs" of these churches to the character in Gilbert and Sullivan's operetta, *The Mikado,* who constantly thought in terms of bureaucratic power.

A move by the United Church of Christ a few weeks before the Princeton sessions inspired this type of criticism from other Princeton delegates. United Church of Christ leaders staged a press conference proposing immediate union in certain functional areas such as missionary efforts, race-relations activities, and the recruitment of ministers. Because they did not coordinate the proposal in advance with the leaders of the other delegations, the United Church of Christ was accused of trying to corner credit for the idea.

A more sophisticated criticism attacks the tenor of the Blake plan. "The basis of union appears to be a property and trade agreement to be made for the benefit of visitors, stockholders, and a wider public, rather than a confession of faith, repentance, and praise," complained Markus Barth, son of theologian Karl Barth, in the journal Christianity and Crisis.

Other Protestants fear a mighty, monolithic church, one they contend would be a renewal of the monolithic structure of Sixteenth Century Roman Catholicism against which their forebears revolted. "We rejoice in the growth of the ecumenical movement and in the development of the ecumenical spirit," proclaimed Methodist Bishop Gerald Kennedy of Los Angeles in his episcopal address to the 1964 Methodist convention. "But we are not sure that God wills the churches of the Reformation to become one organic union. We believe that our pluralism has produced much good fruit, not the least of which has been freedom."

The Rev. Dr. Blake insists that a united church would be decentralized and would be unalterably local in its emphasis. "What we're looking at—what we're concerned about—is what the Christian church looks like on Main Street," he says.

In the final analysis, it's how Main Street views a merger, not how merger advocates view Main Street, that will determine whether a merger goes through. If and when delegates of the denominations come up with a specific merger plan, the denominations themselves will have to ratify it.

Here inertia, more than open resistance, will threaten any merger proposal. But resistance will be there, too. Warns Bishop Kennedy in *The Challenge to Reunion:* "I have found that many will shout 'hosanna' to the vision but cry out 'crucify it' when they see what it costs." ♦

The World's Major Religions

How They Rank By Members (Estimated)

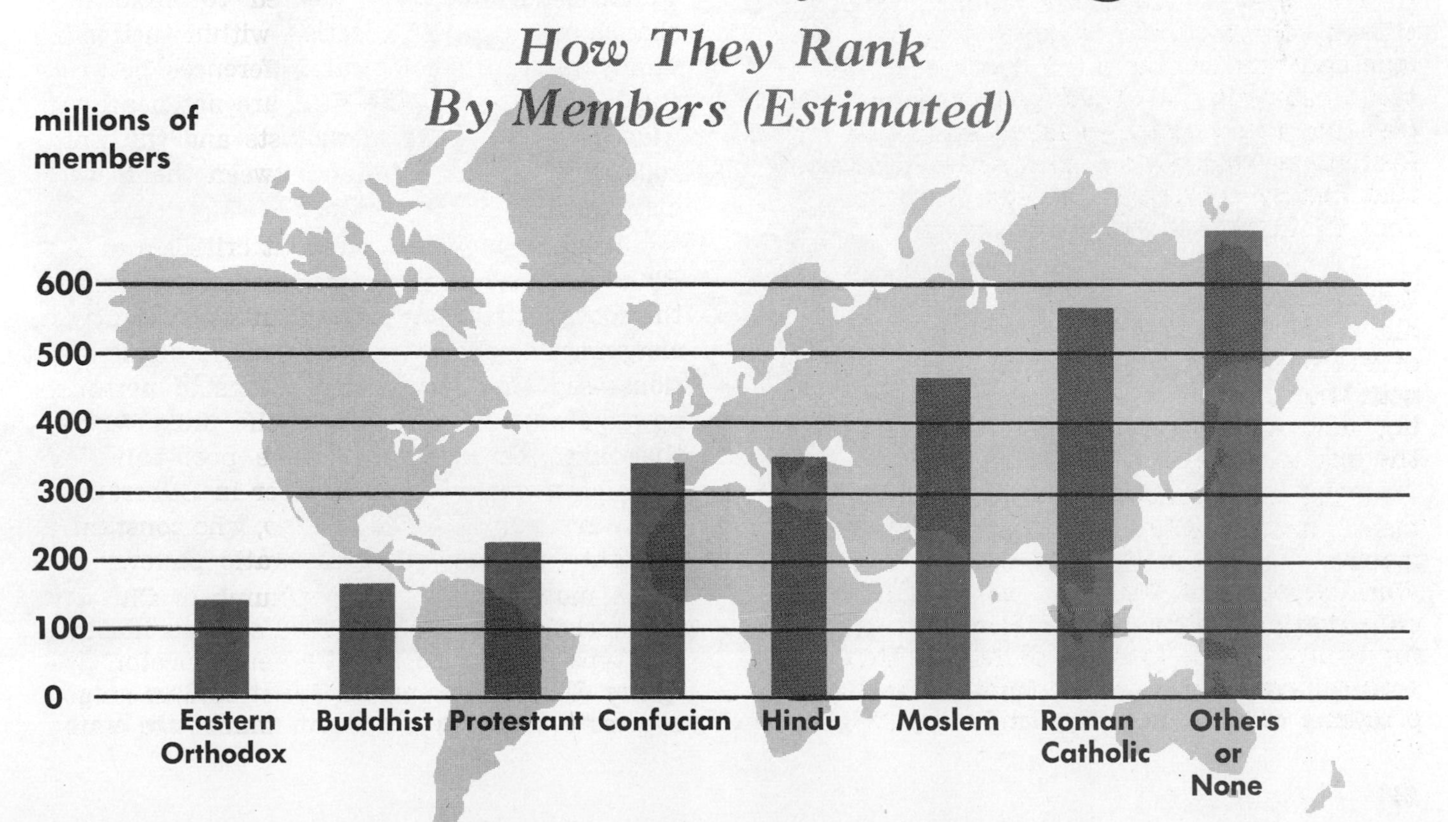

Within Protestantism, the differences are wide—and easily visible to the naked eye. Above, the simplicity of a Southern Baptist Sunday. Right, the elegance of an Episcopal service in the Middle West.

The Methodists

Go to the people: The watchword of the young Methodist minister—don't wait for them. In Louisville, Kentucky, a Methodist conducts a service at a parking lot.

Recovery of a Heritage

Hampered by Signs of Complacency, Methodists Search For a Way Back to the Fervor of an Earlier Day

PITTSBURGH.

"WHERE'S the prophetic leadership of the Methodist Church today?" asked the president of a leading Protestant seminary over an after-dinner cup of coffee. "Where's the Methodists' strong tradition of social concern?"

Methodists in recent years have become, in the caustic phrase of Methodist Bishop F. Gerald Ensley of Ohio, "chaplains of the middle class." As the circuit-riding frontier days have vanished and the poor of earlier times have climbed into the middle class, Methodism's evangelistic fervor has diminished.

Methodist membership growth has slowed to less than 1 per cent a year; once by far the nation's largest Protestant denomination, Methodists now are playing statistical tag with the Southern Baptists at just over 10,000,000 members. Church school attendance is falling off 1 per cent a year. Of 46 denominations surveyed by the National Council of Churches on per capita financial giving, Methodists ranked 43rd.

John Wesley, the Church of England priest who founded Methodism two centuries ago, once warned: "I am not afraid that the people called Methodists should ever cease to exist, either in Europe or America. But I am afraid lest they should exist only as a dead sect, having the form of religion without the power."

Stung by frequent criticism that they have succumbed to the status quo, Methodists are working in many directions to preserve the power of religion as well as its form. They are sharpening up their theology, revitalizing their evangelism, and slowly but convincingly excising a condition that has plagued them since they united in 1939—racial segregation within the church.

Methodists themselves are fueling the engines of change; their heritage of free-wheeling dissent emboldens them to become their own best critics. Proclaimed the Methodist Board of Evangelism in 1964: "We need a renewal in the Methodist Church—a revival." The board referred not so much to enlisting new members as to deepening the convictions of the old. "The weakness of the church today," it declared, "lies in the partial commitment of its members."

To help correct this weakness, a fledgling Department of Evangelists has stepped up the number of "crusades" in local churches from 25 in 1960 to several times that number now. Young Methodist ministers around the nation are engaging in "unconventional evangelism" at drag strips, drive-in movie theaters, county fairs, and boat docks. The Division of World Missions is starting to send missionary task forces overseas whose members pledge not to marry for three years; the first 16-man group went to the Congo in the summer of 1964.

The object of all this is not to improve statistics but deepen convictions. "The basic motive of the past 5 or 10 years has been to gain members," says the Rev. Lawrence Guderian of Albany, Oregon. "But we haven't been engrafting them into the body of Christ. We got their names, but we didn't get them." Numbers shouldn't count, insists Mr. Guderian. "After all, J. C. only had 12 men, and one of those was a rat. What are we griping about?"

Many Methodists believe, however, that as long as racial segregation persists in the church, the church betrays its Christian message. And

Methodist Faces:

John Wesley, founder of Methodism.

The Rev. A. Dudley Ward, a young Methodist leader.

segregation is built into the structure of the Methodist Church in the form of the all-Negro Central Jurisdiction, an institution unique in America's major denominations.

"The Central Jurisdiction is actual evidence of segregation—racism, if you will—within the church," declares the Rev. A. Dudley Ward, general secretary of the Methodist Board of Christian Social Concerns. "Its very presence diminishes the clarity and soundness of our witness in today's world."

The Central Jurisdiction was formed in 1939, when the century-old North-South breach in the Methodist Church was healed. The merged church was divided into six jurisdictions —five geographic and one (the Central Jurisdiction) all-Negro. The Central Jurisdiction cut across boundary lines of the five geographic jurisdictions, with churches in each. It has elected its own bishops and overseen its own conferences (groups of churches). Of the 400,000 Negroes in the Methodist Church at the beginning of 1964, some 373,000 belonged to churches in the Central Jurisdiction.

The question for years has not been whether to abolish the Central Jurisdiction, but how. Should it be eradicated in one sweep or eliminated gradually? Should integration of Negro bishops and churches into white conferences be mandatory or voluntary?

Chats with Negroes as well as whites confirm that the battle lines on the issue, clear in 1939, have become fuzzy. In 1939 the Negroes opposed the segregated structure so strongly that they voted against the merger; they accepted the Central Jurisdiction only when faced with being left out of the church entirely. More recently, however, many Negroes have feared being stranded on islands of segregation, isolated from fellow Negroes with common problems. They have feared, too, that they will lose power and prestige if they are absorbed in larger, mostly white jurisdictions. "Ambition," says retired Negro Bishop Matthew W. Clair, Jr., of St. Louis, "is the same in any race."

The Central Jurisdiction issue hung heavy

Bishop Prince A. Taylor, Jr., president-designate of the Council of Bishops.

Charles C. Parlin, a lay force in the Church.

Bishop Gerald Kennedy, dynamic preacher and evangelist.

over the Methodists' quadrennial convention at Pittsburgh's silver-domed Civic Arena in 1964. Machinery for voluntary integration, in existence for six years, had proved ineffective; only 27 local Negro churches and no conferences had transferred into the geographic jurisdictions. A group called Methodists for Church Renewal, composed largely of young ministers and theological students, mobilized their forces at Pittsburgh to protest "racial injustice" within the church. They attracted 1,600 persons to an all-night vigil at two downtown Pittsburgh churches, placed placard-carrying pickets outside the Civic Arena, and staged a "kneel-in" on the Civic Arena steps as a dramatic counterpoint to the oratory inside.

The delegates reaffirmed the voluntary approach. But they gave it teeth by declaring that an all-Negro jurisdiction could not continue to exist after the Methodists unite with the 760,000-member Evangelical United Brethren, a merger expected to occur in 1968. They added moral weight against church segregation by directing Methodist churches to admit anyone regardless of race (though no practical penalties exist for noncompliance) and by deploring racial discrimination in such areas as church employment and church hospitals. The Council of Bishops, in addition, for the first time, elected a Negro bishop, Prince A. Taylor, Jr., its president-designate.

Pittsburgh opened many doors. Within months large groups of Negro churches were transferring lock, stock, and bishop to white jurisdictions. Negro bishops took over the predominantly white, state-wide conferences of New Jersey and Iowa; one-third of the Negro membership was transferred to areas headed by white bishops.

If the Central Jurisdiction of the Methodist Church is unique, so is the condition that has permitted it to endure—the church's united, truly national character. The Presbyterians and Baptists remain divided along Northern and Southern lines; the Lutherans, Episcopalians, and Roman Catholics have comparatively few

Church Center for the United Nations. Built with Methodist funds and imagination, it brings together under one roof all UN-related church agencies, regardless of denomination.

churches in the South. One-third of the nation's Methodists, by contrast, live in the South.

This has tended to blunt the sharp edge of Methodism on the racial issue. The Council of Bishops remained silent on civil rights until long after most denominations had spoken out forcefully on the topic. When they did speak in December 1963, the Methodist officials admitted inaction: "We confess with deep penitence that our performance as a church has not kept pace with our profession."

Actually, many individual Methodists already had sacrificed heavily in the civil-rights cause. An Alabama delegate to the General Conference in 1960 challenged the stand expected of him; as one Methodist puts it, "He wound up in Rhodesia." After the University of Mississippi riots in late 1962, 28 Methodist ministers in Mississippi published a statement quoting the Methodist *Discipline* that Jesus "permits no discrimination because of race, color, or creed"; more than half have been forced out of their pulpits.

Emphasis on Social

But the failure of the bishops to speak out earlier troubled many Methodists. For Methodists historically have considered it an obligation to stand in the forefront on social questions. "The Gospel of Christ knows no religion but social," John Wesley had declared; "no holiness but social holiness."

Wesley made it his mission to preach to miners, to prisoners, to paupers—to the kind of Englishmen that Charles Dickens was to write about a century later. For his social warfare, a modern-day scholar has conferred on him perhaps the supreme accolade for a Christian: "The life of John Wesley was an extension of the Resurrection into history."

Methodism was cut from a cloth fit for the American frontier. In line with Wesley's recollection that "my heart was strangely warmed," it stresses personal conversion to Christ. In line with Wesley's works in England, it stresses hope for the underdog.

From humble origins in the Revolutionary era, Methodism grew to immense influence in Nineteenth Century America. During the Civil War, one-fifth of all church members belonged to the Methodist Church. "It is no fault in others," wrote Abraham Lincoln in tribute to Northern Methodists, "that the Methodist

Church sends more soldiers to the field, more nurses to the hospitals, and more prayers to heaven than any."

The "soft" policies of Andrew Johnson toward the defeated South brought criticism, then direct hostility, from Northern Methodists. Their fervor became so intense that their 1868 General Conference, convened during the impeachment trial of President Johnson, set aside an hour of prayer asking God to deliver the nation from the "corrupt influences" that were being exerted to prevent his conviction.

In the Twentieth Century, Methodists have campaigned vigorously on many of the great social issues. They helped lead the fight for Prohibition. They urged economic reform in the early days of the Depression. They articulated pacifism in the interval between the two World Wars.

In New York, across First Avenue from the United Nations building, a new 13-story glass and aluminum structure testifies to Methodism's continuing concern for social action. It's the Church Center for the United Nations—so important a gesture, says the Rev. Mr. Ward, that "it's the one place in the entire social action operation that we've been willing to go into debt." Some 10,000 Methodist ministers and laymen stream into the $3,000,000 structure each year for four-day seminars on international issues and Christian attitudes. The center also is conducting an experimental international nursery school, with 20 students from nearly as many nations. Owned by the Methodist Church, it's used also by several other denominations.

From his tan-carpeted office in Washington looking out on the Capitol, the Rev. Mr. Ward oversees many areas of Methodist activity in his capacity as head of Methodism's Board of Social Concerns: Legislative work (for such measures as the Civil Rights Act and migrant workers legislation), a new drive against gambling, a rapidly growing program of "schools of moral concern" to give leadership training to youths who lead discussions in their home churches on such topics as the Christian attitude toward sex and the meaning of personality. Convinced that the "social action of the church must be sound Biblically

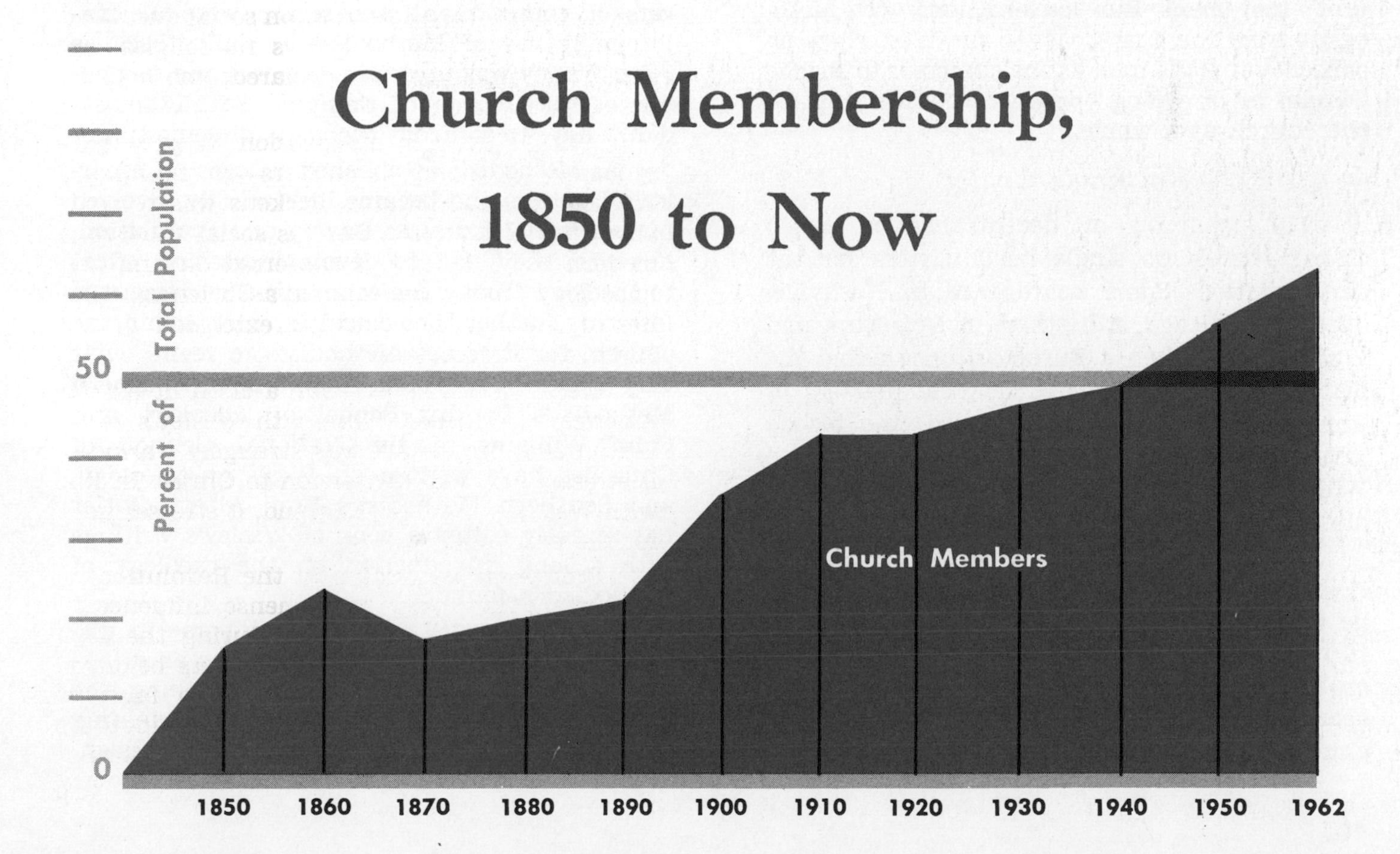

as well as sociologically," the Rev. Mr. Ward is directing a research project that has already produced half a shelf of books.

Through all of this, the Methodist voice is rarely one. Outspoken though many Methodist leaders are, the church's strong tradition of individual conscience mutes the over-all effect.

Each of the 60 bishops wields immense power in his own conference. "There's only one bishop that tops us in authority—and that's Rome's," says one wryly. Outside their conferences, however, they have no power and usually have little influence.

Now and then in the flow of Methodist history a bishop has emerged as a *primus inter pares,* a first among equals. The late G. Bromley Oxnam, a dynamic bishop remembered most for his attacks on McCarthyism in the early 1950s, achieved such stature. As yet, no bishop has built a similar following. Bishop Lloyd C. Wicke of New York commands wide respect and is 1964-65 president of the Council of Bishops, but this one-year post gives its occupant temporary prestige more than permanent influence. Bishop Gerald Kennedy of Los Angeles, a prolific author, is acclaimed by many as Methodism's greatest preacher and Ohio's Bishop Ensley as its most able spokesman in the Protestant unity movement. But conversations with Methodists from the East Coast to the West show no consensus on one man as the successor to Bishop Oxnam in providing "prophetic" leadership for the church as a whole.

No Single Center

The tradition of decentralization is so strong there's no single headquarters for the denomination. Some boards are in Nashville, others in Chicago, still others in New York and Washington. When a European once asked the bishop of Chicago where the headquarters of American Methodism was located, the bishop jokingly replied: "Chicago." Retorted Bishop William C. Martin of Dallas: "Pardon me. I always thought it was in Dallas."

Theologically, Bishop James K. Mathews of Boston may have been on firm ground when he argued, after he and a Negro bishop were turned away by a Jackson, Mississippi, church on Easter 1964, that Methodist bishops are "responsible to the whole church for the whole church." But tradition dies hard. Few Methodists in Mississippi will listen to Bishop Mathews —as, indeed, few Methodists in Massachusetts would listen to the Bishop of Mississippi.

In the view of many Methodists, the merger that brought Methodism in Massachusetts and Mississippi together crippled its theology of social concerns. They worry that, in doing so, it crippled Methodism itself.

Methodists have developed little in the way of theology, at least in the formal sense. "Theology?" goes a popular quip. "The Methodists have no theology." Acknowledges one Methodist clergyman: "We don't know our theology—most of our people don't."

Technically, Methodist theology is contained in 25 Articles of Religion, borrowed for the most part from the 39 Articles of the Church of England. In practice, however, Methodists have avoided building theological walls to keep Christians out, stressing instead the common ground of Protestantism. They insist, for example, on open communion, available to all "that do truly and earnestly repent of your sins."

Little Theology

Says Prof. Jaroslav Pelikan of Yale Divinity School, an expert on Methodist history: "Conversion, commitment, and service were the major emphases of Methodism initially, because John Wesley was protesting against the formalism of the Church of England. So Methodists didn't have to confront theology for some time."

As Methodists established colleges on America's frontiers and became increasingly involved in such social issues as slavery and Prohibition, however, they had to devote increasing effort to theology. Today the ecumenical movement is fostering further theological interest within the church, for it forces Methodists to recite what they believe. Prof. John Deschner of Southern Methodist's Perkins School of Theology and Colin Williams of the National Council of Churches have written on Wesleyan theology, and Southern Methodist's Prof. Albert Outler has recently edited a book of Wesley's writings with a long introduction on the theology of Methodism's founder.

Methodists still feel more at home in discussing such down-to-earth questions as drinking, however, than they do in plumbing the murky depths of theology. And on drinking, despite a minor skirmish at their 1964 conven-

Flowing robes, clerical collars, the confession of sins—all are part of "the liturgical revival," a movement toward formality within Methodism.

tion, they remain adamant: All church members are expected to abstain, and all lay officers must pledge they will do so.

Many Methodists believe such a rigid stance encourages hypocrisy. A 1958 study in Iowa showed that 49 per cent of the state's Methodists drink alcoholic beverages, and a 1962 poll in a suburban Philadelphia church indicated that 67 per cent do so. Still, the convention delegates refused to affirm that "sincere Christians differ" on drinking.

Social drinking is perhaps one evidence of Methodism having gone middle-class. So, in a way, is another controversial development in Methodism: The revival of more formal worship practices. Clerical collars, long shunned, are appearing more and more. The confession of sins is returning to the liturgy, and a few new Methodist churches have even installed kneelers for prayer.

Perhaps the liturgical revival represents a rebuttal of the rambling verbiage of the old-time preaching service. Or perhaps, as the Rev. Edmund W. Robb of Midland, Texas, put it in Christianity Today, the added liturgy is causing the church to lose the common man: "These things simply do not speak to the average church member. . . . He can see through the pride, pretense, and sham of substituting form for experience."

The crucial point is whether added liturgy helps or hinders the Methodist's awareness of Christ. For it is "the ever-present feeling about Christ that makes Methodism meaningful," says Dr. Charles F. Marsh, president of South Carolina's Wofford College. "The faith that He's with us all the time, and that He's worth keeping with us."

To remind Christians of Christ's presence, Methodists believe in fervent preaching. "Preaching. This is our heritage," says Dr. Marsh. "Evangelistic preaching. Prophetic preaching."

In the episcopal address at the opening of the 1964 convention, Methodists heard evangelistic, prophetic preaching by one of the masters. "We do not share the current pessimism which speaks of a 'post-Protestant era,'" declared Los Angeles' Bishop Kennedy emphatically. "Let the Methodist Church proclaim that so far as it is concerned, we are not post-anything, and the best is yet to be." ♦

The Baptists

—Robert de Gast

The signs are many. . . .

A New Sophistication

Crosses, Choral Responses, Pastor's Robes, Urbanization: These Are Signs of Change in a Huge, Varied Faith

ATLANTIC CITY.

A NEW sophistication is beginning to filter through the Baptist movement.

The new breed of Baptist shuns the "hell-fire-and-brimstone" approach, preferring a more dignified style of preaching. He studies the message of the Bible instead of merely memorizing its verses. If he takes to the sawdust trail, he forsakes the "here today, gone tomorrow" tradition for a program of intensive preparation and follow-up.

"Country preachers" still predominate in the Baptist movement. But Baptist ministers, like the people they minister to, are becoming more attuned to urban society. In May 1964, Baptist ministers and laymen from all over the nation and Baptist missionaries from all over the world converged on Atlantic City to commemorate 150 years of organized Baptist work in North America. They represented more than 20,000,000 Baptists — one-third of America's Protestants and one-fifth of the nation's church members of all faiths.

The Baptist Jubilee symbolized the growing awareness in diverse Baptist groups of the theology and heritage they share. Equally symbolic, and perhaps more significant for the future of the Baptist movement, the Southern Baptist Convention and the American Baptist Convention held concurrent pre-jubilee annual meetings in Convention Hall here. Not since 1936 had the Southern Baptists and their Northern brethren met under the same roof at the same time.

True, few believe the nation's 10,400,000 Southern Baptists and 1,500,000 American Baptists will merge in the next decade, if indeed in the next century. But merger advocates in the two groups held unofficial discussions for the third year in a row, and here and there the casual boardwalk stroller would spot a lapel badge proclaiming "Baptist Unity: I'm For It."

True, the Southern Baptists again elected a "conservative" pastor—the Rev. Wayne Dehoney, of Jackson, Tennessee—as their new president. But the Rev. Theodore F. Adams of Richmond, Virginia, an advocate of more dignified worship and spiritual unity among Christians, survived the balloting until the runoff and then lost by a mere four-to-three margin.

True, the Southern Baptists refused by a close vote to affiliate with a proposed North American Baptist Fellowship that had been warmly endorsed by most other Baptist groups. But Southern Baptist leaders, surprised by the action, attributed it to traditional Southern Baptist suspicion of merger moves and confessed they had done little in advance to allay these fears.

Baptists in America already cooperate in the Baptist World Alliance, a loose-knit body formed in 1905 to discuss the great themes and problems of the Baptist community. The most influential Baptist denominations all support the Baptist Joint Committee on Public Affairs, which vigorously defends the Baptist principle of church-state separation on Capitol Hill.

That Baptists co-exist even to this degree is, to outsiders, more than mildly surprising. For Baptists are a diverse people with diverse beliefs.

The Baptist movement embraces Nelson Rockefeller and Martin Luther King. It embraces Mississippi's Ross Barnett.

It has produced a Billy Graham to ignite the spark of conviction in the hearts of hundreds of thousands. It has produced a Walter

The Baptist look of tomorrow: The city church serving city needs.

Rauschenbusch, a turn-of-the-century prophet of the "social gospel," to tell Christians the way to act on their conviction is to immerse themselves in social reforms.

A Baptist church may be as fashionable as First Baptist in Memphis, with its society weddings, or as homespun as Salem-Seminole Baptist of Donalsonville, Georgia, with its rattlesnake hunts. It may be as liturgy-conscious as Riverside Church in New York (operated with the United Church of Christ) or as informal as First Baptist of Brownsville, Texas. It may be as huge as 12,900-member First Baptist of Dallas or as tiny as one-room Okfuscee Baptist in McIntosh County, Oklahoma.

Amble past a Baptist church on a Sunday morning. Perhaps you'll hear *The Old Rugged Cross,* sung with great enthusiasm by a congregation very much off key. Or you might hear Handel's *Largo* or an aria by Bach.

Step into the classroom of a Baptist seminary. Students may be debating the "demythologizing" theology of Rudolph Bultmann and the "ground of all being" theories of Paul Tillich. Or they may be listening to a lecture defending the literal meaning of the "Book of Revelation."

Millions of Baptists oppose any association with the National Council of Churches or the World Council of Churches, fearing that participation might dilute Baptist theology or dampen the traditional Baptist evangelistic fervor. Many Baptists, in fact, are convinced the National Council is heavily infiltrated by Communists. Yet an American Baptist, the Rev. R. H. Edwin Espy, is general secretary of the National Council.

Despite the diversity and despite the contradictions, Baptists the nation over agree they are entering a new age.

For the 7,000,000 members of Negro Baptist denominations, the new age represents little more than an awareness by their leaders of the importance of a seminary education. American Baptists, at the other extreme, see it as a challenge to speak boldly and to act with a daring not usually seen in an "established" church. In

—Godsey-Monkmeyer

Baptist roots, however, are in rural churches that have served their people well for generations. The Sycamore Log Church, above, built for a total cost of $18, is staffed by visiting preachers.

the South the transformation from an agrarian to an urban society is producing the "new" Southern Baptist.

For most Southern Baptist preachers, the new age means little more than an acknowledgment that times are changing. The Rev. K. Owen White of Houston, retiring president of the Southern Baptists, sipped a Coke behind the Convention Hall stage here and said he sees "a degree of sophistication and maturity among Baptists that is evidence that we're moving forward and trying to keep up with the world we're living in." But the Rev. Dr. White, a self-styled "conservative, Bible-believing Baptist," warned that "if we become too sophisticated, too intent on conforming to modern thought patterns, an element of coolness will dampen the fires of evangelism."

Thundered the Rev. W. A. Criswell of Dallas at the Southern Baptist Pastors' Conference here: "The land is becoming more paganized." The only answer, he said, is "every preacher in every pulpit on fire for God." The Rev. Enoch C. Brown of Columbia, South Carolina, urged Southern Baptist preachers to "point the way to Christ not by social and economic reform but through lives made new in Christ."

Such convictions still prevail in the overwhelming majority of Southern Baptist churches. But they are beginning to be challenged.

"A whole new breed of Southern Baptist pastors is pushing up through the ranks," declares W. C. Fields, public relations secretary of the Southern Baptist Convention. "They're not really visible yet to the rank and file because they're assistant pastors in large city churches or just getting started in churches in medium-sized towns. But they're there."

They're there because the six Southern Baptist seminaries are producing a graduate quite different from the graduate of 25 years ago. He, like most clergymen, is becoming more tolerant of other faiths, better grounded in his own. He tends to be more impatient than longtime pastors to "solve" the racial problem, as his predecessor of a generation ago tended to be impatient to "solve" the problem of war and peace.

For the first time, more Southern Baptist seminary students are coming from an urban rather than a rural background. What's more, fewer and fewer are graduates of Southern Baptist colleges and universities. The inevitable result: A greater respect for other faiths.

"You can't really be violently anti-Catholic if you went to a state university," says the Rev. Duke McCall, president of Southern Baptist Theological Seminary in Louisville. "You knew Catholics, and they were fine people. You probably even belonged to clubs or fraternities with them."

Baptist seminary students today are digging into new subjects, and doing it in new ways. Baptist seminaries have pioneered in the field of pastoral psychology; Southern Baptist Seminary's Prof. Wayne Oates ranks among the foremost in the field today. They're strengthening course work in Biblical archeology, music, and many other subjects.

Debating Develops

Just as important, they're encouraging students to think things through themselves rather than to learn by rote. In what the Rev. Dr. McCall terms "the most exciting development" he has seen in seminary education, students at Southern Baptist in Louisville have begun holding spontaneous debates on their own volition. Other students and even professors listen and sometimes enter the debate themselves.

The Rev. Dr. McCall denies that there has been any perceptible shift in the theology taught in Southern Baptist schools. But it's taught in different terms, he says.

"When I went to seminary, 'Biblical emphasis' meant studying Greek words in the New Testament," he says. "Now you don't ask so much, 'What is the root meaning of a certain word?' but 'What is the author saying?' "

Gone are the days—in seminaries, anyway—of the "proof text," the practice of quoting one verse and then another and ignoring the fact that they're being quoted out of context. Instead, seminary students learn the classic parody of the proof-text practice: "And Judas went out and hanged himself. . . . go thou and do likewise. . . . and that which thou doest, do quickly."

Just as Southern Baptists in the past have been accused of succumbing all too frequently to the temptations of the "proof text," so have they been charged with caring more for statistics than for souls. They're trying to remove this stigma, too.

"A million more in '54," proclaimed a Southern Baptist slogan a decade ago that would be out of fashion today. Still, there's some playing of the numbers game. The Foreign Mission Board, enthused over its success in tripling the number of its missionaries in the past 16 years, called here for a tripling in the number again by 1980. Complained Prof. Kenneth Chaffin of Southwestern Baptist Theological Seminary in Fort Worth: "We have become a denomination of midwives, so concerned with the birth of new Christians that we have forgotten about helping our church members to grow and mature spiritually."

A New Evangelism

Professor Chaffin exaggerates, but the tendency today is to agree with the point he makes. "There'll always be a place for the tent and brush arbor," contends the Rev. James L. Sullivan, executive secretary of the Southern Baptist Sunday School Board. "But the evangelism we're emphasizing now is a more thorough evangelism, and I think a more intelligent one."

It stresses the individual "witness" by ministers and teachers who have the respect of the person they're trying to convert. Unlike the old-time evangelist who moved on to the next town, they follow up the "conversion" experience in succeeding months and years.

Baptist officials admit the new approach contributes to the declining rate of Southern Baptist growth (19 per cent in the past seven years against 29 per cent between 1949 and 1956). But they say they have fewer "dropouts," and they're confident a more dedicated membership will soon pay off in a faster growth rate.

Southern Baptist officials believe their members are not only more dedicated, but also—as educational levels rise—more demanding intellectually. And they say members of their urban churches insist now on less impromptu preaching "from the heart" and more preaching from the heart and mind.

Crosses are coming into vogue. "Please," pleads one Southern Baptist, "let's take the weathervane off the church and put a cross on it. We don't want the church to be a weathervane of popular trends." Choral responses are becoming more popular; so are pastor's robes.

The desire for more dignified worship is spreading through other Baptist groups. "We're becoming more and more aware that we need to meet God in our worship service, not just have a chatty time of it," says the Rev. Herbert Gezork, president of American Baptist-affiliated Andover-Newton Theological School in Massachusetts. The Rev. Dr. Gezork sees evidence in his own church of the new trends in worship: Until its renovation several years ago, it followed the old Baptist tradition of having simply a pulpit in the middle of the chapel; now it has the pulpit on one side, the lectern on the other,

A rarity one decade ago, not uncommon now: A Baptist pastor in robes.

and a communion table and a hanging cross in the middle.

American Baptists in 1964 introduced a refreshing format for their convention. They tapped outspoken experts to write papers on race, peace, and Christian unity, then chose equally frank experts to rebut them; in the afternoon, delegates gathered in smaller forums to sound off on the issues.

The technique, say the American Baptists, is in the best tradition of the Baptist insistence on free expression. But the Rev. Edwin H. Tuller, their executive secretary, admits they couldn't have tried it a few years ago. "We'd have split right down the middle if we had done it in the '40s," he says.

Mission to America

American Baptists are pioneering in mission concepts as in convention formats. Not only do they send American missionaries abroad; they're beginning to bring foreign "missionaries" to the United States. A Burmese couple recently spent several months "witnessing for Christ" in Massachusetts churches, and a Filipino couple is there now. A South Indian group is going to Ohio with a similar assignment. "These days, you just can't talk about the little guy in the African jungle who's dying without Christ," declares one American Baptist. "You've got to talk about the smug, lethargic Christian in America who's dying without knowing what it's like in the other half of the world."

It was missionary work that first brought Baptist churches in the United States together in 1814. En route to Burma, three Congregational missionaries converted to the Baptist faith. But the Baptists had no national organization that could support missionaries, only loose regional associations. One of the three Burma-bound missionaries returned to the United States to stir up support for a national group. He succeeded, and soon obtained missionary support for his associates in Burma.

Missionary activity has helped sustain, perhaps even dominated the Baptist movement for the past 150 years. But for more than 300 years, Baptists have shared common theological roots and Biblical insights.

Baptists believe that a direct fellowship exists between God and man. "God controls the universe; He intervenes in human affairs," says the Rev. Dr. McCall. Man is a response to God, and is responsible to Him.

Baptists contend that no institution—no church, no state—comes between God and man. "If it did, then a priesthood would be in order," says the Rev. C. Emanuel Carlson, executive director of the Baptist Joint Committee on Public Affairs. "But the Baptist, the individual, has to come to God, confess his sins, experience his own salvation. Then he goes out and organizes the church."

Out of this concept flow the Baptist doctrines of salvation, church organization, and religious freedom.

Salvation comes when an individual, of his free will, confesses his sins and declares his faith in God.

Baptism for Adults

An infant obviously can't experience this kind of conversion. So Baptists insist that only responsible persons who have made a personal commitment to Christ be baptized. Baptism, which Baptists perform by immersing the person in water in line with what they consider the true New Testament tradition, is the graphic portrayal of the person's commitment and "new life."

Many Baptist preachers expound the "once saved—always saved" concept from the pulpit. Prof. Wayne E. Ward of Southern Baptist Theological Seminary criticizes this approach. "Like a rocket leaving the launching pad, (they believe) if they can muster up enough faith to blast off, the momentum of the initial experience will carry them through to Heaven," he says. "What these people do not realize is that the Christian life is a powered flight all the way. It is not a matter of one big bang and you are in orbit."

The direct God-to-man relationship leads also to the Baptist insistence on the autonomy of the local church. No one outside the local church exercises any control over its affairs. Churches "cooperate with" the Southern Baptist Convention, but they're not bound by its decisions. They send "messengers," not delegates, to their annual conventions. No one, not even the national president, speaks for the local church or for the Southern Baptist Convention as a whole.

Nor is religious liberty an accidental appendage of Baptist doctrine. For Baptists, re-

Nowhere is the diversity within the Baptist faith—of mood and of belief—better illustrated than in its members. Above, Gov. and Mrs. Nelson Rockefeller of New York. Below, ex-Gov. Ross Barnett of Mississippi.

ligious liberty is not something "in which we also believe" but something "in which we inherently believe."

Painful though it may be, most scripture-conscious, God-fearing Baptists support recent Supreme Court decisions on prayers and Bible readings in public schools. As advocates of a strict separation of church and state, they agree government should refrain from formulating or promoting devotional exercises in schools.

They agree, too, in principle on the danger of accepting Federal aid for Baptist schools, hospitals, and other institutions. But by the end of 1963, 22 Baptist hospitals occupied facilities built in part with Hill-Burton Act funds. And after President Johnson signed the $1.2 billion aid-to-education bill, many Baptist educators were starting to study the route to the White House door.

In the best traditions of Roger Williams, the Baptist apostle of religious liberty and founder of Providence, Rhode Island, the 1964-65 president of the Southern Baptist Pastors' Conference warns of the danger institutions that accept Federal aid face. "Some day the White House will feed them," scoffs the Rev. Jess C. Moody of West Palm Beach, Florida, "then make them chop wood for their new master."

Freedom aside, most Baptists hold "conservative" theological views. "Extreme liberals in

Baptists have their "conservative" and "liberal" wings, too. The Rev. Wayne Dehoney, above, president of the Southern Baptist Convention, is comparatively "conservative." The Rev. Duke McCall, right, rallies "liberals."

the Southern Baptist Convention would be called conservative within the larger context of the Christian community," says the Rev. Dr. McCall of Louisville. The same is true in the Negro Baptist conventions.

Almost to a man, Baptists hold that the Bible represents the unique, divine revelation of the word of God. Theological arguments rage not over the divine revelation of the Bible, but over the intent of the divinely inspired authors.

The fundamentalist insists on accepting every story recorded in the Bible as a historical event, every prophecy as a literal prediction.

But the Rev. Dr. McCall, like other comparatively "liberal" Southern Baptists, looks at the writer's style and other clues in search of the author's intent. Books of the Bible written as poetry, he contends, should be read differently from the Ten Commandments.

The story of the Good Samaritan is almost universally considered an imaginary story, a story Jesus concocted to illustrate a point. The story of Jesus' Resurrection is quite different; the authors of the New Testament obviously intended that it be considered true. "I will use the word heretic if you deny the Resurrection," says the Rev. Dr. McCall. "For you're now reserving to yourself the right to decide what parts of the Bible are true. You're saying that whatever you choose to believe is true, no matter what the writers believed."

Baptists divide not so much over theology as over more practical matters. Matters such as race and cooperation with other Christians.

"I feel much closer to Roman Catholic tradition than to some of the more liberal Protestants," declared the Rev. Billy Graham, as the evangelist emerged from a 45-minute chat with Richard Cardinal Cushing of Boston in October 1964. Yet the Rev. G. Earl Guinn, president of Louisiana College, the same year termed "Communism, Catholicism, and secularism" the primary threats to freedom of religion, and the Rev. Mr. Moody of West Palm Beach labeled the unity movement "a retirement center for superannuated, drowsy, non-relevant denominations."

In the racial area the American Baptists, often accused of having spoken softly and carried a little stick in the civil-rights struggle, have organized Baptist Action for Racial Brotherhood (BARB) to prick the conscience of their members on racial equality. They have taken in several Southern Baptist pastors forced out of their pulpits in the South for racial stands. In November 1963 they installed a professor at Andover-Newton *in absentia* as he sat in a North Carolina jail for participation in a racial demonstration. And at their Atlantic City meeting they urged participation in nonviolent direct action where necessary and pointedly awarded the first Edwin T. Dahlberg Peace Award to Martin Luther King.

On the floor below, however, the Southern Baptists rejected a pledge to support "laws designed to guarantee the legal rights of Negroes" and refused to commend the few Southern Baptist churches that have opened their doors to Negro worshipers and members. Instead, they adopted a milder resolution sponsored by a coalition of messengers from Alabama, Mississippi, and Louisiana that urged Southern Baptists to work for "a peaceful Christian solution" to racial problems.

Passage of the Civil Rights Act did bring calls for compliance from prominent Southern Baptist voices. The Rev. Wayne Dehoney, president of the Southern Baptists, told his Jackson, Tennessee, congregation that "as Christian citizens, we are charged by the word of God to give voluntary, peaceful obedience to every letter of this law." E. S. James, of Dallas, editor of the influential Baptist Standard, said that if Southern Baptists failed to take the lead in adhering to the law, "this may be their last chance to be the determining voice of the Southland."

The racial issue, the chief issue that caused the split between Southern and Northern Baptists in 1845, remains the biggest barrier to eventual reunion. But regionalism is eroding. Southern Baptists, with the recent formation of a church in Vermont, now operate in all 50 states. American Baptists are following industry and retired people into the South. "It may be that we'll see a new alignment in the Baptist family some day soon," asserts the American Baptists' Dr. Tuller. "The issues, as I see them, would be evangelism, cooperative Christianity, and race."

Perhaps so. But any realignment would be painful. And it just might deprive the struggling Baptist churches in the small towns and rural areas of the type of leadership they're finally in sight of getting. ♦

The Lutherans

A Lutheran classroom. A boy, enraptured.

Imagination in School and Policy

Jazz, Visual Aids, the Drawing Board—Lutherans Use Them All to Modernize the Christian Message

NEW YORK CITY.

TO MANY, "Christian education" means Sunday School. And "Sunday School," in the memories of millions of adults, means an hour of prime play time preempted by Bible stories with moral punchlines.

Look again. Churchmen now are marshaling psychology, science, and modern art to devise new approaches to Christian education. Some of the most imaginative work in the field is being done by Lutherans, who pride themselves on their historic emphasis on education.

The Lutheran Church in America (LCA), the largest of the nation's Lutheran bodies, in the fall of 1964 introduced a spire-to-home, cradle-to-grave curriculum. At the same time the American Lutheran Church (ALC), almost as large as the LCA, introduced the first segment of a similar curriculum that will be offered in ALC parishes at all age levels by 1970.

The inner vitality of Lutheranism in America, so evident in the ambitious new curricula, has long been apparent in other areas. Lutheranism has, for example, produced an impressive group of young theologians. Jaroslav Pelikan and George Lindbeck of Yale Divinity School, Joseph Sittler and Martin Marty of the University of Chicago Divinity School, Warren Quanbeck of Luther Theological Seminary in St. Paul—these and other Lutheran thinkers have influenced Catholics as well as Protestants in the United States.

The young theologians differ on details, but they agree on several important strands of thought. They base their arguments on scripture but go beyond the literalism fashionable in earlier days. They articulate the "post-Protestant" view of religion in America, which emphasizes recognition of all faiths. They espouse the current interfaith interest in Christian unity.

Wrote Professor Pelikan in Christian Century: "Whatever is worth salvaging from the Lutheran tradition ought to be tough enough to survive in an interdenominational milieu. We have nothing to lose but our isolation."

Prodded by their theologians and led by their experts on worship, Lutherans have played an important role in the liturgical renewal that is spreading through Christianity.

In this "perpetual quest to express 'God loves you,'" as one Lutheran describes the interest in liturgy, Lutherans criticize themselves vigorously at times. Professor Pelikan, for example, has scoffed at the music heard in some Lutheran churches: "Lutherans have sometimes exchanged their birthright of hymnody for a mess of Gospel songs."

But a revised service of worship introduced in the late 1950s by several denominations that later united to form two church bodies, the ALC (formed in 1961) and the LCA (1963), has been accepted with surprisingly little resistance. More than 2,200,000 new hymnals containing the revised service have been sold to churches with an adult membership of 3,900,000. The revised Lutheran service parallels changes in the new English-language Mass of the Roman Catholic Church.

Liturgical scholars continue to search for new evidence that will help inject the spirit of the early Christian church into the Lutheran liturgy. A Lutheran Society for Worship, Music, and the Arts promotes cultural creativity within the church. "The society teetered on the edge of the esoteric for a while," says a prominent

—The Lutheran

Jazz is a prescribed course of study for the Rev. John Gensel (left), pastor of New York City's Evangelical Lutheran Church of the Advent. His congregation is filled with jazz musicians. Above, they accompany him at a service.

Lutheran pastor interested in the arts, "but it's on solid ground now."

Lutherans, like most other large faiths, are experimenting with new ways to reach people. A Manhattan pastor spends his evenings and early mornings with jazz musicians in night spots and sponsors jazz liturgies in his sanctuary. An Iowa pastor in 1964 began holding outdoor "drive-in" services at a local drive-in theater to combat summer apathy toward religion. Annual seminars for Lutherans in high Government positions, which started in 1959, have proved one of the most successful forms of special ministry to Government personnel.

For 65 years the Lutheran Church—Missouri Synod, the third of the Lutheran "big three," has ministered to the deaf through sign language and other means; it now has more than 250 congregations and preaching stations for the deaf and supports schools for the deaf in Detroit and on Long Island. In addition, the Missouri Synod operates a parochial school system second only to the Roman Catholic system in size in the United States. Missouri Synod elementary schools, which now have nearly 160,000 pupils, more than doubled in the decade and a half after World War II; the number of schools has leveled off since 1962, partly because an upgrading of teacher standards has required higher expenditures for salaries.

"Inner-city" work, aimed at improving the lot of unfortunates in the cities, is commanding more and more attention among Lutherans. Since the late 1950s, Lutheran subsidies to downtown parishes have climbed from next to nothing to $2,000,000 a year. Lutherans are cooperating in Chicago's new Urban Training Center for Christian Mission. Lutheran studies of inner-city problems and what Lutherans can do to alleviate them have been conducted or are being planned in Milwaukee, Pittsburgh, Chicago, Detroit, and Washington, D. C.

Emphasis on Parish

Unlike some denominations, Lutherans keep their ministry parish-centered. They estimate they will start between 6 and 10 new congregations in inner-city situations in 1965; where they work in existing situations, they work on local parish staffs. At the First Lutheran Church in Pittsburgh's "Golden Triangle," for example, a full-time staff counselor conducts his own program rather than referring persons to social agencies of the church or to local secular agencies.

"The parish-centered ministry fits the norm of the Lutheran approach," explains the Rev. Franklin Clark Fry, president of the LCA and former president of the Lutheran World Federation. "*Seelsorge.* The care of souls. The duty of the church is to care for souls, to nurture them, to edify them, to instruct them."

The Rev. Dr. Fry, in prestige the reigning patriarch of Protestantism, rests an elbow on the desk of his third-floor office in the old J. P. Morgan mansion on Madison Avenue. "We work through the congregation not because it has any sacredness in itself but because it's an agency for the true preaching of the Word and the right administration of the sacraments."

Just as the parish approach governs Lutheran activity in inner-city work, it guides Lutheran conduct in social action. Lutherans play down the national proclamation and play up the local pastor.

Eschewing the scattershot approach to social issues, Lutheran bodies tend to make thorough studies on a few selected topics. A statement on atomic testing, for example, was debated for several days at a Lutheran convention in 1960. The LCA acted on only three social action statements at its July 1964 convention (on race relations, religious exercises in public schools, and marriage and the family), but it spent an unusually long time—eight hours—debating the race relations statement.

"It's not the function of the church to deal with every last issue that comes down the pike," declares the Rev. Harold Haas, executive secretary of the LCA's board of social ministry. Yet the Rev. Dr. Haas believes the church can no longer view itself as an ecclesiastical community involved in social issues only to the degree that it encourages its members to involve themselves individually.

"We live in a political age," he says. "One of the dilemmas of the church today is that political issues are moral issues. Many of the things the church has traditionally been concerned with—poverty, race—have moved into the political arena."

Heretics and Catholics

Lutherans occupy a curious position in the religious spectrum. Catholics traditionally have viewed them scornfully as followers of a Sixteenth Century "heretic," Martin Luther. Protestants have regarded them with equal suspicion for being too "Catholic" in their liturgy and vestments.

Professor Pelikan of Yale subtitled his book *Obedient Rebels, Catholic Substance and Protestant Principle.* Lutherans, he declares in the book, cherish the "substance" of the Catholic faith while insisting on the Protestant "principle" that everything be judged by the Word of God as spoken through Christ. Luther contended that the Bible, not the Roman Catholic Church or its priests, had final authority over a person's conscience. But this was not to mean that Lutherans should worship the Bible. "The Bible is the manger in which the Christ Child lies," said Luther. "And we do not worship the manger; we worship the Christ!"

Unlike the Episcopalians and most other Protestant churches, the Lutherans do not be-

Dr. Franklin Clark Fry, president of the Lutheran Church in America, and a national Protestant leader: "The duty of the church is to care for souls. . . ."

lieve in allowing a wide divergence of doctrinal belief. Like Roman Catholics, they espouse the concept of *consensus doctrina,* under which doctrine widely agreed upon by the theologians and church leaders is to be adhered to. Their differences with Catholicism arise over doctrine itself. Three examples: Their belief that a person can be freed from the penalty of sin by faith alone; their conviction that the Lord revealed Himself in the Bible and not in the Bible plus later church tradition; their acceptance of only two sacraments, or rites ordained by Jesus (baptism and the Lord's Supper) instead of the seven recognized by Catholics.

All Lutherans consider themselves "evangelical," in the sense that they believe God "saves" men through faith in Christ. They have a tradition of being "evangelistic" too, of aggressively preaching the gospel.

Through a new radio station in Ethiopia the 73,000,000-member world Lutheran movement, the world's largest Protestant group, can reach more people in a half-hour than the Apostle Paul reached during his entire ministry. In the United States, Luther Film Productions a decade ago produced a film, *Martin Luther,* that proved so popular it required 3,000 prints and is still being shown.

The United States' three largest Lutheran bodies, almost equal in membership, have 95 per cent of the nation's 8,400,000 Lutherans. The Missouri Synod is the most evangelistic of the three bodies; for six years in a row, it has had the largest percentage gain in membership.

By ecumenical standards, the Rev. Dr. Fry's LCA is the most liberal of the three denominations; it belongs to both the World Council of Churches and the National Council of Churches, and he is chairman of the World Council's central committee. The ALC belongs to the World Council but not the National Council. The Missouri Synod belongs to neither.

Maturation

Traditionally suspicious of unity movements, the Missouri Synod has long taken the position that it must not enter co-operative bodies unless the other denominations agree completely with it on all doctrinal matters. But the Missouri Synod is undergoing what the Roman Catholics term an *aggiornamento,* a bringing-up-to-date of the church. Its members are beginning to learn, says one Missouri Synod theologian, that "expressing a scriptural truth in a different way is not necessarily heretical."

Some Missouri Synod education officials regret privately that their denomination did not work with the LCA or the ALC, or both, in the development of the new Christian education curricula. In the late 1950s the antecedent denominations to the LCA and the ALC explored together a "long-range plan" for Christian education. They did not continue working together after the mergers, largely because ALC leaders believed they would in effect be merging the boards of parish education of the two new denominations.

The concepts of Christian education in the new curricula, however, proved quite similar. "Our paths have been parallel," says the Rev. C. Richard Evenson, director of parish education of the ALC. "We walked part of the path together, then went our own ways. Now we're

Lutherans demonstrate in behalf of civil rights in Washington, D.C.

starting to get back on the same path by meeting now and then to explore new ideas."

To get a wide-angle view of current trends in Christian education, examine the new curriculum of the LCA.

Sunday School remains the chief vehicle—the "nuclear school," in LCA parlance—for instilling Christian beliefs. Church camps, vacation church schools, and catechism classes for children about to become confirmed members supplement the Sunday sessions.

The LCA is plowing untilled land in two fields that have long resisted Christian education. To entice adults and senior high students to broaden their Christian perspective, the LCA is trying church-sponsored courses in religion, week-end study conferences, and guided reading programs. To help parents impart Christian education in the home, which Lutherans consider especially important in the light of the Supreme Court decisions on prayer and Bible reading in public schools, the denomination is conducting classes for parents in churches.

Careful Planning

Eight years of planning and $1,500,000 in research and development have resulted in a curriculum with no unplanned repetition or overlapping. What the child or adult learns at home, at camp, or in catechism class reinforces but does not duplicate what he learns on Sundays.

In line with modern educational techniques, the curriculum emphasizes the dynamic rather than the static. "Christian maturity is not a fixed point at which one may arrive and stop," says the Rev. W. Kent Gilbert, executive secretary of the LCA's board of parish education. "For the Christian there is always a tension between being and becoming."

Instead of studying rigid subjects, says the Rev. Dr. Gilbert, Lutheran children are exposed to many topics gradually. The Christian attitude toward race relations, for example, is introduced subtly in the third-grade course, "Fellow Workers for God," rather than abruptly as a separate unit at, say, the junior high level. Television introduces children to the "tensions of society" early, reasons the Rev. Dr. Gilbert's staff; churches must help create healthy attitudes toward them at an equally early age.

Bible studies, from the fifth grade through the adult level, stress the importance of modern scholarship in providing new insights into the Bible. "We want people to see the Bible as a variety of kinds of literature—that God is speaking through it, it's true, but that not everything in it was intended to be understood in literal fashion," says the Rev. Dr. Gilbert.

Experimental teaching of an adult course, "The Mighty Acts of God," has already proved the value of emphasizing scriptural scholarship. "People had gotten the impression that they had to park their intelligence outside the church," the Rev. Dr. Gilbert recalls. "They suddenly breathed a sigh of relief to learn that this or that isn't what the church believes either."

To illustrate the books used by students, the LCA commissioned 50 artists at a cost of more than $100,000. To illustrate teachers' handbooks, it took a different approach; it searched for drawings done by children of the age level being taught.

Skeptics wonder whether the Lutheran curriculum will prove more successful than the curricula introduced by the Episcopalians, Presbyterians, and Congregationalists in recent years, or by the Methodists at the nursery-through-sixth-grade levels in September 1964. "It's hard to distinguish between how much is really 'new' in these things and how much is just pretty covers," warns a veteran executive of another denomination.

Sunday session attendance picked up an average of only 1 per cent in 62 LCA congregations field-tested for the new program over a three-year period. The sharpest increase occurred at the level of most serious concern—senior high school, up 12 per cent—but the low initial attendance there makes any increase look good in percentage terms.

Refine and Rework

Attendance, of course, is not the only basis for judging the value of a new approach to Christian education. From weekly suggestions from field-tested congregations, planners continually refined the curriculum in their search for the most effective content and methods.

The elaborate field-test programs used by both the LCA and the ALC may prove the Lutherans' most significant contribution to the future shape of Christian education. Early in their research, LCA planners ran an analysis of every sixth LCA congregation in terms of

Through the eyes of a child: Lutheran youngsters draw a pastor, left, "Paul Preaching on a Hill," above.

size, members' occupations, environment (urban-surburban-rural), and so on. From these 1,000 churches they chose 62 that most accurately represented the types of congregations in the LCA.

Field-test editions of books were illustrated, printed, and bound, then completely revised and published again. The field testing affected major concepts as well as details; the amount of individual homework was reduced, for example, because teachers reported that homework assignments were being neglected.

Extensive field-testing, a dynamic curriculum, "nuclear" Sunday schools with additional courses throughout the week—these are part of the legacy in Christian education that Lutherans of this generation are creating. That it is a rich legacy is not surprising.

For Lutherans like to recall that it was a university professor and ordained priest, Martin Luther, who inspired the Protestant Reformation by nailing his 95 theses to a church door in Wittenberg, Germany, that served as a sort of university bulletin board. "The Lutheran Church," goes an old Lutheran saying, "was born in a university." ♦

The Presbyterians

A new era, when church and society will reach out to each other.

Prophets of a New Era

One Bold Step After Another Puts the Presbyterians In Forefront of Churches Working with Social Problems

DES MOINES.

FOR Christians to argue that religious exercises—Bible readings, for example, or prescribed prayers—have no place in the public schools seems self-defeating to some, almost heretical to others.

For Christians to say, as well, that their tax-exempt churches should make voluntary contributions to their communities strikes many as strictly suicidal.

Yet the United Presbyterian Church, the nation's fifth-largest Protestant denomination with more than 3,200,000 members, has taken just such positions. By their avant-garde stance on these and other important issues, the Presbyterians have become widely regarded as prophets of a new era in American religion.

The new era would be an era of direct action by the churches in such social areas as race relations and poverty. It would be an era of strenuous efforts toward Christian unity. Most dramatic of all, it would be an era when the church would scrape away special privileges that tend to corrode its most precious commodity, its sense of spiritual mission.

To some degree, of course, the new era has already begun. Where it has, Presbyterians almost invariably have helped lead the way.

At their May 1963 general assembly at the Veterans Memorial Auditorium here, the United Presbyterians became the first large Protestant denomination to speak as a body against devotional services in public schools. Their statement helped reduce a whiplash of public anger against a Supreme Court decision less than a month later that declared these exercises unconstitutional. Over the next several months other large Protestant, Catholic, and Jewish bodies, as well as hundreds of prominent churchmen, made similar statements; many congressmen described these statements as the decisive factor in the House of Representatives' refusal to approve a prayer amendment to the Constitution in early 1964.

At the Des Moines general assembly, too, the United Presbyterians broke new ground on the tax-exemption question. They voted to seek repeal of the Federal exemption on profits of church-owned businesses not directly related to the church's mission, and they urged local churches to make token payments to local governments for such services as police and fire protection. The move inspired no Presbyterian stampede on tax collectors' offices. But at least one church, Central Presbyterian in Des Moines, decided to make a token payment in lieu of taxes to its city government for municipal services; in 1964 Central Presbyterian, which would pay $4,100 in city taxes were it not tax-exempt, paid the city $500.

In 1964 the United Presbyterians placed their weight behind a proposed solution to the perennial controversy over public aid to parochial schools; again they were the first major denomination to support a concept many churchmen consider a foretaste of the future. This time the concept was the "shared-time" plan for schools, under which parochial and private school children would receive some instruction in the public schools.

Presbyterians have long supported "cooperative Christianity." The Rev. Eugene Carson Blake, stated clerk of the United Presbyterian Church (largely Northern Presbyterians), was president of the National Council of Churches from 1954 to 1957, and the Presbyterian Church in the U.S. (Southern Presbyterians) is the only predominantly Southern white denomination in the National Council.

Presbyterians have stumbled several times in their efforts to reunite their own church, torn apart by the Civil War, but merger within the next 10 or 20 years is considered a definite possibility. The predominantly Northern branch of Presbyterianism was studying a possible merger with the Episcopalians as early as 30 years ago, and more recently it has been exploring common ground with Lutherans. Finally, the Rev. Dr. Blake struck the first spark that led to the current discussions of a possible merger of six large Protestant denominations.

Like most churchmen, Presbyterians have been working quietly for decades to help alleviate the problems of the poor. When the United Mine Workers of America announced that mounting deficits were forcing it to close 10 hospitals in the Appalachian Mountains, however, the United Presbyterians acted promptly to keep them open—months before "poverty" became a breakfast table byword and a political issue. Many of the patients served each year by the hospitals could not have received hospital care had not the Presbyterians, with Federal financial aid, purchased the hospitals.

Disobedience, Yes

As early as 1960, the United Presbyterians were taking a strong position in favor of civil disobedience on racial matters: "Some laws and customs requiring racial discrimination are, in our judgment, such serious violations of the law of God as to justify peaceable and orderly disobedience or disregard of these laws."

Three years later, as churchmen in many denominations and in many regions of the country were beginning to feel the sting of conscience for inaction on civil rights, the United Presbyterians formed one of the first denominational commissions on religion and race. Supplied with $500,000 and a wide mandate, the commission began working on such matters as voter registration, neighborhood desegregation, and equal job opportunities.

The Presbyterian fervor for racial integration continued undiminished despite popular talk of a "white backlash." At their May 1964 general assembly, United Presbyterians took a step unprecedented in Protestantism by electing a Negro minister from New York City, the Rev. Edler G. Hawkins, as moderator—nominally the highest position in the church. Good-natured critics in other churches promptly tagged them "V.I.P.'s"—"Very Integrated Presbyterians."

The shift in United Presbyterian emphasis in recent years has not received unanimous acclaim within the church. The Rev. Robert H. Stephens, retiring chairman of the church's evangelism commission, in 1964 noted that the church's annual membership growth in percentage terms had slipped from more than 3 per cent in 1954 to less than 1 per cent in 1963 and wondered whether it was because the church, having done many good things for people, had possibly "done everything for them except offering them Christ."

Critic Speaks Out

An Idaho physician argued in a letter to Presbyterian Life that "the emphasis given to social and economic issues to the exclusion of the primary mission of the church, i.e., the spreading of the gospel, makes us more of a political organization than a segment of the true church." He expressed a fear that Presbyterians would become merely "clanging cymbals" unless they corrected wrongs first in their own church. "Why not sit-ins in our segregated churches, rather than in business houses?" he asked. "Why not ask our members to share their wealth with the poor, rather than ask the Government to lead the way?"

But an effort to censure the Rev. Dr. Blake at the 1964 general assembly for "openly defying and notoriously violating" Maryland laws during a 1963 demonstration at the segregated Gwynn Oak Amusement Park turned into a tribute. Only four scattered "No's" objected to a commendation of the Rev. Dr. Blake "for his courageous action and witness in the area of race relations."

A few days before, at a breakfast of the activist Presbyterian Interracial Council, the Rev. Dr. Blake had stated his case. "Fellow jailbirds," he had begun audaciously, "the more I think about the wide publicity which I received as a result of my participation in the Baltimore demonstration last year, the more troubled I become about the Church of Jesus Christ. It is tragic that the secular press finds so much news when a Christian does what he says."

Southern Presbyterians, quite naturally,

The Rev. Eugene Carson Blake, highest Presbyterian official, as he stepped into a police patrol wagon in 1963. He was arrested at Gwynn Oak Amusement Park in Maryland for demonstrating against the park's white-only admission policy.

have been less enthusiastic about racial demonstrations. Though they declared their sympathy with the objectives of the March on Washington in August 1963, they refused to support it because they did not consider it the proper province of the church to bless demonstrations.

Still, the Southern Presbyterians repeatedly have condemned discrimination within their 940,000-member church. At their 1964 general assembly, they resisted efforts to have them withdraw from the National Council of Churches because of the National Council's civil-rights activities. In the spring of 1964, nearly 800 influential Southern Presbyterians, including two Mississippi ministers and Gov. Edward T. Breathitt of Kentucky, signed a letter to Senate members urging passage of the Civil Rights Bill. "These men and women have nothing to gain by taking this stand except the freedom which integrity of conscience provides," declared the Rev. John Randolph Taylor of Washington, D.C., who helped obtain the signatures. "Some have much to lose."

Why do Presbyterians present the image of the activist, of the prophet of a new day?

Partly, no doubt, because of imaginative leadership. The United Presbyterians' Dr. Blake, an aggressive guard for Princeton's Tigers in his undergraduate days (Class of '28), thinks with the imagination of a Knute Rockne and acts with the finesse of a Red Grange. Two of the many ideas he has set in motion: A united Protestant church "truly catholic, truly reformed, and truly evangelical," and the voluntary payment of taxes by churches.

The image arises partly, too, from Presbyterian success in enlisting laymen in its work. A Presbyterian atomic scientist on loan from General Electric helped direct their campaign against repeal of a California fair-housing law in 1964. About 40 volunteer laymen—doctors, therapists, teachers, secretaries, business consultants—go abroad each year for tours of service in mission fields of from three months to two years.

Most important, perhaps, the Presbyterian heritage teaches that a dynamic church can reform society. Not that Presbyterians entertain naive hopes of establishing a utopian Kingdom of God on earth. But, as the late philosopher H. Richard Niebuhr noted, some religious traditions flee from society and some leave society alone, while the Calvinist tradition of the Presbyterians holds that religion can transform society.

John Calvin, the Sixteenth Century Frenchman who laid the foundations for Presbyterianism, immersed himself deeply in social and political affairs. He dealt with legal and economic issues as well as religious matters while helping to govern Geneva, his adopted city; he founded the university there; he established democratic governments in both church and state.

In Calvin's theology lay the germ that ultimately destroyed the doctrine of the divine right of kings. He taught that God alone is the sovereign of a man's conscience; with men subject only to God, they cannot be subservient to any other man. To Calvin, salvation was a free gift of God and not a reward for having faith or for doing good works, as in some other traditions. The new dignity Calvin gave to man finished off feudalism and set the spiritual tone for freedom and capitalism.

A city street, an open door.

Calvin's theology leaped to Holland, France, England, Ireland, and Scotland. A century after he lived a group of Scots and Englishmen, sitting in the Westminster Assembly of Divines, resolved to have "no bishop, and no king." This Westminster Assembly, which sat from 1643 to 1648, cleared the way for Cromwell's ousting of the king and the establishment of a commonwealth; it also produced the Westminster Confession of Faith, which became a major doctrinal standard of Scottish, British, and American Presbyterianism.

The United Presbyterians in 1965 will debate a new document, seven years in preparation, that could occupy a place alongside the Westminster Confession. The committee that drafted it proposes a "book of confessions," from the Nicene Creed through the Westminster Confession, the Barmen Declaration, and the new document. The committee sees in the Barmen Declaration, composed by German churchmen in the 1930s against Nazism, a modern precedent for a confession restating the word of God in a new dimension.

The new "confession" would not be a comprehensive theological statement, but would be "a call to reconciliation in a divided world and a divided church, where nations, races, families, and individual lives are torn by strife and enmity." Based upon the Apostle Paul's statement that "God through Christ reconciled us to Himself and gave us the ministry of reconciliation," it would relate this ministry to such questions as poverty, war, and race.

Clear Language

Some of its language would be theological and abstract, some remarkably specific. "When some persons are led across racial lines into the intimacy of courtship and marriage," one draft read at one point, "they should not find themselves therefore rejected but rather supported by the church." Grumbles one opponent of the document: "The whole business of civil rights is the most trivial first step."

Thus, in the proposed "confession," there is evidence of the Presbyterians' dynamic view of the church—a church that redefines its mission in terms of modern needs, a church that believes in attempting to reform society. Further evidence exists in the Presbyterians' positions on tax exemption and school prayers.

Tax-exempt real property in the United States has climbed from 12 per cent of all real property three decades ago to 30 per cent today. Government property ranks first. But churches and other religious groups come next, accounting for one-third of the exempt property.

If this pattern continues, the Rev. Dr. Blake warned in Christianity Today magazine in 1959, it may within a century "present the state with problems of such magnitude that their only solution will be revolutionary expropriation of church properties. . . . The growing wealth and property of the churches was partially responsible for revolutionary expropriations of church property in England in the Sixteenth Century, in France in the Eighteenth Century, in Italy in the Nineteenth Century, and in Mexico, Russia, Czechoslovakia, and Hungary (to name a few examples) in the Twentieth Century." Increasing economic power in churches, he argues, also creates envy and resentment among non-members. What's worse, tax exemption can corrupt the church if the church should mute its criticism of government in order to continue receiving tax privileges.

No one—not even the most ardent foe of tax privileges for churches—believes churches should pay full taxes for property used for worship, religious education, and similar activities central to religion.

True, the churches receive services from the Government they don't pay for. "But how many more drunkards would there be if it weren't for the church?" asks the Rev. C. Emanuel Carlson, executive director of the Baptist Joint Committee on Public Affairs. "How much more juvenile delinquency would you have? How much more gambling? How much more lost time at work?"

The Logic of Exemption

A Roman Catholic legal expert stresses that this is the chief reason behind Western civilization's long tradition of exempting churches from taxation. In medieval days, rulers refrained from taxing church lands because the church aided the rulers by ministering to the spiritual and welfare needs of their subjects. The principle became rooted in English common law, and from there it was transplanted to America.

If the churches' work is curtailed because its resources are drained off, the lawyer argues, the Government will have to step into the welfare area more and more.

Nor is it clear that the size of tax-exempt church properties is reaching the danger point. In 1875, President Grant warned Congress of "an evil that, if permitted to continue, will probably lead to great trouble in our land before the close of the Nineteenth Century. It is the accumulation of vast amounts of untaxed church property," which he said could "lead to sequestration without constitutional authority and through blood." He proposed a constitutional amendment eliminating tax exemption of church property.

Another important argument for tax exemption is expressed by Chief Justice John Marshall's famous pronouncement, quoted so often it has become a cliche: "The power to tax involves the power to destroy." Taxation could become a weapon to destroy the vitality of the churches.

A Subtle Weapon

But tax exemption can be used as a weapon, too. California adopted a constitutional amendment in 1952 requiring that churches sign loyalty affidavits as a condition of tax exemption. Religious groups protested, saying this amounted to ideological control by the state as a price for preferred treatment. The California supreme court has declared the law unconstitutional.

Two Episcopal ministers in Detroit stirred up similar sentiment when they proposed that the Government deny tax exemption to all-white churches in crowded sections of Detroit. Chided a Christian Century editorial: "The power to levy taxes is given to the Government for the purpose of raising necessary revenues; it is not given as a punitive instrument for the disciplining of the people. Governments should neither reward churches for being 'good' nor punish them for being 'bad.' "

What would taxes do to church budgets? The effect would vary widely, depending upon tax rates and a church's financial health. Most churches, however, must strain hard to raise money and then to pare planned expenditures so they do not spend more than they receive. By the time they complete the process, their financial boards are not in a mood to give money to governments that don't require it.

Some persons in the large and comparatively wealthy Bower Hill Community Presbyterian Church in Mt. Lebanon Township in western Pennsylvania, for example, pursued the matter far enough to learn from tax assessors that their church would pay about $16,000 a year on its property if it paid its full share of taxes. Although this would be only a small percentage of the church's annual budget of about $180,000, church officers quickly dismissed the idea as, in the words of one, "way out."

Prof. Elwyn A. Smith: He pushed Presbyterian statement against prayer services in public schools.

The high cost of paying taxes simply to adhere to a principle may prove the most persuasive argument of all against the Presbyterian recommendation. This argument could overwhelm the arguments of churchmen such as the Rev. Dr. Blake and Methodist Bishop John Wesley Lord of Washington, D. C., another prominent churchman who worries about church privileges in American culture.

"How often the church accepts the dubious role of the 'pampered darling' of a sin-sick society," bemoans Bishop Lord. "How often it seeks and accepts privileges for itself as it perpetuates and entrenches its own holdings and interests."

Not surprisingly, Bishop Lord agrees with the Presbyterian position on school prayers. The Presbyterian position urges that devotional services "never" be conducted in public schools. As the Supreme Court took pains to point out in its 1963 decision, prohibiting religious exercises does not rule out reading the Bible in connection with academic courses. But prayers and Bible readings as devotions, the Presbyterians declared, "tend toward indoctrination or meaningless ritual and should be omitted. . . ."

Prof. Franklin H. Littell: His book provided background for prayer statement.

The Presbyterian prayer statement, so timely in 1963, actually had been submitted to the 1962 general assembly for approval. A nine-man church-state committee under Prof. Elwyn A. Smith of Pittsburgh Theological Seminary presented its recommendations that year, only to have the general assembly refer them to local congregations and presbyteries (groups of congregations) for detailed study.

The delay proved providential. More than half the denomination's presbyteries and one-tenth of its individual churches studied the report (a Grosse Point, Michigan, church alone reported some 50 hours discussing it) and sent their comments back to the committee. Though the committee dabbled with the language of the recommendations here and there, it didn't change them substantially.

The procedure consumed time. But when the committee went before the 1963 assembly, it was able to claim that the report had been studied widely by local clergymen and lay leaders. Just as important, it could say that even on the most controversial issue, Bible reading and prayer, its supporters outnumbered its opponents by two to one.

Worry Unfounded

"If we tear out the guts of this report," a worried committee member said before the vote, "we repudiate the wishes of the presbyteries."

His fears were unfounded. The Bible-and-prayer position won the approval of 527 of the assembly's 840 delegates. The rest of the report swept through by such a large margin that votes weren't even counted.

Corridor talk here indicated that a good many Presbyterians, though outnumbered by the convention vote, felt strongly that religious exercises should be permitted in public schools. "A neutral position is a position against God," said the Rev. Frederick C. Fowler of Duluth, Minnesota, a member of the national advisory council of the Protestants and Other Americans United for the Separation of Church and State. "In the United States, 95 per cent of the people believe in God. Why should 5 per cent tell them they can't speak of God in public institutions?"

Persons sympathetic to this view argued that the United States throughout its history has been a God-conscious country. Atheism and secularism have been nibbling away at cherished parts of the nation's religious heritage, they said, so Christians should struggle to preserve remaining symbols of God-consciousness.

But Professor Smith and his band contended that it is an "illusion" to believe that having religious practices in public schools makes the United States a godly country. He insisted that full responsibility for inculcating religious values lies with the church and the family.

The nine committee members, divided when they began discussing church-state relations in 1960 but united in 1963, drew heavily upon the writing of Prof. Franklin H. Littell of Chicago Theological Seminary.

In *From State Church to Pluralism,* published in 1962, Professor Littell stated that the United States never was a "Christian" nation. During the Revolutionary War, a mere 5 per cent of the people belonged to churches, and by 1850 the figure had risen only to 16 per cent. Nineteenth Century revivalists fostered this "myth of a Christian America," the committee said, when they appealed to people "to return to the faith of their fathers, although those of their fathers who had faith were a small minority."

Critics of the Littell view note that statistics were not as accurate in earlier years as they are today. They contend, too, that the number of church members is not an accurate measurement of the prevalence of faith.

The Presbyterians made it clear that they believe that "God is sovereign over all the nations," that "the people of the nations forget God at their peril." But since the first waves of Irish Catholic immigrants began to reach America's shores in the 1830s, they said, religious pluralism—the existence of many faiths, the predominance of none—has been part of the American tradition. Yet, grumbled Professor Smith, "churches still cling to the old view that we're a Protestant country."

To Presbyterian lay delegate Ralph Kennedy, a soft-spoken aircraft company engineer from Fullerton, California, the church-state report was significant because it "struck at the jugular vein of the Protestant preferred position." The report's backers admitted that this has its practical side: They don't want to see religious observances in public schools become a ball bounced by whichever faith happens to control the school board; the honest way to disapprove of this is to withdraw their own right to bounce the ball.

The Presbyterians don't propose that every vestige of religious faith be stripped from public life. They admit it's carrying consistency too far, for instance, to erase "In God We Trust" from coins or to pull the Bible out of the courtroom. "We're interested in a reasonable and just application of the doctrine of the separation of church and state," said Professor Smith, who wrote his doctoral dissertation on Sixteenth Century church-state relations in John Calvin's Geneva.

"Some say this is a retreat," acknowledged Professor Smith. "We say we're grateful. A church is a body called to witness to Jesus Christ. Witnessing will show forth more clearly now"—with the church divorced from its "preferred" position.

Religious beliefs, the report asserted, should bring "no civil advantage. If profession of religion becomes such an advantage, danger of impure love for Christ is increased."

More than a year after the report was adopted—after the arrest at Gwynn Oak, after the defeat of the school prayer amendment, after a press leak of the proposed new "confession"—the Rev. Dr. Blake took a moment from a busy day of meetings in a Southern city to assess the status of religion today.

"The church is being transformed," he said. "It's changing from merely the religious decoration of a secular culture to the dynamic creator of a new—and I hope more Christian—culture." ♦

A time-honored duty: Presbyterian minister visits with a prisoner.

—Presbyterian Life

The Episcopalians

Episcopalians march for civil rights in Washington, D.C., demonstration.

The Death of an Image

New Vibrancy Infuses Old-Line American Faith; Social Action Is Today's Gospel—For Nearly All

ST. LOUIS.

"IT'S JUST not true any more," said the Very Rev. Charles Harris, dean of Seabury-Western Theological Seminary in Evanston, Illinois. "You can no longer aptly refer to the Episcopal Church as the Republican Party at prayer."

"Around the turn of the century," he continued, shifting in his chair for emphasis, "financier J. P. Morgan dominated our annual convention. They say he would pull up in his plush private railroad car, march into convention headquarters and start talking. And what J. P. said had weight.

"That era's over. The Episcopal Church is actively striving to erase the image of the church of the affluent, the church of the cultured upper stratum."

The image never was totally accurate. In many cities, true, the "society" church has been the Episcopal Church downtown. But more often than not its fellow Episcopal churches nearby have blended with the social landscape of their neighborhoods.

Now, in fact, many of the former "society" churches have become centers of imaginative Episcopalian "inner-city" work. "Inner city," in the euphemistic vocabulary of the world of religion, means "slum."

In New York City, ministers and members of Episcopalian "society" churches are devoting hours each month to cultivating the confidence and friendship of underprivileged children on city playgrounds. In Washington, D.C., an Episcopal clergyman in a downtown church holds regular worship services in a tiny restaurant for a loyal and growing "church" community of poor. In suburbs outside the nation's capital—outside many cities, in fact—men and women in wealthy Episcopal churches make weekly pilgrimages to run-down rural homes miles away to tutor Negro children having difficulty in school.

In the new emphasis on the "inner city" among the nation's faiths, the Episcopal Church has supplied ideas and leadership far out of proportion to its size. The first two directors of the Urban Training Center for Christian Mission, an interdenominational training school in Chicago, have been Episcopalians. The Rt. Rev. Paul Moore, Jr., suffragan bishop of Washington, D.C., has written a recent book on urban church work that has attracted wide attention, *The Church Reclaims the City*.

Bishop Moore, an ex-Marine in his mid-40s who won the Navy Cross and Silver Star in World War II, typifies the new species of Episcopalian. Born into a wealthy family and educated at Yale, he has spent most of his years while a priest working in blighted areas of New York City and Jersey City. Since being consecrated as a bishop in early 1964, he has worked frequently among Washington's poor.

At the Episcopal Church's triennial convention in Kiel Auditorium here in October 1964, the church decided to devote even more money and energy to the "inner-city" movement and other social causes. Over the next three years it will spend record amounts as a denomination on such projects as work in the inner city, increased civil-rights activity, and programs designed to offset the harmful effects of automation on displaced workers.

For such activities in the past, the Episcopal Church has gained a reputation as an "activist" church, almost a daring church. It moved swiftly as the churches began mobilizing in mid-1963 for a strong civil-rights campaign; a pastoral letter on the subject from the Rt.

Rev. Arthur Lichtenberger, presiding bishop at the time, was one of the first decisive moves by a major denomination in the civil-rights field. In a different area, the 1964 convention boldly decided the church should push forward on work on a liturgy for the physically and mentally ill; the work could lead to a restoration of "healing" as a function of the church.

"The church must change," the Rt. Rev. John E. Hines, former bishop of Texas, declared here hours before he was elected to succeed Bishop Lichtenberger as presiding bishop. "It has been changing, and it must continue to do so despite protest and lamenting. The church must develop new strategies to meet the challenge of the urban revolution. It must serve as a catalyst in society to reduce racial tension, misunderstanding, and enmity."

The Youngest Ever

Bishop Hines, 54 when elected, was the youngest man ever chosen presiding bishop. Barring disability, he will serve until the mandatory retirement age of 68. His position calls for him to serve, in words he chose in an informal chat before his election, as "the unofficial official spokesman of the Episcopal Church." The official spokesman: The general convention.

Though the presiding bishop's office brings great challenge and responsibility, it offers little authority. In functioning as administrative head of the church, the presiding bishop cannot order other bishops around. He can cajole, and he can depend on the fact that Episcopalians respect the office he holds. Yet the slap on the back, the cheery greeting, and the tactfully worded pastoral letter constitute his only weapons.

The biggest obstacle any presiding bishop faces is his church's diversity. The bishops themselves best illustrate the dissimilarity in the church. They straggle into sessions in the House of Bishops wearing everything from black suits with wine-red vests and clerical collars to subdued sport jackets and ties. Only the purple amethyst ring definitely marks a man as a bishop—and even the rings vary.

Theological opinions differ as much as the bishops' attire. At one extreme is the Rt. Rev. James Pike of San Francisco, a controversial former lawyer who has questioned such fundamental beliefs as the virgin birth of Christ and, more recently, the Trinity (the Father, the Son, and the Holy Spirit). The Trinity, he declared in a New York City sermon in August 1964, is "one of the nonessentials of Christian belief"; on the morning the convention opened, he called for an end to "outdated, incomprehensible, and nonessential doctrinal statements, traditions, and codes." Several days later the Episcopal House of Bishops rebuked Bishop Pike for his views, though it tempered its statement by not mentioning him by name.

At the other extreme from Bishop Pike is the Rt. Rev. Walter Conrad Klein, bishop of Northern Indiana and former scripture professor at Nashotah House, a Wisconsin seminary. Bishop Klein defends conservative theological tenets, including the virgin birth. He is close to Roman Catholic tradition.

The church encompasses laymen as different in their views as Barry Goldwater and William Stringfellow, a New York lawyer and lay theologian who set the convention buzzing when he flew into St. Louis and made an anti-Goldwater "statement of conscience" to the press. More than 725 Episcopalians in 41 states backed the statement, which in effect charged the Presidential candidate with making use of white prejudice against the Negroes to gain votes.

Pipes vs. Preachers

But the differences don't end at theology and politics. There remain the pipe-smoking priests who spend their days preparing Sunday's sermons in the quiet of their studies and who regard their parishes as tight little clubs. And there are the young, gray-uniformed laymen in the Episcopalians' "Church Army," which sends out men to preach on street corners and to parade through the streets with drums calling on everyone to attend services.

The staid priest who stays in his study belongs to a vanishing breed. More and more the clergy consists of men such as the Rev. Malcolm Boyd, an avant-garde priest who spent part of the summer of 1964 in Mississippi in civil-rights work and part of the convention in coffee houses in St. Louis' Gaslight Square among youths who rarely enter a church. More and more the seminaries are producing men such as the Rev. Hugh White, who founded the Detroit Industrial Mission in 1956 to help relate religion to daily work. Malcolm Boyd and Hugh White work by a theology that regards

The procession of bishops at the 1964 convention of the Protestant Episcopal Church in St. Louis.

the world as a parish—a theology for which there is room in the Episcopal Church.

There are, of course, theological limits beyond which the Episcopalian cannot go and still remain in the church, though as a practical matter these limits may not be observed. A document drawn up by various Anglican officials at Lambeth Palace in London in 1888 sums up the dogmas a church must profess to remain in the loose federation of churches called the Anglican Communion. It also provides an accurate summary of the doctrines to which the 3,600,000 American Episcopalians subscribe. The document, called the Lambeth Quadrilateral, declares that the church has two "necessary" sacraments, baptism and eucharist (communion). It says that the Apostles Creed is the statement of Episcopal faith and that Episcopalians must accept the episcopate—bishops, priests, and deacons, acknowledging these ministers as direct successors to the apostles. Finally, it decrees all must believe in the Bible as a fundamental source of revelation that contains the word of God and all things necessary to salvation.

The Low and the High

Within this doctrinal corral there is a lot of room to stomp around. Yet the church is pulling in the fences. Once the difference between the "low" and "high" churchmen was wide. Now it is narrowing.

Both high and low churchmen use vestments and the other accouterments of church ritual. They use them, however, in varying degrees. Low churchmen disdain the use of incense and ornate ceremonial garb; high churchmen relish these. High churchmen also advocate the practice of private confession, as Roman Catholics do; low churchmen are satisfied with a prescribed general congregational confession.

Pulling these diverse elements together is a small book entitled the *Book of Common Prayer*. The whole devotional-theological system of the church rests on it and on the church's constitution and canons (administrative provisions roughly equivalent to the bylaws of secular organizations).

High and low churchmen alike use the *Book of Common Prayer*. In a typical pocket-size edition the book runs 600 pages, about the size of a Roman Catholic's missal. It contains prescribed prayers and rubrics for communion, the formula for morning and evening prayers, a catechism, articles of religion, and the forms of rituals for "making, ordaining, and consecrating bishops, priests, and deacons." It also incorporates the psalter and, among other things, the form to be used in administering the sacrament of matrimony.

The widespread movement for Christian unity has helped minimize differences within the Episcopal Church. As one church lady at the convention here put it, "We don't like to talk about the high and low business any more."

The Episcopal Church of the United States had its tentative beginning when Sir Walter

The last stone is put in place on the tower of the National Cathedral in Washington, D.C.—a triumph of Episcopalian architecture.

—Living Church

Raleigh tried to establish a colony in the New World. Later, when Capt. John Smith arrived in Virginia, he brought Chaplain Robert Hunt and the church came to stay.

The transplanted Church of England dominated the South. Prominent leaders in the region—George Washington, John Randolph, Robert Morris, Richard Henry Lee, John Jay—belonged to the church.

With the Revolution, however, came distress. The church smacked too much of England to satisfy patriots. The intense patriots drove out most of the church's clergy. It was not until 1783 that the remaining church leaders assembled in Annapolis, Maryland, where they adopted the name Protestant Episcopal Church—"Protestant" to set it apart from the Roman church; "Episcopal" to distinguish it from the Presbyterian and the Congregationalist churches.

American Independence

Also in 1783 the clergy in Connecticut elected Samuel Seabury as their prospective bishop. He was consecrated in Scotland in 1784. Five years later the Protestant Episcopal Church adopted a constitution and revised the *Book of Common Prayer*. From then on the American church was on its own.

Because the church traces its origins to the Church of England, it maintains ties to the English or Anglican Church. So do the churches of Uganda and Canada and 15 other nations in which the churches sprang from the Church of England. Along with the Church of England these separated churches form the Anglican Communion, which resembles the British Commonwealth. Each of the churches in the communion exists as a self-governing entity, yet all cooperate with the Church of England.

Through a "Mutual Responsibility and Interdependence" plan, approved in St. Louis, the American church will demonstrate its ties to the Anglican Communion by sharing money and talents with other churches in the communion. But because "Mutual Responsibility" involves money, it involves problems.

Neither the finances nor the membership of the Episcopal Church have been growing as rapidly as in the past. During 1963 it experienced its smallest membership increase since the Depression of the 1930s. Laments the Rev. Robert B. Appleyard, rector of Christ Church in Greenwich, Connecticut: "This can mean we're a static, status-quo church."

More shocking yet was a disclosure in St. Louis by the Rt. Rev. Thomas H. Wright, bishop of East Carolina. If every Episcopalian in the United States were on public relief and tithed (donated 10 per cent of his income) based on this public relief, Bishop Wright computed, the income of the Episcopal Church would rise by 50 per cent.

Episcopalian executives have been looking for financial evidence of increased dedication among the church's members, but so far they have looked largely in vain. In 1961 the church resolved that parishes should allocate 50 per cent of their total receipts to work outside the parish. In 1963 the church as a whole was devoting just 13.3 per cent of its total revenues to outside work, a meager improvement from the 12.1 per cent in 1961. Says the Rev. Mr. Appleyard: "Obviously the church is a long way from achieving its goals."

What are the goals of the Episcopal Church? Like everything else about Episcopalians, the goals are diverse.

To Meet Science

Dean Harris of Seabury-Western ("West Jesus U." to theological wags in the church) sees a strong need for church unity and for answers to the dilemmas posed by automation. But he is equally concerned about the fact that "scientists today think the church has nothing to say to them." He insists one of the church's goals should be to reach these scientists.

Episcopalians already have addressed themselves to the problem. Within a few years they may establish houses near prominent scientific centers such as Massachusetts Institute of Technology and California Institute of Technology. Graduate students pursuing science degrees would live and study there. An Episcopalian priest would live with them, answering moral questions that crop up in the course of the students' studies, and serving as a symbol of the fact that the men committed to God are committed to the men of science, too.

A larger goal of the church is a goal everyone shares. Bishop Wright expresses it best. The goal of the Episcopal Church, he says, is to meet the needs of people—to keep priests from "answering questions nobody is asking." ◆

The Roman Catholics

In Rome, American Bishops Influence Major Decisions; In San Diego, the Faithful React—For and Against

A VATICAN Ecumenical Council is many stories. It is a story of pageantry and a story of debate, a story of study and a story of action. Most compelling of all, it is a story of people—the people who shape it and the people who are shaped by it.

Americans are part of this story. A few American clergymen have been going to Rome to participate in the decisions of the Vatican Council. Millions more, people like the Roman Catholic parishioners at Immaculate Conception Church in San Diego, are finding their lives and their faith affected by what the official Latin calls *"Concilio Ecumenico Vaticano II."*

Have the Americans in Rome really influenced the course of the Vatican Council? Conversations in the Eternal City with bishops of several nations indicate that the Americans' influence, largely submerged during the first two sessions in 1962 and 1963, surged to the surface in the third session in late 1964. Their influence may be felt even more in the final session in 1965 or later.

"In the beginning, it was not possible to see very well the influence of your American bishops," declares Bishop Emile Josef De Smedt of Belgium, one of the two vice-presidents of the important Secretariat for Promoting Christian Unity. "But the American bishops have a very great influence in the progressive direction of the Council."

Albert Cardinal Meyer of Chicago emerged as a "giant" of the Council, a man whose logic, sense of history, and knowledge of the scriptures gives him immense influence every time he speaks. Bishop John J. Wright of Pittsburgh, another persuasive speaker on the Council floor, has also made what one European colleague calls an "exhilarating" impact within the strategic Doctrinal Commission of the Council. An American "expert" at the Council, the Rev. John Courtney Murray of Woodstock College in Maryland, is doing as much as any one man to shape the Council's stand on religious liberty.

Americans are influencing the Council as a group, too, while they are in Rome for Council sessions or commission meetings. Occasionally they unite formally on a specific subject, as they did when all of the American bishops at the Council in late October 1964—about 175 of the 240 members of the American hierarchy—united to urge a "forthright and unequivocal condemnation" by the Council of the "cancerous evil of racial injustice." Day in and day out they have exerted influence informally, as Council fathers from other lands pump them with questions while they stroll down the Via Della Conciliazione toward the Tiber River or sip coffee in the coffee bars of St. Peter's Basilica.

"Perhaps it's not the right thing for a Christian to say," chuckled the jovial Abbot Christopher Butler of England as he relaxed in a cloistered Benedictine college on Aventino Hill in Rome, "but I think your bishops at first were perhaps a bit too humble." He buried his arms in his black habit swami-style. "For the longest time they listened to bishops from insignificant little sees as though the Europeans had the right to speak and the Americans the obligation to listen and obey."

Now the Americans are speaking as well as listening. They speak not with the brashness of the "ugly Americans" of tourist fame, but with the calm confidence that they have much to share.

American Catholics do have much to share, say Catholic prelates from Europe, Africa, and

At the Council, In the Parish

San Diego's Immaculate Conception Church and its pastor, Rev. Talmage Glazier.

Asia. On the major issues of the first two sessions, the Catholic liturgy and the nature of the Catholic Church, American Catholics brought with them no unique competence. But the world listened eagerly to what Americans had to say on the issues that preoccupied the third session—religious liberty, for example, and such contemporary problems as nuclear weapons, birth control, and poverty. These issues, and others like them, also will predominate at the fourth and final session.

American Catholics do differ, after all, from Italian Catholics, or from French Catholics, or from Catholics nurtured spiritually in the missionary churches of central Africa.

Not that all American Catholics are alike. The American Catholic can be as progressive in his approach as Joseph Cardinal Ritter of St. Louis or as conservative as James Francis Cardinal McIntyre of Los Angeles. If he has been raised in New England, he comes from a Catholic heritage largely Irish in its orientation; if in the Midwest, from a German Catholic heritage; if in the New Orleans area, Napoleonic French; if in the Far West, Spanish. He may himself bear the distinctive marks of a foreign nationality; one-half of all American Catholic adults are either immigrants or the children of immigrants.

Yet American Catholics share a common heritage. Most have been trained in American schools. They have lived most or all of their lives as members of a minority faith in a culture with many faiths; about 25 per cent of the American people are Roman Catholics.

A New Reputation

The American bishops drink of this common heritage. Before the Council opened, it was widely assumed that the American hierarchy would be among the most conservative at the Council; many of the bishops had received theological training in Rome, the argument went, and Rome has no more obedient sons than in Ireland and in the United States. Now, however, the Americans for the most part are considered progressives. Of the 28 American speeches at the second session, only 5 were considered conservative in tone. More than one prominent American bishop disputes the idea that theological training in Rome has made "super-Romans" of most Americans; argues one: "Cardinal Ritter, a progressive, studied in Rome, and Cardinal McIntyre, the most outrageously conservative of the American bishops, never studied in Rome at all."

The bishops of the United States, then, think as Americans and act as Americans. Unlike the bishops of such countries as Italy and Spain, they have disdained bloc politics at the Council. Bishops in many countries are accustomed to meeting frequently at home, think of themselves as a collective entity (for largely protective reasons), and participate in their nation's power politics. The American bishops, on the other hand, consider themselves as anything but a collective entity. They met only twice in the 130 years from the founding of the Republic until 1919, and since 1919 they have met just once a year. American bishops can join or refuse to join the national body of the bishops, the National Catholic Welfare Conference, as they wish; some in the past have refused to join it.

Heritage of Freedom

Religious freedom in the United States has spawned this free-wheeling attitude of American Catholic bishops, and it is precisely in the field of religious freedom that the American bishops are making their greatest single contribution to the Vatican Council.

"When it comes to religious liberty," says Bishop Robert F. Joyce of Vermont, "Americans can not only preach the theory but exemplify the fact." Experience has shown that churches can exist under a constitutional government that guarantees freedom of religion, but it has shown more than this—that they can flourish under it.

Bishop after American bishop therefore rose in the Council hall to defend a document stating that freedom of religion is the right of every person. Americans take this for granted. But in some countries the authorities still hold to the medieval view, once held by every Christian church, that the prince (the government) has a duty to protect the one true religion and to outlaw religions he considers false. The sentiment the Council has displayed on religious liberty has already emboldened the Catholic hierarchy in Spain to go along with a proposed relaxation of restrictions against Protestants in Spain.

A related factor, America's success in religious pluralism (the existence of many faiths, the predominance of none), also has colored the direction of the Vatican Council. American bishops argued forthrightly for the strong Council stand in favor of greater understanding among faiths. They argued, too, for the clear statement absolving Jews of special responsibility for the crucifixion of Christ.

American Catholics, it is apparent in Rome, are not yet regarded as powerhouses or innovators in most fields of theology. But they are highly esteemed for their "bricks-and-mortar" success in building an impressive educational system and in instilling a sense of vital Christianity into their parishes. When prelates from other countries want to take a reading on practical questions, therefore, they turn frequently to the American bishops.

"Some of my Italian friends will ask, 'How do you Americans read this?' " said Pittsburgh's Bishop Wright, pacing his Rome living quarters in his black cassock with purple buttons and purple piping along the seams. "If this were largely a doctrinal council, as Vatican I was in 1869 and 1870, this reputation would be a limitation. Since it's largely a pastoral council, it's an advantage."

Influence, then, is exerted in many ways at this world council of Catholicism. It is exerted in informal conversations far from the Council floor and in formal meetings of the various Council commissions, which serve much the same function as congressional committees on Capitol Hill.

It is exerted also in written statements by individual Council fathers, addressed to Council commissions preparing documents for debate. "We little fellows working with the commissions have to pay just as much attention to the written interventions as to the oral ones on the floor—and there are many more of them," says one of the most influential Council "experts." Finally, influence can be exerted in the speeches on the Council floor, speeches that sometimes sink in with the Council fathers but just as often do nothing more than get a bishop's name in home-town newspapers.

It is the speeches, however, that win the public's attention. And from the speeches alone, the American public would deduce that the American bishops made almost no impact on the Vatican Council until 1964. In 1962, the U.S. bishops and archbishops appeared quite willing to let the five American cardinals do their talking. The American hierarchy did better in 1963, though they still delivered less than one-twentieth of the speeches. Only in 1964 did their proportion of Council speeches approach their numerical proportion among the Council fathers—nearly one-tenth.

"From the very beginning," contends one American bishop, "the American hierarchy has

Two outstanding American voices at Rome: Bishop John J. Wright, left, Albert Cardinal Meyer, right.

played a much greater role than most Catholic writers—in their eagerness to have their men make a 'good show'—have been willing to admit." Most American bishops who served on preparatory commissions before the Council opened were retained when the permanent Council commissions were formed, he notes; most European and African bishops were replaced. Additional evidence that the Americans have been proving valuable members of the commissions: Of the 43 bishops chosen in 1964 to augment the various commissions, 7 were Americans.

Who are some of the most influential Americans at the Vatican Council?

They can be cardinals, though not all American cardinals exert real influence at the Council. They can be bishops, "experts," even laymen.

Chicago's Cardinal Meyer has built a huge following on the strength of his speeches on nearly every important topic before the Council. "If I haven't made up my mind on some subject and Cardinal Meyer takes a stand on it," says one bishop, "I'll follow him."

Cardinal Ritter has impressed many bishops, too, though some complain that he weakens his progressive stance by arguing invariably from a pragmatic rather than a theoretical viewpoint. When he proposed in 1964 that the declaration on religious liberty be stripped of its theological basis, he found himself abandoned by his fellow progressives and allied, to the distress of his friends, with Council conservatives. Arguing only the practical may prove wise in a legislative assembly, say Council fathers, but the practical cannot be shorn of principles in trying to enumerate church doctrine.

Richard Cardinal Cushing of Boston captured applause in the Council hall and headlines in American newspapers when he spoke early in the third session on religious liberty and again on the document on the Jews, but he does not pretend to have the power in the Council of Cardinal Meyer or even Cardinal Ritter. "Just as he promised, he thundered into the microphone so he could be heard across the Tiber," says one prelate. "People still remember his two speeches, but he didn't change a vote. Their minds were already made up."

Cardinal Cushing, ailing, left for Boston well before the end of each of the three sessions, making no secret of the fact that he understands little Latin. He once said of Latin: "I didn't know whether it was Chinese or Eskimo." When he went to the late Pope John XXIII to complain of his language troubles in the first session, Pope John asked: "Are you a theologian?" Replied Cardinal Cushing: "I only know what I learned in my catechism." Pope John grinned. "Shake hands," he said. Then he gave

Richard Cardinal Cushing: For religious liberty.

Joseph Cardinal Ritter: A pragmatic stance.

Cardinal Cushing approval to return to Boston.

Bishop Wright of Pittsburgh has impressed the Council fathers from many countries with his intellect and wit, both on and off the Council floor. A man of imposing physical stature, he sprinkles crisp images through a brogue that sometimes has a poetic swing about it.

Archbishop John F. Dearden of Detroit, the other American member of the Doctrinal Commission, also has made a strong impression on the commission; he and Bishop Wright were two of the five commission members chosen to report parts of the important document on "The Church in the Modern World" to the Council as a whole.

Many American Hands

Archbishop Paul J. Hallinan of Atlanta, unable to attend the third session because of illness, made valuable contributions to the Council on the liturgy. Bishop Ernest Primeau of New Hampshire, widely known in Rome because he spent several years here before being consecrated a bishop, has made important speeches to the Council on laymen and on religious liberty; laymen, he once urged, must be permitted to do more than "obey, pray, and pay." With Archbishop Lawrence J. Shehan of Baltimore and Bishop Charles H. Helmsing of Kansas City, Bishop Primeau serves on the Secretariat for Promoting Christian Unity.

Father Murray of Woodstock College, perhaps the foremost Catholic theologian in America, was the first to develop a theological rationale for Catholicism in America's pluralistic society. In a sense, therefore, he contributed to the Vatican Council long before it first convened. He continues to contribute, doing his private study while in Rome at his Council residence across the Ville Romania from the Church of St. Robert Bellarmine—named, appropriately, in honor of a Sixteenth Century Catholic who opposed royal absolutism and advocated a form of limited government.

Other Catholic "experts" at the Council have exerted intellectual influence—among them the Rev. Godfrey Diekmann of Worship magazine on liturgy, the Very Rev. George Higgins of the National Catholic Welfare Conference on the layman and on economic affairs, and the late Gustave Weigel of Woodstock College on Christian unity.

Even the American lay auditor, James J. Norris of the International Catholic Migration Commission, has made a mark at the Council. Speaking in almost flawless Latin in St. Peter's one Thursday in November 1964, he urged the Council fathers to create a secretariat in the church to coordinate the church's attack on world poverty. A follow-up speech by Joseph Cardinal Frings of Germany provided evidence that the Norris proposal had broad support.

Just as Americans in Rome have influenced the Council, the Council has influenced these Americans. It has instilled in the American bishops an alertness toward theology that many have never had before. It has quickened their awareness of their common heritage. It has enhanced their sense of a common mission in the United States.

Perhaps, depending on one's viewpoint, it has revised their attitude toward Rome as well. "Because they were a pioneer church in a Protestant environment," says a European cardinal, "Americans had looked to Rome and acquired a mental attitude of undue subservience. I suspect they will not be subservient in the future."

And what of the people of Immaculate Conception in San Diego? How does the Vatican Council affect Mrs. Alexander Aunchman, a housewife? How does it affect the Rev. Talmage Glazier, a parish priest?

In the Parish

Rich in its history, diverse in its membership, Immaculate Conception qualifies as well as any parish as a group representative of American Catholics. Its 300 member families live in $50,000 homes high on the bluff above the church and in ramshackle frame structures in the shadow of a blocks-long Convair plant. They include graduates of medical schools and graduates of no schools, old-timers who helped build the church in 1917 and newcomers seeking sun and success in the Far West, Mexicans who speak little English and "Anglos" who speak nothing else.

In San Diego's Old Town, home of Immaculate Conception parish, three Carmelite priests recited the first Mass in what is now California 363 years ago. In Old Town the Rev. Antonio Ubach, "Father Gaspara" of Helen Hunt Jackson's romantic novel *Ramona,* lived and ministered a century ago to the early permanent settlers of San Diego.

One recent Tuesday, as darkness blotted

out the brilliant sunset over San Diego Bay, 21 parishioners filtered into Immaculate Conception for the daily 5:15 Mass. Six or seven who had brought their missals followed the Mass in parallel columns of Latin and English; the others listened to the Latin, watched, and prayed.

Emerging from the Mass, Navy civilian employe John McGee pinpointed the prevailing attitude in the parish toward one of the big decisions of the Council—permission to recite the Mass in the vernacular.

"Did you ever bring a guy or a girl to Mass and try to explain what all that Latin is all about?" he said. "It's like pulling teeth." Then, remembering the wonders of the modern age, he added: "Without novocain."

Across the Gap

The modern age. It was the need for a *balzo in avanti,* a "leap into modernity," that inspired the late Pope John XXIII to issue the call for the first world-wide council of bishops since 1870.

In a red-carpeted office 6,400 miles from St. Peter's Basilica, Father Glazier, pastor of Immaculate Conception, puffed on a cigaret and assessed the significance of the liturgical changes made by the Council: "We had to face the fact that we just were not getting the message across."

The new liturgy, says Father Glazier, is "a revelation for our people, not a problem. They're learning, not re-learning."

For the most part, he explains, the people in his parish have developed an emotional, spiritual involvement in the Catholic faith, but not an intellectual one. Thus Father Glazier welcomes the opportunity to recite the Mass in English—an opportunity Catholic priests around the country first had on November 29, 1964.

As early as 1962, Father Glazier invited a priest of an Eastern rite to sing the liturgy of St. John Chrysostom in English at Immaculate Conception. Several Eastern rites, numerically small branches of the Roman Catholic Church, have long been permitted to recite the Mass in the vernacular. The reaction in Immaculate Conception to this early use of English in worship, Father Glazier recalls, was "very, very favorable."

Father Glazier has dark, wavy hair and an aquiline nose—the ideal profile for a classic Greek bust. His eyes dance expressively with humor and understanding as he describes the difficulties priests faced when they had to read their breviary, a book of daily scripture readings and prayers, entirely in Latin.

"We read Psalms, Proverbs, the Gospels every day," he says. "Yet it was our separated brethren (Protestant ministers) who were capable of quoting, quoting, quoting. You just don't go to a banquet and start reeling off *'In illo tempore: Erat quidam regulus. . . .'* "

Now, thanks to Vatican Council action, priests can read their breviaries in English.

If any part of the Council's work has excited as much interest at Immaculate Conception as the moves toward the vernacular, it has been the new emphasis the Council is placing on good will toward non-Catholics. In the opening address of Pope Paul VI at the second session, the spiritual leader of the world's Catholics told observers from other Christian communions of the hope their presence stirred in his heart and of the sadness he felt over their separation. "If we are to blame in any way for that separation," he said, "we humbly beg God's forgiveness, and ask pardon, too, of our brethren who feel themselves to have been injured by us."

Few parishioners at Immaculate Conception have read the words of Paul, words that were unprecedented for a Pope to utter. But nearly all have sensed the new attitude toward non-Catholics, partly through reading, partly through the sermons of their pastor.

Long Wait

"We let 500 years go by before we started to apologize," exclaims Father Glazier. "And we're Christians!"

In the parish, memories remain fresh of priests who took quite a different approach. "When I was a Campfire Girl in Vermont," recalls Mrs. Aunchman, "we met once in the basement of the Congregational Church. The priest came around afterwards and talked to our mothers. You'd think we had committed a mortal sin. Talk about bigotry!"

A minority in Immaculate Conception have feared that the Council would downgrade the place of the Virgin Mary in church doctrine. Catholics in Latin lands, including Mexico, tend more than other Catholics to center their faith on Mary. Mexican members of Immaculate Conception are no exception.

H. A. Contreras, a swarthy, coverall-clothed

John McGee: Wants an English Mass.

H. A. Contreras: Keep the leading lady.

Mrs. Alexander Aunchman: Against bigotry.

Mexican with a gray stubble of beard, expressed this fear as he poked around in the engine of his old car: "They took the Virgin down from the altar over at the church and put her in the hall. Our church was built for service to her, mostly. If they vote over in Rome to not keep her as the leading lady, it'll disillusion a lot of us."

Mr. Contreras has nothing to fear. The Council will not diminish Mary's stature in the church; the dogmas of the Immaculate Conception and of Mary's bodily assumption into heaven will remain intact. But neither is Mary's stature being greatly exalted, as a minority in the church had hoped.

Other fears have crept into the minds of many Catholic residents of Old Town. Some of the fears have stemmed from ignorance, others from confusion.

One well-read parishioner has allowed the fear that priests will be permitted to marry to color her whole attitude toward the Council. "You'll find a lot of Catholics turning into 'home Baptists' if they let that happen," she promises.

"These priests—they want the sheltered life and the life of the world, too. They can't have both." Echoes her husband: "The priest has enough problems without taking on more."

Again, the parishioners of Immaculate Conception need not worry. From every indication in Rome, Immaculate Conception will not have a married priest for decades or perhaps centuries, if ever.

Father Glazier stresses repeatedly that the Vatican Council will do nothing to alter the essence of the Catholic faith. "The virgin birth is the virgin birth," he says. "The Immaculate Conception is the Immaculate Conception. The Trinity is the Trinity."

But he believes firmly, possibly more firmly than any of his parishioners, in the need for change in the church's approach to the world. Perhaps this is as it should be. It is, after all, the duty of the pastor, the shepherd, to lead—not follow—his flock.

It is this duty—the duty to lead—that the bishops of the church are discharging as they deliberate and decide, in St. Peter's Basilica, upon matters that affect Catholics the world over. ♦

The Eastern Orthodox

The Most Rev. Iakovos, archbishop of the Greek Orthodox Church in North and South America.

The Fourth Major Faith?

Steeped in Mysticism, the Eastern Church Thrives In Pragmatic America, Spurs Drive for Church Unity

NEW YORK CITY.

THE Eastern Orthodox churches, with a membership in the United States that nearly equals that of the Episcopalians, are seeking recognition as America's "fourth major faith."

Rich in their liturgy and in their historical traditions, the Orthodox are the leading Christian denomination of Eastern Europe and the Middle East. They have 139,000,000 members throughout the world—nearly two-thirds as many as all Protestant churches—and 3,000,000 members in the United States. Yet, as one Orthodox priest complains, it's not uncommon to spend an entire half-hour in the barber's chair explaining how a person can be a Christian without being either a Protestant or a Roman Catholic.

The Orthodox are making progress in their drive for recognition. Since World War II the armed services have added "Orthodox" to "Catholic," "Protestant," and "Jew" as accepted identification tag symbols. Orthodox priests have entered the service as chaplains. Greek Orthodox archbishops began participating in Presidential inauguration ceremonies under President Eisenhower.

Misunderstanding of this historic faith remains widespread, however. "The Greeks are puzzled by the fact that while so many Americans . . . are at great pains to recognize Western civilization's indebtedness to Greece, they pay little attention to the Christian form of Greek civilization," wrote Prof. John S. Romanides of the Greek Orthodox Theological School in Massachusetts in Christian Century magazine. "Some Greeks jokingly suggest that had they remained faithful to the gods of Mount Olympus Greek paganism might have long since been recognized as the fourth major faith in the United States."

Orthodoxy arrived early in Alaska, but late in the continental United States. Until quite recently, the Orthodox have been too sparse and too wedded to their Old World origins to make a real impact on American culture.

Eight Russian Orthodox monks entered Alaska, then a Russian preserve, in 1792. They baptized 12,000 natives of Alaska within two years, and they built at Sitka the first Orthodox cathedral in what is now the United States.

Only in the 1890s, though, did Orthodox members begin emigrating in any numbers to the United States proper. Greeks, Russians, Rumanians, Serbs, and other Europeans entered the country in the great immigration waves at the turn of the century.

The immigrants preserved close ties with their national groups. When the Greeks formed the Greek Orthodox Archdiocese of North and South America in 1922, for example, they did not declare their independence but placed themselves under the supervision of the patriarch of Constantinople.

Inevitably, the Orthodox in America have been affected by political turmoil in their homelands. Communist take-overs have wrenched religious loyalties in many directions.

The Russian Orthodox, for example, have split into three separate groups. One group accepts the full authority of the Moscow patriarchate, which has been forced to go along with the atheist Soviet government. A second refuses all contact with Moscow, contending the patriarch has forfeited his right to represent Orthodoxy. The third, by far the largest of the Russian groups, with about 750,000 members, would declare its spiritual loyalty to the Moscow patriarch if he would recognize its administrative autonomy; so far neither the American church nor the Moscow patriarch will yield.

Restricted immigration is helping the Orthodox communities to assimilate into American life. American-born Orthodox now make up 80 per cent of the total American membership; with tight immigration quotas in force, the percentage of foreign-born will dwindle even more.

Orthodox members have begun to assume an important place in America's leadership. Russian Orthodox member Igor Sikorsky is a successful aircraft executive. Active Greek Orthodox laymen include movie executive Spyros Skouras and George Christopher, a former mayor of San Francisco.

English Takes Precedence

English has become the most commonly used language for preaching and church school teaching in Orthodox churches in America. In worship services in Russian, Bulgarian, and Serbian churches, English is gradually replacing Old Slavonic—a dead language in the sense that Chaucerian English is dead. In July 1964, the Greek Orthodox Archdiocese authorized for the first time the use of English in parts of the liturgy and the sacraments.

As ethnic distinctions disappear, sentiment grows for formation of a single Orthodox group in the United States. In 1960 the Orthodox set up the Standing Committee of Orthodox Bishops that could form the framework of eventual union. Personal jealousies persist among the bishops, and cultural traditions endure. But the Orthodox know that union would bring greater recognition as a major American faith.

Most Orthodox churches have long cooperated closely with other Christian faiths. Eastern Orthodox churches participate in such joint religious organizations as the World Council of Churches and, in the United States, the National Council of Churches.

Archbishop Iakovos, leader of the 1,500,000 Greek Orthodox in the United States, glanced at a tiny portrait of the spiritual leader of all of Orthodoxy, Patriarch Athenagoras I of Constantinople, in his New York office one day and spoke of the Orthodox interest in Christian cooperation. "We have never felt," he said, "that stretching your arm to find or greet your brethren would be prohibited on the grounds that you may betray your faith or be contaminated with the other faith."

Because of centuries-old suspicions, Orthodoxy reacted slowly to the first overtures toward Christian unity from the Roman Catholic faith. Only the Russian church sent observers to the first two sessions of the Vatican Ecumenical Council, held in 1962 and 1963.

But at a Pan-Orthodox conference on the island of Rhodes in late 1963, Orthodox leaders agreed to hold a "dialog" with Rome on Christian unity. Patriarch Athenagoras and Pope Paul VI prayed together in the Holy Land shortly afterward, renewing high-level contact between East and West that had been broken for centuries. In the fall of 1964, two Greek Orthodox theologians from the United States served as observers at the Vatican Council for Patriarch Athenagoras.

"We Orthodox don't believe that unity should be based on one single church leader," says Archbishop Iakovos. "Unity, if it's ever reached, must be the unity the Roman Catholic St. Vincent described some five centuries ago: Unity in essentials, freedom in nonessentials, charity in all."

Deference to the Pope

The Orthodox are not taking an adamant stand in the unity discussions. Patriarch Athenagoras in late 1963 suggested that Pope Paul, "as the first bishop of the church," convene a Pan-Christian conference for leaders of all Christian faiths to consider how to rebuff the threat of their "common enemy, atheism and tyranny." The proposal died quietly, but the significance of the patriarch's wording was not overlooked. The phrase "first bishop of the church" accorded the pope a place of honor the East was unwilling to grant at the time of the great schism that divided Orthodoxy and Roman Catholicism nine centuries ago. At the same time it preserved the East's insistence that no one man should govern the entire church.

The structure of the church was the underlying issue over which the East and West split in 1054. It is the issue that divides the church today.

Christianity, almost from the beginning,

Patriarch Athenagoras I, spiritual leader of Orthodoxy (left), and Pope Paul VI meet in Jerusalem, breaking a silence between the two churches that had lasted for centuries.

developed different traditions in different parts of the world. St. Andrew, a disciple of Jesus, taught and applied Christianity in one way as he roamed Asia Minor and Greece; the Orthodox consider him the founder of the church in the East. St. Peter, who was first introduced to Jesus by Peter's brother, Andrew, traveled in other lands; he's considered the founder of the church in the West.

With divergence in traditions came misunderstanding. Disputes arose on many issues. In doctrine, for example, the West adopted the view that the Holy Spirit emanates from both the Father and the Son; the East held that it comes only from the Father. In worship, the East began using leavened bread; the West, unleavened. The power struggle between the political empires of the East and West ensnared the churches. Ecclesiastical jealousies emerged.

In 1054 the pope excommunicated the patriarch of Constantinople, and the patriarch excommunicated the pope. A Fifteenth Century effort to reunite the church, undertaken at the Council of Florence, collapsed. After the West failed to aid the East in the Turkish take-over of Constantinople, Eastern Christians coined the caustic saying: "We would rather see the turban of a Turk than the tiara (crown) of a pope."

Suspicions do linger. The Orthodox resent Roman Catholic efforts to convert their members and to establish new churches in their areas. The Greeks, the only ethnic group of Orthodoxy that refrained from supporting Patriarch Athenagoras' encounter with the pope in the Holy Land, smart at the permanent pres-

A procession of Rumanian Orthodox prelates in Bucharest.

ence of a Roman Catholic "archbishop of Athens" in their capital.

Unlike the centralized Roman Catholic Church, the world Orthodox communion is organized along the lines of national or regional churches. Patriarchs guide the largest and most influential ethnic groups; metropolitans (or others of bishop rank) lead the smaller ones.

Each ethnic leader exercises authority over his own group of Orthodox. None reports to any other, but all regard the patriarch of Constantinople as "first among equals." This title derives from the world influence of the patriarch's area; if East and West ever reunite, say the Orthodox, they could easily accept Rome as "first among equals."

Orthodox doctrine differs little from the doctrine of the Vatican. Both churches accept the Nicene Creed, adopted in the year 325, though they differ on a clause on the Holy Spirit. Both believe in the virgin birth, express devotion to the Virgin Mary, and revere saints.

Like Roman Catholicism, Orthodoxy recognizes seven sacraments, or rites ordained by Jesus—baptism, confirmation, communion, penance, holy orders, marriage, and holy unction.

Concepts of the sacraments vary somewhat. In Orthodoxy, for example, holy unction is performed each year for everyone to heal their bodily and spiritual ills. In Catholicism, extreme unction ("last rites") in practice has usually been performed only for dying persons —though a new term for the sacrament, "anointing of the sick," was adopted by the Vatican Council to stress that it can be administered also to people who are not in danger of dying.

Confirmation practices differ, too. In the Western church, a person is baptized as an infant and is confirmed only upon reaching a certain maturity, usually at about age 12. The bishop himself administers the holy oil in the confirmation. In Orthodoxy, the infant is both baptized and confirmed on the same day, and the rite can be performed by a priest.

Priests hear confessions in Orthodox churches, but they're not hidden from sight as in Roman Catholic confessional boxes. Married persons can be accepted into the priesthood; nearly 90 per cent of the Orthodox clergy in the United States are married. But priests can't

Easter vesper services at the Russian Orthodox church in Philadelphia.

marry after they've been ordained, and no married priest can become a bishop. Veils worn by priests and bishops indicate they have taken the vows of celibacy.

To the Westerner attending an Orthodox worship service, perhaps the most apparent difference is the liturgy. All Orthodox churches use a liturgy composed by St. James, the first bishop of Jerusalem, as arranged in the Fourth Century by St. John Chrysostom. The oldest liturgy now in use in Christendom, it is longer than the Roman Catholic Mass and, even to many Catholic eyes, more beautiful.

This difference, though, is not significant. In fact, some Roman Catholic churches—the so-called "Eastern Rite" churches—use the same liturgy as the Orthodox. These churches recognize the pope as the supreme head of the church, but they have not only a different liturgy but different laws and customs from the mainstream of Roman Catholicism. Of the 12,000,000 Eastern Rite Catholics throughout the world, some 700,000 live in the United States. Like the Orthodox, the Americans of the Eastern Rite are subject to the jurisdiction of Eastern patriarchs, though these patriarchs belong to the Roman Catholic Church.

Orthodox churchmen in the United States have been far less vocal than their Protestant and Catholic brethren on the great social issues of the day. For one thing, they are devoting much of their energy to drawing world attention to Patriarch Athenagoras' precarious position in Turkey, which is related to the Greek-Turkish political dispute over Cyprus. For another, they come not from the pragmatic tradition of the West, but from the mystical tradition of the East.

The mysticism of the East, in fact, may provide the Orthodox with their most important single weapon in their struggle for recognition in America. Protestants and Catholics alike are placing a new emphasis on the value of the mystical in Christianity.

Dr. Howard Schomer, president of Chicago Theological Seminary and a Congregationalist, urged the Greek Orthodox at their biennial congress in July 1964 to share their heritage of mystical Christianity. "Reach out," he said, "and help us all draw together in a Christ-centered mysticism." ♦

The Jews

—Robert de Gast

From grandfather to father to son the trend grows. . . .

A Question of Identity

From Grandfather to Father to Son the Trend Grows: As Americanization Sets In, Judaism Loses Its Hold

WASHINGTON, D.C.

IS the American melting pot a greater long-range threat to Jewish identity than the Russian ghetto or even the Nazi extermination camp?

Some Jews think so. "For the first time in history, Jews no longer have to be Jews," declares Rabbi Joachim Prinz, president of the American Jewish Congress. Today it's easier to be a Jew, for oppression is absent and anti-Semitism, though present, is diminishing. Yet, at the same time, in the curious ways of a free society, it's more difficult to be a Jew—more difficult to preserve a Jewish identity.

Jews, like Catholics, are finding that the American dream for religions is finally coming true. "We've made it. We're 'in,'" says Rabbi Richard G. Hirsch, youthful director of the Reform Jews' Religious Action Center here. "Kosher is A-Okay, and you can't understand comedians unless you know a few words of Yiddish. We have synagogues that are as beautiful as cathedrals, and we join everybody else in our 'edifice' complex."

At the same time, many Jews have fled their Jewish heritage as they have traveled to the "promised land" of suburbia. Immigration laws bar any large-scale infusion of immigrants, shutting off an earlier source of Jewish growth. Intermarriage drains off many Jews; a recent survey of Washington, D.C., found that 13 per cent of the Jews here marry outside their faith, and that more than 70 per cent of the children of these families identify with no Jewish group. In less concentrated areas the statistics are even more startling; 42 per cent of the Jews in Iowa marry outside their faith.

Alarm is widespread. With the number of Jews in the United States remaining almost static at 5,585,000 while the total population surges upward, nearly every Jewish leader urges a "renewed commitment to Jewish values." A few even clamor for zealous missionary activity among non-Jews—a tactic that, if adopted, would mark a major departure from the tradition of the centuries.

Yet Jews tend to splinter even when common interests are involved. No fewer than three Jewish "defense agencies" devote most of their energies to fighting anti-Semitism in the United States. In other areas—Washington lobbying, day-school education, humanitarian service—many more groups charge into the lists.

"Jewish life in this country cannot survive the jungle of organizational competition for credit and publicity, the jockeying for power, the babel of voices drowning each other out, and the inexcusable waste of needed resources in arrant duplication of programs," declared Rabbi Maurice N. Eisendrath, president of the Union of American Hebrew Congregations (Reform), not long ago. "Yet that is, roughly, the situation of American Jewry."

Who speaks for American Jews? Everyone, really, and yet no one. Judaism is, in the simplest terms, excruciatingly complex. Jews hold widely different beliefs, even on the basic question: "What is a Jew?"

A fifth-grade Jewish student once answered this question with "A Jew is a man who lived a long time ago and had a beard." Today, if he travels to Tel Aviv, he might answer, "A Jew is an Israeli youth with blond hair and blue eyes."

A Jew can be a blond Hungarian with a flaxen mustache or a hatchet-faced Argentine with coal-black hair. He can speak Old-World

"We've made it," says Rabbi Hirsch, speaking of the Jews' solid place in American life. In proof are these three successful political leaders: Democratic Sen. Abraham Ribicoff, left, of Connecticut; Supreme Court Justice Arthur Goldberg, center; Republican Sen. Jacob Javits, right, of New York.

Yiddish or New-World English flavored with the accents of Flatbush, the Midwest, or the Deep South. He can be an atheist, a skeptic who attends synagogue "for the good of the children," or an ardent believer in any one of several varieties of Judaism.

The emigrations and intermarriages of the centuries have made every Jew typical, and none typical. Jews have been described as a people of destiny, a community with a memory, a civilization. Most accurately, perhaps, they are a people with a faith.

A faith, ideally, not a religion of worship and prayer, strictly defined. A faith rather that embraces all of life—a faith that insists on regulating the secular areas of life as well as the man-to-God relationship.

"Subtract religion from Jewish peoplehood," Philip M. Klutznick, former president of B'nai B'rith, the largest Jewish service organization, writes in *No Easy Answers,* "and you remove the heartbeat."

Yet even the heartbeat pumps differently for different people. When Jews lived in closed ghettos, as they did until the Age of Enlightenment and the Industrial Revolution, they maintained a certain unity of faith essential to their survival. But with the intellectual and scientific ferment and the spirit of freedom of the past two centuries, Jews who have chosen to remain Jews have had two choices: To resist the challenge to the ancient tradition or adapt that

tradition to the modern spirit.

Efforts to adjust Judaism first took place in Germany. But only in America, where religion from the start was free from government interference, did the new approaches to Judaism flourish and become full-scale religious movements.

A wave of German immigration after the unsuccessful 1848 revolution brought Reform Judaism to the United States on a large scale. Reform (or liberal) Jews predominated until a huge Orthodox Jewish immigration from Eastern Europe began in the 1880s. Soon a growing number of American Jews began to consider Reform Judaism spiritually wanting and Orthodox Judaism rigorously formal. The founding of the Jewish Theological Seminary by this group in 1886 marked the beginning of the Conservative movement, dedicated to "conserving" the tradition but transmitting it to the new generations in understandable terms.

All three movements today prosper within Judaism. Each has its own rabbinical bodies and unions of congregations. Each maintains its own seminaries, and nearly every all-day school—schools that resemble Roman Catholic or Lutheran parochial schools—bears the distinct stamp of one of the three movements.

In theory the three movements, which have nearly equal strength, seem quite different.

The Orthodox, who preserve the theology and traditions of the ages, believe in faithfully observing biblical dietary laws and traditional holy days. Orthodox Jews use the Hebrew language in their synagogue prayers and English in their sermons, and Orthodox rabbis wear the *yarmulke* (skull cap) to keep their heads covered at all times.

Reform Jews believe much of this isolates Jews from modern mankind and makes it more difficult to instill spiritual awareness in Jews; the Reform movement has simplified the Jewish ritual and adapted it to modern customs.

Conservative Jews, finding their haven in a sort of halfway house, believe that "The old will be renewed, the new become sanctified"; thus Conservative Jews oppose extreme changes in Jewish tradition but do, for example, use English in some synagogue prayers and permit men and women to sit together during worship.

The Reconstructionist Movement

Cutting across all three movements is Reconstructionism, more a school of thought than a movement. Born in 1934 with the publication of Rabbi Mordecai Kaplan's classic *Judaism as a Civilization,* Reconstructionism views Judaism not alone as a faith but as a complete civilization. Dr. Kaplan, still a powerful influence in Jewish thought, though now in his 80s, rejects belief in a personal Messiah, in the divine revelation of the Torah (in the broadest sense, the whole body of Jewish religious teachings), and in the concept of Jews as a "chosen people"—all fundamental tenets of Orthodoxy. Yet Reconstructionist followers are found among Orthodox as well as Reform and Conservative Jews.

Removed from the textbook and applied to

real life, Judaism has no rigid divisions. Like Protestants in the mobile American society of 1964, Jews often skip across denominational lines for the familiar catalog of reasons: They like the rabbi, for example, or Temple Shalom is closer to their home, or perhaps the atmosphere is "warmer" there. Rabbis themselves, in fact, often cross the lines, for each synagogue has complete authority over its affairs. One example of many is Orthodox Rabbi Stanley Wagner, who serves a Conservative congregation in Baldwin, N. Y.

In Hillel Foundation chapters of Jewish youth on college campuses, in the chaplaincy in the armed forces, in fund-raising ventures, Jews have submerged their doctrinal differences. Now and then Jews pull together on issues that threaten fellow Jews, even though their own beliefs aren't in jeopardy; New York humane societies protesting the slaughter method insisted on by Orthodox Jews encountered opposition from Reform and Conservative groups, too.

From Unity, Strength

Jews have made progress in uniting on the broadest issues. A decade ago a State Department expert on the Near East complained that a different Jewish delegation had visited him every day for six days, and that each had merely parroted the other's arguments. This gentle rebuke led to formation of the Conference of Presidents of Major American Jewish Organizations.

Through the initiative of the Conference of Presidents, leaders of 24 major Jewish organizations gathered here in Washington, D.C., in April 1964 for an "American Jewish Conference on the Soviet Jews." The conference, which attracted the broadest representation of American Jews since a similar conference on Nazi Germany two decades earlier, planned strategy aimed at arousing public indignation over Soviet oppression.

Jewish suffering under Communist rule follows a pattern all too familiar in the centuries of Jewish history. Russian authorities have closed more than 350 synagogues in the past several years; fewer than 100 remain open. The government permits no facilities for the religious education of Jewish children and harasses rabbis and synagogues with special taxes. The Soviet press often pictures Jews as unscrupulous money-worshipers and synagogues as dens of drunkenness and dishonest business. Each year the government forbids the public baking and sale of matzo, the unleavened bread that is used in observing Passover.

"Under the Nazis we lost 6,000,000 persons —one third of our Jewish people—in physical genocide," says Rabbi David H. Panitz, a suave, influential leader in Conservative Judaism. "Now we face the loss of 3,000,000 Russian Jews —one-fourth of our world-wide religious community—through the Soviet program of religious and cultural genocide. Is it any wonder we're so agitated?"

Ribicoff Does the Job

The Washington conference appealed to Soviet officials to eradicate anti-Semitism and restore the Jews' religious and cultural rights, and implored every synagogue to observe a national day of prayer for Soviet Jews. Sympathy generated by the conference and later regional conferences helped Sen. Abraham Ribicoff corral votes for a U.S. Senate condemnation of Russia's persecution of Jews. The Senate approved the condemnation by a 60-to-1 vote.

Still another significant show of unity could come soon. The Synagogue Council of America, a loosely organized body of all three Jewish movements, hopes to create enthusiasm for a national conference on intermarriage.

Intermarriage for years was a problem Jews had identified but preferred to ignore. They can ignore it no longer. Only about 2,500 non-Jews convert to Judaism each year, while a far larger number of Jews become Christians.

"And what about the children in mixed marriages? How will they be reared?" asks Rabbi Philip Hiat, executive vice president of the Synagogue Council of America. "Perhaps Barry Goldwater is the best example of what usually happens." Senator Goldwater's part-Jewish ancestry inspired the famous crack by author-humorist Harry Golden: "I always knew the first Jewish President would be an Episcopalian."

The Jews' increasing assimilation into the American culture has proved but a partial blessing. On the one hand the Jewish community of the 1960s, as Rabbi Hirsch has noted, could merely blink at the fact that Jack Ruby, alias

Rabbi Maurice N. Eisendrath: "Jewish life . . . cannot survive . . . jockeying for power. . . ."

Prof. Mordecai M. Kaplan: Architect of Reconstructionism.

Rabbi Richard G. Hirsch: "Kosher is A-Okay."

Rubenstein, is a Jew; the community of the 1950s squirmed self-consciously over the Jewishness of atom spies Ethel and Julius Rosenberg. Yet the decline of anti-Semitism has erased a powerful justification for Jewish institutions. Discrimination against Jewish doctors, for example, long served as an excuse for the existence of Jewish hospitals.

More alarming, population trends point toward a diminishing Jewish influence in the years ahead. The percentage of Jews to the total population has dropped to 2.9 per cent from a high of 3.7 per cent in 1937. At current rates, it will plunge to 2.1 per cent in 1980 and 1.6 per cent in the year 2000.

Jews, like other minority groups, have found that the American melting pot has shaped them into a predominantly "Anglo-Saxon" mold and has submerged the various elements that made them "different." All the elements, that is, but one: The immigrant's religion. Or so goes the thesis of sociologist Will Herberg, a thesis most Jewish thinkers accept.

"Only Judaism the religion, in the final analysis, cements one Jew to another and all Jews to all other Jews, to assure their survival as Jews," wrote Arthur T. Jacobs, administrative secretary of the Union of American Hebrew Congregations, in American Judaism magazine.

Not Enough Rabbis

Yet Judaism as a faith faces unenviable problems. It has an acute shortage of rabbis—1,000 rabbinical posts remain unfilled—and not a few Jews find the caliber of the average rabbi woefully weak. "Time is running out on the rabbis," declares C. Bezalel Sherman, author of *The Jew Within American Society* and a Jew himself. "If they fail to assert their leadership now that the majority of the Jewish population is within their reach, they will not get a second chance."

Judaism suffers from another malady common to religion in America: A suspected shallowness of faith masked by the membership and building boom in the postwar era. Some Jews join synagogues as they join a country club; if the spiritual or material tariff gets too high, they get out. Several families in a Mississippi town, for example, recently joined the Unitarian church when their temple assessed its members for a building program.

More common—and perhaps more danger-

Jews see the preservation of Hebrew as a key to the preservation of Judaism itself. Here a professor at Yeshiva University in New York carries on the tradition.

ous for Judaism—is the Jew who remains a Jew, but in name only. Rabbi Hirsch calls them "alimony Jews—they're willing to pay for it, but they're not willing to live with it."

A recent B'nai B'rith survey of Jewish college students provides little hope for improvement. A full 91 per cent indicated they have a high regard for the synagogue, but only 5 per cent attend services more than once a month.

Concludes gloomy Rabbi Arthur Hertzberg, author and Columbia professor: "As ways of belief, our contemporary sects have failed, without exception, to produce either an answer that compels the perplexed to believe or a source of emotional power that touches their hearts."

What do Jews believe? They believe, first, in an omnipotent God. They believe, second, in practicing the teachings of the Torah.

Jews see two events related in the Torah as central to their history: The exodus from slavery in Egypt and God's handing down of the law on Mount Sinai. The one marked the creation of a people, the second the founding of a faith.

"Theologically, our whole Jewish tradition is built upon the experience of slavery," says Rabbi Hirsch. Unlike Christians, "a Jew can't attain salvation in an 'hour of decision.' He has to live a lifetime of commitment, and even then he doesn't achieve salvation." Jews can be "saved" only when all mankind reaches a state of perfection. Until this "messianic era" arrives, Jews are to remind themselves of their heritage of slavery; in the Haggadah, a narrative of the Exodus read in the Passover season, rabbis recite: "In every generation every Jew shall look upon himself as if he had been a slave like in Egypt."

The coming of the Messiah, Jews believe, will signal the beginning of mankind's state of perfection. Some Jews expect him to be an actual person, while others see the "Messiah" in terms of a "messianic era." But Jews don't accept Jesus as the Messiah for two theological reasons: First, Jesus failed to fulfill the Jewish conditions of a Messiah because he didn't bring lasting peace. Second, in being divine, Jesus became more than he was supposed to be. "No Jew ever said the Messiah was going to be more than a human being," says Rabbi Hirsch. "The idea of the Trinity—the Father, Son, and Holy Ghost—this Jews really rebel against."

Jews stress the here-and-now rather than the hereafter. They consider their faith "this-world oriented" and think little about an afterlife; thus they emphasize the need to labor for a Kingdom of God on earth. "A rabbi breathing 'hell-fire and brimstone' from the pulpit would be inconceivable," asserts the wife of an Orthodox rabbi.

Jews find in the Torah the outline of ethical practices by which to consecrate their daily lives to God. Wrote R. T. Herford in *The Truth About the Pharisees:* "The cornerstone of Judaism was the deed, not the dogma."

Action Now, Not Words

In their new-found status in America, Jews are making bold moves to demonstrate their emphasis on deeds. From local community relations councils to Rabbi Hirsch's Religious Action Center, Jews are sounding off as never before on social and political issues.

"Until recently most Jewish groups employed the 'TV approach' to social action," says Rabbi Hirsch. "We selected our own channels of activity." The activity centered on issues that directly concern Jews—relations with Israel, civil rights, church-state separation.

Dropping into a chair beneath a cast-iron statue of Isaiah beating swords into plowshares, Rabbi Hirsch stresses that Jews must now speak out on all moral issues—on disarmament, on poverty, on migrant worker problems, on civil rights.

"The Bible says, 'Seek good and not evil, that ye may live,' " he says. "If the Jewish community doesn't seek good, it's not going to live—except in name only." To most Jews, the Civil Rights Act fits the definition of "good"; hence the rabbinical and congregational wings of all three Jewish movements empowered Rabbi Hirsch to speak for the bill for them as it moved through Congress.

Social struggles may help renew and strengthen fervor for the Jewish faith. But education is perhaps most crucial in implanting it in the first place. Formal Jewish education, says Hillel Foundations official Norman E. Frimer, "indubitably is the Waterloo for Jewish survival and creativity."

Jews freely employ a classic Mark Twain phrase to describe Jewish education: "A mile wide and an inch deep." Of some 600,000 children receiving at least some Jewish instruction, only 9 per cent attend all-day schools.

Yet Jewish schools have improved markedly over the past decade. Enrolment has risen by 75 per cent while the total Jewish population has grown by a mere 11 per cent. Quality has kept pace, perhaps even forged ahead.

Jews speak proudly of mushrooming summer camps for religious education; Rabbi Panitz, lighting up a Newport, enthusiastically talks about the Conservative-operated Hebrew Camping Movement: "The boys play ball in Hebrew. They even pass the butter in Hebrew." Jews are pleased, too, with promising efforts by a few campus groups, such as the intercollegiate Orthodox organization's providing facilities for kosher food on a dozen Eastern campuses.

Interest in Judaism

The fever is spreading among adults. B'nai B'rith and several other Jewish organizations sponsor week-end or five-day institutes for adults during the summer, using the twin attractions of a vacation setting and controversial scholars. Profession-oriented education groups, such as the Association of Orthodox Scientists, have begun to spring up. Hundreds of synagogues sponsor evening classes; a Danish Lutheran pastor active in the World War II underground, for example, spent two months lecturing in the United States under the adult education program of B'nai B'rith.

The reviving interest in Jewish values among adults heartens Jewish leaders. "You can't transmit to the kids what you don't have yourselves," says one.

What the parents are getting, it's apparent, is an image of Judaism that's largely religious. If Judaism survives in the United States, it will survive as a faith.

"If it survives. . . ." The words tumble off the lips of not a few Jews. Yet, just as assimilation persists, the Jewish faith also persists.

A paradox? Indeed it is. But Jewish life, in the words of a Yiddish aphorism, somehow seems to thrive on its own paradoxes. ♦

The Unitarians

—Robert de Gast

Unitarians at issue.

The Intellectual Advance Guard

Unitarians Argue, Debate, Rethink All Doctrines, Including Their Own, Lead the Way in Many Areas

BOSTON.

TO most Americans, nothing could be more important to a religious denomination than deciding whether it's Christian or non-Christian. The question seems basic.

But ask a Unitarian whether or not he's a Christian. He may say he is, or he may say he isn't. Most likely he will say it makes little difference.

"We have great diversity within a very narrow framework," says the Rev. Raymond C. Hopkins, executive vice president of the 260,000-member Unitarian Universalist Association (UUA). Even the most conservative Unitarians wouldn't be considered Christians by the average Christian, he explains, for they don't believe in the divinity of Christ. The question debated by Unitarians, who believe Jesus was a man and not the Son of God, centers on the extent to which they should emphasize the importance of Jesus' teachings.

Each year they squabble at their general assembly over how far they should stray from the Christianity in which their religion was born and nurtured. A constitutional clause, adopted after an all-night fight on the convention floor when Unitarians and Universalists merged in 1959, asserts that they seek "to cherish and spread the universal truths . . . immemorially summarized in the Judeo-Christian heritage as love to God and love to man."

In what has become an annual ritual, some delegates ask the assembly to strengthen the group's ties with Christianity by declaring their faith "in the spiritual leadership of Jesus." Others would move in the other direction, striking out even the current reference to their "Judeo-Christian heritage."

The issue no longer interests the old hands. "Most of us react with an 'O Lord, not that again!' when it comes up now," says one veteran of several assemblies. "We'd much rather fight over something else."

Fight they do. Not over resolutions for promoting nuclear disarmament, pushing civil rights, or relaxing abortion laws; such positions, which would produce convulsions within most denominations, sail through almost without opposition. Instead, they fight over internal matters of principle, matters such as a proposed change in their constitution to prohibit racial discrimination in admitting members.

Nearly every Unitarian advocates open membership. But few want the association telling local congregations what to do. To avoid an impasse at the 1964 assembly, Unitarians bucked the issue to a board that approves membership applications by churches; it's understood, but not spelled out, that the board will admit no church that discriminates in membership.

This hand-wringing over principles helps to explain why this small denomination finds itself in the middle of more than its share of large controversies.

Sherri Finkbine, a Phoenix television personality and a Unitarian, dramatized rigid abortion statutes in 1962 after learning she had taken the deforming drug, thalidomide. Mrs. Finkbine tried to have an abortion performed in the United States, but finally gave up and went to Sweden for the operation.

A Unitarian family, the Edward Schempps of Pennsylvania's Abington Township, brought to the courts the case that resulted in the Supreme Court's landmark decision of 1963 forbidding states from requiring Bible readings in public schools.

In 1964, nearly 50 Unitarians participated in the 600-man Mississippi Summer Project on

Unitarians in the news: Mr. and Mrs. Edward Schempp and family before the Supreme Court building, where they took a case that led to Court decisions opposing Bible readings and prayer services in public schools.

civil rights. The UUA offered reward money for the apprehension of the killers of three civil-rights workers in Mississippi before any other organization.

Unitarians eschew dogma. But as their position on these three issues shows, they place great emphasis on faith in man. The Rev. Dana McLean Greeley, UUA president, leans back in his third-story office next to Massachusetts' gold-domed state house here and explains why.

"Scientists are recognizing that there's absolutely no limit to man's scientific potential, yet theologians caution that we mustn't go too far," he says, adjusting the smart black vest that hides his red-striped tie. Man's scientific achievements, he argues, prove his vast potential in other areas. "Religion will rise or fall on its faith in man as a child of God—not as a sinner, not as a being of very limited potential."

Unitarian-Universalists pride themselves on having no established creed, insisting they believe only what each individual chooses to believe. They draw freely upon the religious teachings of all of the world's great religions.

At the Charles Street Universalist Meeting House here, for example, the Bible of Christianity shares its place of honor with the Torah of Judaism, the Koran of Mohammedanism, and various Buddhist holy works. New York City's Community Church for years has held services of non-Christian faiths during seasons of special significance. A new Unitarian hymnal has Taoist, Christian, Confucianist, Jewish, Hindu, Buddhist, and "humanist" hymns and scripture readings.

The doctrinal rejection of Jesus' divinity, so important in the Unitarian heritage, first appeared among European Christians in the Sixteenth Century. Boston's historic King's Chapel, the first Episcopal church in New England, struck all references to the Trinity of the Father, Son, and Holy Ghost from its *Book of Common Prayer* in 1785. Nine years later scientist-theologian Joseph Priestley, discoverer of oxygen, founded the first church in America to bear the Unitarian name in Northumberland, Pennsylvania.

Unitarian beliefs flourished in post-Revolutionary America. John Adams, Thomas Paine, John Marshall—in fact, one-third of the original members of the Hall of Fame for great

Americans at New York University (founded in 1900)—were Unitarians. Declared Thomas Jefferson: "I trust there is not a young man now living in the United States who will not die a Unitarian."

Jefferson's enthusiasm proved greater than his foresight. A century and a half later, on the eve of the merger, Unitarians numbered a mere 107,000. Universalists, whose name comes from their belief that salvation is universal for all of mankind, claimed 43,000 members before the merger.

Since the merger, Unitarian membership has climbed by more than 70 per cent. Though its members still account for only one-tenth of one per cent of the nation's population, they exert a political and social influence in the United States out of all proportion to their number.

"Our strength is our independent-mindedness," says the Rev. Dr. Greeley. Unitarians argue that this tends to produce social activists and political leaders. Unitarian rolls include United Nations Ambassador Adlai Stevenson; Chester Bowles, ambassador to India, and 5 of the 100 United States senators, from liberal Democrat Joseph Clark of Pennsylvania to conservative Republican Roman Hruska of Nebraska.

But it can also be argued that Unitarianism attracts, rather than produces, free thinkers. More than 85 per cent of all Unitarian men were raised in non-Unitarian families. Fully 40 per cent of the Unitarian ministers have been ordained in other denominations, and many other ministers of other faiths apply. The Rev. Dr. Greeley ascribes this phenomenon to the growing orthodoxy, the "leaning to the right," of many denominations.

Not content to let their resolutions do their talking, Unitarians work actively in Washington on the legislative front. Robert E. Jones, director of the Washington office of the Unitarians' department of social responsibility, wheels around the Capital trying to drum up support for Unitarian stands on nuclear disarmament, civil rights, and countless other issues.

"We Unitarians aren't great in numbers," says the casual, crew-cut Mr. Jones, munching on a mid-morning apple. "But we hope to make our influence felt. We try to serve as the leaven to the loaf of reform." ♦

Influential Unitarians on both sides of the political spectrum: Liberal Democratic Sen. Joseph Clark, of Pennsylvania, left; conservative Republican Sen. Roman Hruska, of Nebraska, right.

The Quakers

Quaker worship: The essence of democracy.

The 'Priesthood of All Believers'

The Gentle Friends Look to Theology and to Their Heritage to Reawaken and Recharge Christianity

RICHMOND, IND.

"A Quaker seminary."

The phrase sounds strange. The Religious Society of Friends—or "Quakers"—traditionally has shunned an organized ministry, preaching instead the "priesthood of all believers."

Yet on the tranquil Earlham College campus in Richmond, Indiana, the Quakers have inaugurated a full-fledged theological school. The Earlham School of Religion has inspired new interest in the Friends, long known for their humanitarian service and for their association with pacifism. And it promises to stir the whole caldron of Protestant thought about ministers and laymen.

"We don't want to just stew in our own Quaker juice," says Earlham's Prof. D. Elton Trueblood. "We want to penetrate the world."

Prof. Trueblood, who has written some 20 books on philosophy and theology, has earned a wide reputation as an interpreter of contemporary Quaker thought. A measure of the esteem in which he's held at Quaker-sponsored Earlham College: A one-story Colonial brick building nestled in the trees of the campus contains but one room, Dr. Trueblood's study.

Prof. Trueblood moves from desk to easy chair to 2,000-volume bookshelf in his wood-paneled study as he talks about the new Earlham School of Religion. Like the other men instrumental in its founding, he stresses it's not intended to become "just another seminary" in a day when many seminaries are having trouble recruiting qualified students.

Instead, Earlham will emphasize a fresh concept of the ministry, a concept rooted in the teachings of the early Quakers of the Seventeenth Century but applied with new force to

Prof. D. Elton Trueblood: "We want to penetrate the world."

Twentieth Century society. It's a concept designed to combat apathy among Christians, a malady common to many denominations.

"Our enemy today is not atheism," explains Dr. Trueblood. "That doesn't bother us a bit. Our enemy is mild religion."

Prof. Trueblood and his colleagues at Earlham will stress that (1) every Christian has a "ministry," and (2) especially gifted persons should be trained to encourage their fellow Christians to find and pursue that "ministry." Some of the gifted persons would be trained to perform a nonpastoral ministry in such fields as teaching, nursing, or operating a business employing handicapped persons.

Quakers trace the idea of a "universal ministry" to their founder, George Fox, who criticized what he called a "hireling ministry" that was educated at class-conscious schools, dressed in distinctive robes, and traveled in "status" society. Fox concluded that God and Jesus Christ speak to men through an "Inner Voice," a voice any man can hear. God calls all men to do His work, making all believers "ministers." But He has given some men the responsibility of being "pastors and teachers"; thus the need arises for an "equipping" ministry, in which some persons help equip others for Christian work.

Quaker Ministers

Dr. Wilmer A. Cooper, dean of the Earlham School of Religion, believes that the idea that "ministers are a different breed of cats from the rest of us" is falling from favor. He detects a growing feeling among many Protestants that ministers are teachers, co-ordinators—catalytic agents working within the congregation.

The Quaker concept permits local Quaker congregations either to employ ministers or not to employ them, as they see fit. Until about 75 years ago, none did. Now two-thirds of the nation's Quaker congregations, largely in the Midwest and Far West, have pastors.

The traditional Quaker practice of holding silent worship meetings also is less prevalent than in earlier days. Some Quaker congregations, chiefly along the Eastern Seaboard, continue to hold only unprogramed services, periods of silence interrupted only when a person—any person—desires to speak. Many of the other congregations, such as the boyhood church of former Vice President Richard M. Nixon in Whittier, California, schedule periods of silent meditation before or after the normal worship service.

In recent years, the feeling grew among Quakers that they needed a school of religion, both to produce Quaker pastors and to prepare Quakers and non-Quakers who want to go into some form of the nonpastoral ministry. Earlham, located in the center of the largest concentration of Friends in the nation, was a logical choice for the site.

Earlham School of Religion attracts many students from outside the Quaker movement. Its student body—30 in 1963-64 and 40 in 1964-65—has included Episcopalians, Methodists, Baptists, and Mennonites. More than half of the students come from other traditions.

Why do non-Quakers choose Earlham? Consider the case of Robert Foster, a Dartmouth graduate and a successful Massachusetts real estate man, who decided to enter the ministry. Mr. Foster admired the work of the Friends in sponsoring spiritual retreats for laymen. Though a Congregationalist, he concluded that studying under Prof. Trueblood and his Earlham associates would provide the type of training he wanted for a nonpastoral ministry.

The Ideal Is Service

Earlham offers an extensive program for persons who, like Robert Foster, want to devote their career to full-time Christian service, though not in a preaching capacity. "We don't believe the only bona fide way to minister is to preach," says Prof. Calvin W. Redekop, a Mennonite on the Earlham faculty.

Under Professor Redekop's guidance, the School of Religion is conducting a "Community Services Internship Program" that involves students in internships in mental hospitals, community development programs, social welfare work, local pastorates, and the like. One student and his wife, for example, live for the entire year in an interracial, low-income area of Richmond; Earlham students gather there frequently for meetings and school-sponsored work projects in the neighborhood. The faculty believes that Earlham orients its classes and internships more heavily to the nonpastoral ministry than does any other seminary.

Earlham has developed another program not usually offered in seminaries. Every Tuesday, all faculty members and students assemble

A new direction for Quakers.

for a luncheon meal and a lecture course by a member of the faculty. Prof. Trueblood lectured one term on "The Philosophy of the Christian Ministry." Prof. Alexander Purdy, one of the nation's most brilliant New Testament scholars and the retired dean of Hartford Theological Seminary, discussed "Christian Discipleship" another term. Prof. Canby Jones, chairman of the religion department at Ohio's Wilmington College, gave a series of lectures on "The Devotional Life." The program has twin attractions for the faculty: The professors become better acquainted with each other's ideas and work, and the lecturers are stimulated by their colleagues' presence to do some especially creative thinking.

Not all of the thinkers agree with each other. The Quakers' whole approach toward religion—toward religious beliefs and toward their organizational structure—encourages diversity.

"Our system has its dangers," comments Dean Cooper. "Sometimes we go so far we have virtual anarchy."

But Quakers prize their freedom of belief,

Quakers picket—in silence—before the Pentagon. The year was 1960; the doctrine behind it was age-old.

and the differences in outlook among different congregations show it. Their attitudes span the theological spectrum from the deep involvement in social causes by some liberal Philadelphia area congregations to the literal interpretation of the Bible by many fundamentalist Kansas and Oregon congregations.

By founding the Earlham School of Religion and providing such Quaker thinkers as Elton Trueblood a new platform from which to speak, Earlham College has stirred the coals of many debates that smolder under the surface among Quakers.

Consider pacifism. Officially, the Quaker position on pacifism has remained the same for 300 years. Quakers first set it forth in 1660 in a statement to Charles II of England, in which they said in essence that they would refuse to bear arms regardless of how worthy the cause might be.

Pacifism a Problem

But Quakers today vigorously disagree over how they should express their pacifism. Lawrence Miller, Jr., general secretary of the Friends General Conference (which includes most congregations in the East), proudly recalls the Quaker vigil in front of the Pentagon several years ago. The vigil attracted hundreds of Friends from around the country. On the other hand, Prof. Trueblood rejects the picketing-and-demonstration approach, which he calls "doctrinaire pacifism." "A man can be a conscientious objector himself," he says, "without thereby claiming that all who enter the armed forces are un-Christian."

The degrees of pacifism and the Quaker encouragement of freedom of conscience make it impossible to measure the percentage of Quakers who are pacifists. Since the late 1600s, Quaker historians agree, true pacifists have been in the minority within the movement. In the opinion of one Earlham staff member, however, Quaker enthusiasm for pacifism has reached a new low during the past several decades. He estimates that a mere 25 per cent of draft-eligible Quakers now seek to be classified as conscientious objectors.

Many Midwestern Quakers also display diminishing enthusiasm for putting heavy emphasis on a second activity for which the Quakers are widely known—service.

No one disputes the importance of the humanitarian work of the Quakers, which won the American Friends Service Committee a Nobel Peace Prize in 1947. "But you can't take the cup of water to the needy and figure you're home clean," says Dean Cooper.

Adds Prof. Trueblood: "Quakerism at its best has always made sure there's a connection between its roots and its fruits. If it stresses only the roots (religious experience), it becomes bogged down in self-indulgence. If it stresses only the fruits (service), it engages in secularized philanthropy."

Prof. Trueblood believes that Quakerism emerged from a quiet 200-year period of relative "self-indulgence" late in the last century. But the pendulum, in his view, then swung too far the other way. Quakers ignored the unique heritage of the "exciting, glorious period" of 1650-1690 and adopted the conventional religious patterns around them. They began to adopt all the trappings of a "hireling" ministry, for example, without even providing the ministers a proper education. They plunged into humanitarian ventures without placing sufficient emphasis on the spiritual "healing" ministry within their own movement.

The Old Ideals

Now, he says, the Earlham School of Religion believes it is helping to usher in a new period, in which Quakerism returns to the ideals of its founders. Far from being concerned about the Quakers' lack of growth in recent years (their U.S. membership has remained relatively static at about 120,000), Prof. Trueblood looks to the day when the Quakers, as a sect, will disappear. That will be a day when "mild religion" has been conquered, when every Christian is himself a "minister."

"Quakerism originally was intended to be a ferment within all of Christianity, not a sect in one part of it," Prof. Trueblood continues. "We wouldn't be denying our heritage then. We'd be recovering it."

In recovering their heritage, in reminding themselves and other Protestants of an earlier century's emphasis upon the Christian layman, Quakers can help recharge other Christian faiths. The new age has already begun. Christian leaders, inspired by Prof. Trueblood and other persuasive advocates of the "priesthood of all believers," are urging—and getting—a deeper commitment from laymen than ever before. ♦

The Moravians

An Eighteenth Century manuscript of "And Jesus Said: It Is Finished," by John Antes, early Moravian composer.

Music and the Ministry

A Pioneer Protestant Faith Augments Its Reputation By Recovering a Rich Era of Early American Music

BETHLEHEM, PA.

THE Moravian Church has an intriguing history of religious pioneering. In a sense, Moravians were the first Protestants; their spiritual forebears united to protest religious abuses 60 years before Martin Luther posted his *95 Theses* in 1517. Moravians were the first Protestants to do missionary work as a church, and two centuries ago they were raising lonely voices on behalf of Christian unity.

Now Moravians in America, who number a mere 60,000, are laboring to revive a rich but almost forgotten era in American musical culture. Tiny pre-Revolutionary settlements of Moravians in Pennsylvania and North Carolina, they proudly recall, produced an astounding quantity of good sacred music.

Since 1950, several Early American Moravian Music Festivals have re-created the musical vitality of Moravians in the Colonies. At the 1964 festival here in Bethlehem, Pennsylvania, seven Moravian works were performed for the first time in two centuries.

The Moravian Music Foundation in 1956 began collecting, cataloging, and publishing early Moravian music. So far it has published about 50 Moravian works; another 11,000 manuscripts lie unpublished, and in many cases unedited, in the underground vault beneath the foundation's headquarters in Winston-Salem, North Carolina.

Enthusiasm for Moravian music is spreading rapidly to other religious groups. Choir directors of many faiths have snapped up more than 300,000 copies of John Frederik Peter's Eighteenth Century anthem, *It Is a Precious Thing*. A Baptist in upstate New York terms it "the finest anthem I've ever sung—any place, any time."

Enthused a clarinetist from the Pablo Casals Conservatory in Puerto Rico at the 1964 festival: "This Moravian stuff is phenomenal for the Eighteenth Century—doubly phenomenal for Colonial America. I've spent a lot of time in Philadelphia, just a couple of hours drive away," he said, pacing back and forth on a Moravian College stage as he practiced tricky fingerings, "and I had never heard of this very rich musical literature of our early times."

A rich musical literature it was. Many Moravian immigrants in the 1700s had brushed shoulders with the musical greats of the day in Europe—with the Bachs and the Mozarts and the Haydns. They brought hundreds of manuscripts with them when they sailed for America, and they wrote often to European friends deeply immersed in the musical currents of the day.

Moravian church music constituted the bulk of the sacred music composed in the United States before the 1830s. Yet, because the Moravians had settled in frontier areas, miles away from heavily traveled routes along the East Coast, they remained isolated from the cultural mainstream of America.

The inevitable result, declares Dr. Thor Johnson, a distinguished conductor and a Moravian, was that "Moravian music had a negligible influence on later American music. It was performed in the local Moravian church, tossed on top of a pile of manuscripts, and left to gather dust in the church attic."

For all their talent, the Moravian composers were no Mozarts. Musicians generally compare them with such "lesser greats" as Rosetti, Danzi, and Reicha. Their music, say the instrumentalists, was neither as profound nor as inventive as Mozart's or Haydn's.

Nearly every Moravian composer in Colonial days was an ordained minister. And, it seemed, almost every minister was a composer. Moravians say facetiously that their early American ministers "not only had to preach the sermon, but also compose the anthem, every week."

A Moravian, John Antes, composed the first chamber music written by an American. The Moravian community of Bethlehem produced the nation's first symphony orchestra, the Collegium Musicum, in 1744. The Moravian Trombone Choir, organized in 1754, contends it has been in continuous existence longer than any other musical group in the United States.

Unlike the more staid denominations in early America, Moravians used brasses, wood winds, and strings for sacred as well as secular music. After a Moravian youth finished some Haydn chamber music one Saturday afternoon, tradition says, a haughty New England clergyman asked, "Will you use the same instruments in church to play sacred music that you used today?" Replied the Moravian: "And shall you, sir, pray with the same mouth tomorrow with which you are now eating sausages?"

Song a Part of Life

Music then was a must for all Moravians. Children may have had to eat off crude wooden tables, but they were taught the flute, the viola da gamba, or the French horn. The town watchman sang a couplet every hour as he made his rounds. Moravians composed hymns for each craft—spinners, shepherds, plowmen, seamstresses, washwomen—and a band of musicians accompanied workers whether they went out to harvest crops, to cut timber, or to build a barn. At one 1755 Moravian worship service, a single hymn was sung in 13 different languages at the same time.

Many Moravians today are trying their talents at writing hymns, anthems, and chorales. But Dr. Johnson concedes that so far "the quality has not been what we're looking for." Moravians may have the interest in music their ancestors had, but they don't have the training.

Indirectly, however, the Moravian music revival has inspired a wave of new religious music in the United States. For the Moravians' 500th anniversary celebration in 1957, they commissioned Vittorio Giannini to write an oratorio, *Canticle of the Martyrs*. Recalls Dr. Johnson, who was chairman of a National Council of Churches music commission at the time: "You could just watch the idea spring around the table from denomination to denomination." The Methodists commissioned an oratorio for a youth conference a year later, and in 1964 a Baptist-commissioned oratorio, *What Is Man?*, was premiered at a large Baptist gathering in Atlantic City.

At times, perhaps, the Moravians' enthusiasm for music has bordered on the fanatical.

Music is a way of life for the old Moravian churches.

But in religious doctrines, they embody the essence of moderation.

The public's association of Moravians with Pennsylvania Dutch sects such as the Amish and the Mennonites bothers Moravian Church leaders. "The people with the Kodachrome film want us to become quaint," says Dr. John R. Weinlick, professor of historical theology at Moravian Theological Seminary here. "We're trying to change the quaint image, to remind people that we're a going Twentieth Century concern."

Moravian beliefs and practices resemble those of the Lutherans and the Episcopalians. They stress that salvation is achieved through faith in Jesus as their personal Savior. They subscribe to the Apostles Creed. The closest thing they have to a denominational creed is the phrase, repeated in several of their liturgies: "Christ, and Him Crucified."

Moravians advocated close interfaith contacts long before the ecumenical movement became fashionable. Count Zinzendorf, a European benefactor who visited America in 1742 and named the city of Bethlehem, first tried to achieve a union of Protestant churches on the Continent, and later in the Colonies. The Moravian Church, a founder of both the National Council of Churches and the World Council of Churches, is starting to explore union with other small denominations.

Early Missionaries

Moravians long have been zealous missionaries, especially among primitive peoples. Sixty years before the modern missionary movement started in England, the Moravians in the 1730s were sending missionaries to Greenland, Latin America, and the Hottentot territory of South Africa. "Many of them honestly believed they had an obligation to prevent these people from being singed over the fires of hell 24 hours a day," says the Rev. Dr. F. P. Stocker, highest administrative officer for Moravian churches in the North.

It was the Moravians' missionary interest in American Indians, in fact, that first brought the Moravians to North America. The first Moravians to settle in the Colonies traveled to Georgia in 1735 aboard the same ship as John and Charles Wesley. The Wesleys came to this country to work among the whites in Georgia, the Moravians to work among the Indians.

Illness and the unpopularity of their pacifist position forced the early Moravian settlers to move. They chose to settle in Quaker-governed Pennsylvania, and to work among Indians there. Two decades later, a large group organized a new settlement in North Carolina.

Moravians retain but one mission to Indians, an all-Indian congregation near Banning, California. They continue a vigorous missionary program among the Eskimos in Alaska, and Moravian missions ring the world from Tibet to Surinam. Two-thirds of the world Moravian membership of 300,000 lives in such missionary areas as southern Africa, South America, and Asia.

Moravians are joined world-wide in the Unitas Fratrum (Unity of the Brethren), organized in 1457 by the followers of the Bohemian martyr, John Huss. At the beginning of the Reformation, the churches of the Unitas Fratrum—which opposed the corruption in the Roman Catholic Church and advocated ethical rather than theological reform—numbered about 200,000 members.

Small in Size

The Moravians have never grown much beyond this number. During the Seventeenth Century, they were driven underground; only through the "hidden seed," a tiny band of Brethren who preserved the traditions of the church, did the church endure. The renewed Unitas Fratrum emerged in 1722, when Count Zinzendorf permitted them to build a town on his estate.

In that era the church first became known as "Moravian," for many of the leaders of the renewal came from Moravia, an area in central Europe that became part of Czechoslovakia in 1918. In that era, too, Moravian ideas began to spread that were later to influence such eminent thinkers as Goethe and Kierkegaard.

Moravians in the United States, who constitute the largest single national group, are divided into two "provinces," north and south. Like the other five Unitas Fratrum provinces, they cherish their independence, yet cooperate in such activities as missionary work and the musical revival.

Moravians elect bishops, though the bishops' powers are spiritual and not administrative. Like the Episcopalians, they follow the apostolic suc-

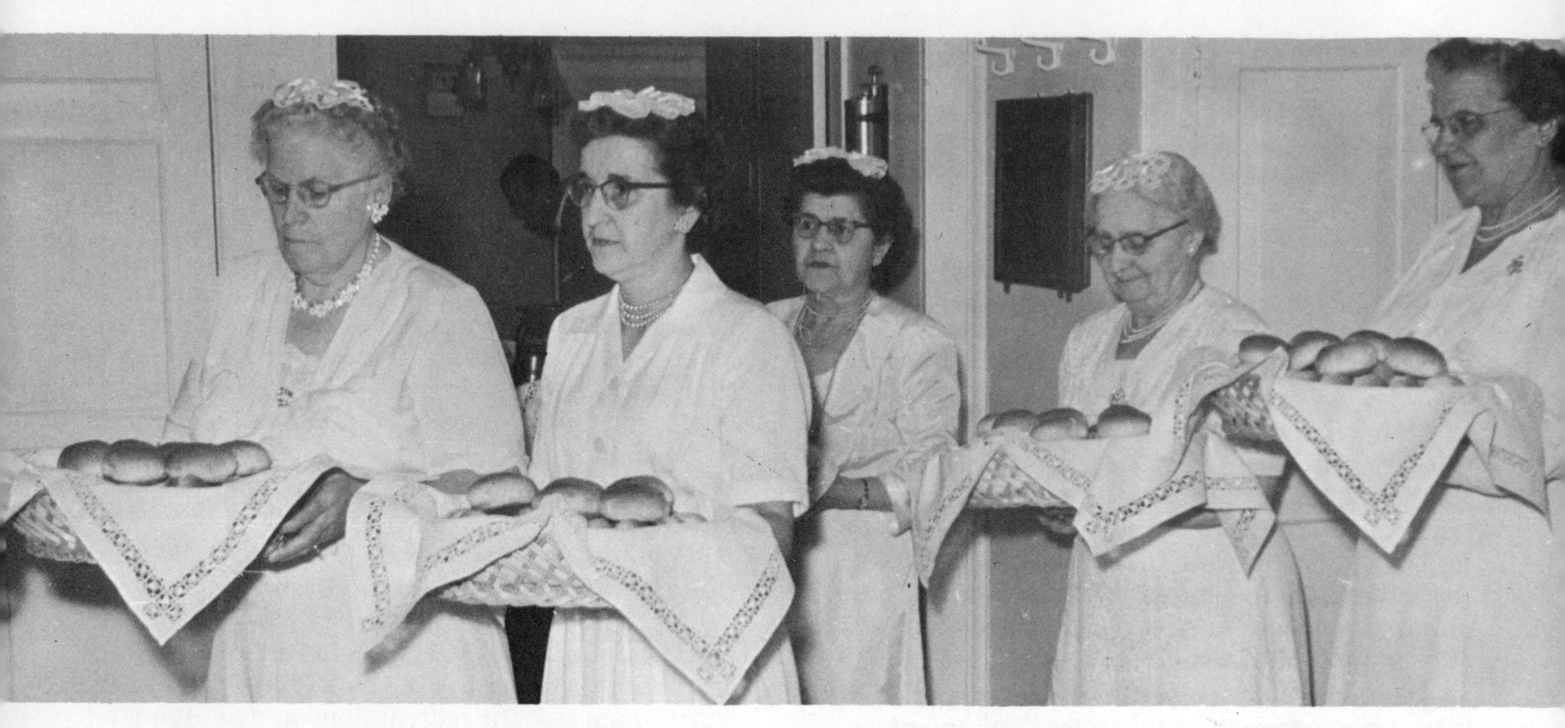

The "love feast," an old Moravian custom, combining worship, songs, coffee, and buns.

cession, the ordination of ministers by the laying on of hands by bishops; unlike the Episcopalians, they don't regard it as an essential doctrine. "If anyone could prove to us that we don't have an unbroken line of succession back to Christ, we wouldn't care," says Professor Weinlick. "We don't believe there's anything sacred in physical contact."

Moravians are afflicted by the familiar catalog of religious problems: Diminishing zeal, a dearth of new ministers, an emphasis on the form instead of the content of Christianity. "Like the great majority of Protestants," says Professor Weinlick, "we are so middle-class that we have become awkward and ineffective in evangelizing the less respectable." The "Inner City," Moravian leaders say, has replaced the Indian territories as the frontier in American life. Yet Moravian leaders argue they have neither the financial resources nor the manpower to undertake a major effort in the cities.

Moravians seem destined to remain a small denomination with only regional influence. The Moravian message differs little from the message of several larger Protestant denominations, and the Moravian attitude toward other faiths makes high-powered recruiting moves unlikely.

Moravians do, however, retain a few of their distinctive customs of earlier days. Their older churches still hold "love feasts"—worship services at which songs are sung, and buns and coffee are served. Moravian families still assemble a *Putz,* or a nativity scene, in their home at Christmas time. The trombone choir still plays, and a "hymnanny" here and there indicates the old *Singstundes,* or songfests, may be returning. But striking features of the early Moravian settlements in America—austere dress, a pacifist posture, a thriving communal society—vanished by the early 1800s. Moravians never regarded these as rigid religious necessities; when the customs became outdated, they abandoned them.

They abandoned, as well, the use of the "lot," an anachronistic test of faith in a highly cultured community. Early Moravians submitted difficult decisions to the lot, convinced that God would speak His will. First they prayed, then they drew a slip of paper marked either "yes," "no," or "no decision." Says Dr. Stocker: "They were sensible enough to give the Lord a little latitude, not to box Him into the corner. A month later, if they didn't like the answer, they phrased the question differently, and submitted it to another lot."

The lot and the communal life are gone, and their loss is not mourned. But Moravian music, given up for dead for decades, is being revived. Moravians and music experts of many other faiths are determined to see that it lives. ♦

America's Largest Religious Groups

Where They Live, By Area

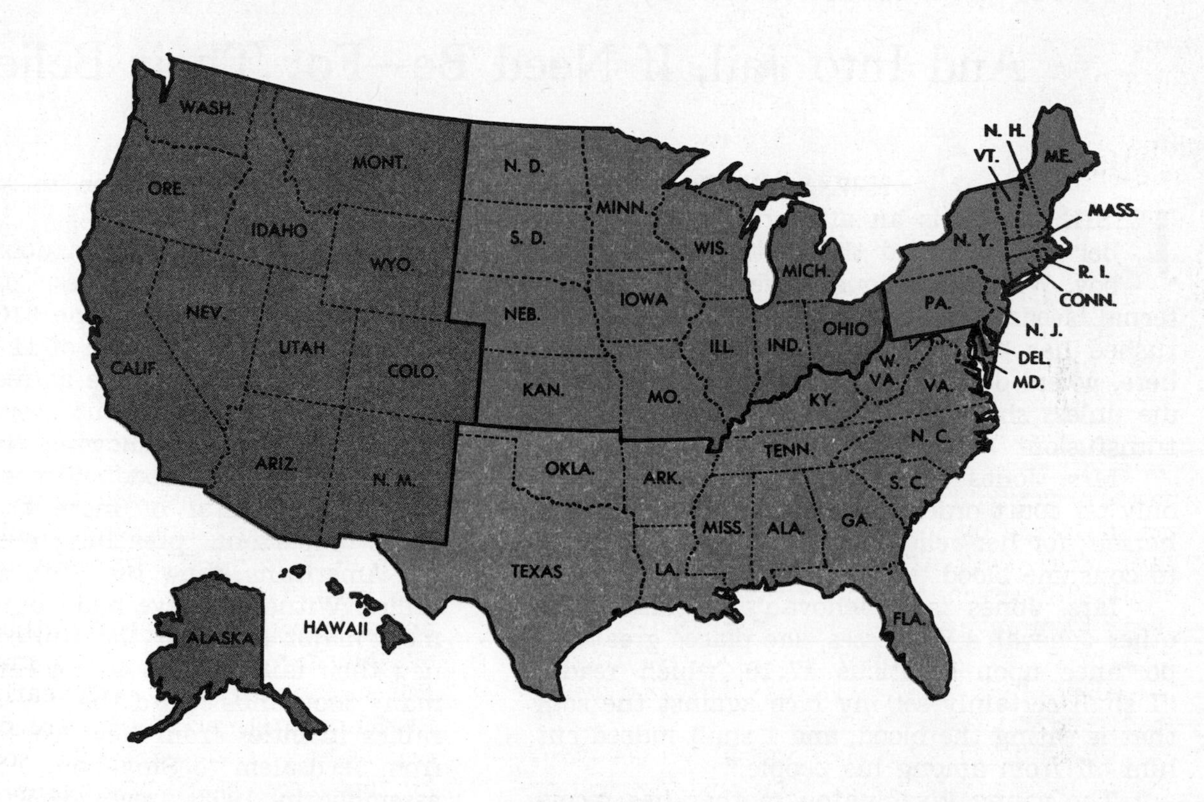

	West	North Central	South	North-east	U.S.
Protestant	14.5%	30.4%	38.3%	16.8%	100%
Roman Catholic	12.1%	28.0%	13.9%	46.0%	100%
Jewish	11.3%	11.9%	7.7%	69.1%	100%
Other Religions	14.2%	26.5%	17.4%	41.9%	100%

Based on *Population of the United States*, by Donald J. Bogue (Glencoe, Illinois, The Free Press). Used by permission of The Free Press.

Jehovah's Witnesses

Active Missionaries, They Go From Door to Door—And Into Jail, If Need Be—For Their Beliefs

WASHINGTON, D. C.

JESSIE JONES is an attractive housewife in her late 20s, and the mother of a young boy. When Mrs. Jones developed severe internal bleeding in September 1963, her husband rushed her to Georgetown University Hospital here, where doctors determined that she would die unless she were given an emergency blood transfusion.

Mrs. Jones received the transfusion, but only on court order. She refused to sanction it herself, for her religion teaches that it is a sin to consume blood.

Mrs. Jones is a Jehovah's Witness. Like other Jehovah's Witnesses, she places great importance upon Leviticus 17:10, which reads: "I shall certainly set my face against the soul that is eating the blood, and I shall indeed cut him off from among his people."

The young Washington mother has recovered fully now, but she insists that if she were faced with the same emergency again, she would again refuse to take blood. "It is better to keep God's law, even in the face of death," she says, "than to compromise one's belief."

Such dedication to faith is not rare among Jehovah's Witnesses. It is, in fact, quite common. This dedication, translated into a missionary zeal with few modern parallels, is the key to understanding the phenomenal growth of this religious movement.

From a small Bible class in 1872 led by Charles Taze Russell, a Pittsburgh haberdasher who was raised a Presbyterian, the movement has grown to a world-wide community of more than 1,000,000 members in 194 countries and territories. Leaders of the movement, which is officially known as the Watch Tower Bible and Tract Society, boast that more than 60,000 Witnesses are being baptized each year.

Americans have come to know the Witnesses in various ways.

They know them from door-to-door evangelism. Armed with Bibles, pamphlets, and sometimes phonographs, the 310,000 American members spend an average of 11 hours a month following Christ's example as recorded in Luke 8:1: "He went throughout every city and village, preaching and showing the glad tidings of the kingdom of God." Witnesses around the world log a total of more than 150,000,000 hours of personal preaching every 12 months.

Americans know the Witnesses from mass rallies. Witnesses have had large gatherings in most major cities in the United States to renew their faith and to accept converts. In 1963, many thousands heard the message at 24 mass rallies in cities from New York to Stockholm, from Jerusalem to Singapore. An international assembly in 1958 drew 254,500 Witnesses to Yankee Stadium and the Polo Grounds in New York for what the Witnesses contend was the largest gathering of any kind ever held in New York City.

Finally, Americans know the Witnesses from books and pamphlets. The Witnesses publish 125,000,000 items of religious literature each year for distribution in homes, on street corners, and at public events. The semimonthly magazine Watchtower, published in 68 languages (including such obscure African dialects as Cinyanja and Xhosa), has a circulation of 4,400,000. More than 17,000,000 copies of *Let God Be True,* the basic doctrinal statement of the Witnesses, have been printed since 1946.

In a recent article in U. S. Catholic, a monthly published by the Claretian Fathers, Prof. William J. Whalen of Purdue University described the "complete commitment" of the Witnesses. Wrote Professor Whalen, a Catholic:

Zealots for Christ

Jehovah's Witnesses pack huge Yankee Stadium to hear the "Everlasting Good News."

"Each Witness—man or woman, adult or child—knows he must become an active missionary. He must establish a set of priorities in his personal life which will reserve first place to missionary work. . . . There is no place in this cult for passive membership."

Witnesses deny they are a cult. They consider themselves a separate religion, the world's only true followers of the Lord, whom they call "Jehovah God." They regard the Bible as a sacred book of prophecy, describing actual events yet to come. Their name comes from Isaiah 43:10: "Ye are my witnesses, saith the Lord, and my servant whom I have chosen."

The Witnesses believe that the end of the world is imminent, and that they have been chosen to warn of its coming. The final struggle between God and Satan will be resolved in the Biblical battle of Armageddon, from which only the faithful—the Witnesses—will survive. They believe that 144,000 Witnesses, including the righteous from all ages, will be picked to rule in heaven. The rest of the faithful will enjoy everlasting life on earth.

Believers reject the concept of hell. A just God, they reason, would not permit eternal torment. The wicked are simply destroyed.

Witnesses also dismiss the concept of the Trinity as "unscriptural," and they do not believe in the immortality of the soul because, they say, the Bible does not say man was given a soul. They emphasize Christ's subservience to God. "Jesus Christ is God's Son," says Pennsylvania-born Nathan H. Knorr, president of the Watch Tower Bible and Tract Society. "But Jesus did not claim to be co-equal with his Father."

The Witnesses' devotion to the future world has often led them to challenge established authority in the present one. Disdaining all governments as evil, most Witnesses refuse to vote, bear arms, or salute the flag, which they consider a "graven image."

No Compromise

Court cases on compulsory flag salutes and on the distribution of religious literature, initiated by Witnesses in the late 1930s and early 1940s, forced the Supreme Court to develop for the first time a consistent constitutional doctrine toward freedom of religion. "By their fanaticism and refusal to compromise with the state," writes Prof. Murray S. Stedman, Jr., of Trinity College in *Religion and Politics in America,* "this marginal and unorthodox religious group managed to spur the Supreme Court into defining (one could even say enlarging) the religious liberties of all Americans."

To Jail for a Cause

Several of the society's leaders, including Charles Taze Russell's successor, Missouri lawyer "Judge" Joseph F. Rutherford, were jailed under the Espionage Act for distributing anti-war leaflets during World War I. Some 10,000 German members were thrown into Hitler's concentration camps 20 years later. In the early days of World War II, Witnesses in several cities were beaten and mobbed for what their opponents described as their lack of patriotism.

Antagonism still lingers. The American Legion of New York State protested the publicity given one rally of the society, which it called "an organization which refused to raise a hand to protect its country." Many Witnesses feed the antagonism by openly displaying contempt for other religions—particularly Roman Catholicism, which Joseph Rutherford once denounced as "the chief visible enemy of God, and therefore the greatest and worst public enemy."

Today's Witnesses, maintains Mr. Knorr, "have no fight with any man because of his religious belief. They seek only to learn the truth from the Bible and then tell it to others."

Mr. Knorr, a quiet, retiring man, has been a full-time Witness since graduating from high school in 1923. He became president upon "Judge" Rutherford's death in 1942, when world membership was a mere 115,200. The society's contempt for worldly luxuries is reflected in Mr. Knorr's manner of living. His home is a modest apartment at Bethel Home, the society's 10-story headquarters in the Columbia Heights section of Brooklyn. He eats the same plain food, much of it grown on Witness farms, as the youngest worker in the society bindery. He receives the same compensation, too: Room, board, and $14 a month.

Unswayed by the material, Witnesses have more time to devote to finding spiritual truths. Boasts Mr. Knorr: "There are more ministers of Jehovah's Witnesses in the world than there are Catholic priests."

The statement is technically true. The Witnesses have no formally ordained clergy; every Witness is considered a minister. More than

The printing plant in Brooklyn, New York, where the Witnesses produce their magazine, The Watchtower, and publish thousands of Bibles.

40,000 Witnesses, called "pioneers," devote more than 100 hours a month to proselytizing. Most gratifying to society leaders is the fact that many of the most active ministers are converts themselves.

Take Mr. and Mrs. Jones of Washington, D. C.

James Jones was raised a Baptist. He had scant knowledge of Witness teachings until the age of 16, when he accompanied a friend to a Bible study class conducted by a member of the society. He then began studying the Bible, which in his view confirmed the message of the Witnesses. Now, a decade later, he carries his Bible to work in a restaurant in a suburb of Washington each day. His speech is sprinkled with Biblical phrases and allusions.

Jessie Jones' father became a Witness when Jessie was five. He often took his daughter to weekly prayer meetings at the neighborhood Kingdom Hall. But Jessie did not fully accept the faith until she was 18. When she did accept it, she moved to New York, where she sought to test her faith by preaching in a strange environment.

Her faith survived, and after she married James, whom she had met at a Kingdom Hall, the two worked together trying to convert others. Until the birth of their son in February 1963, they spent over 100 hours in monthly missionary work in Washington.

The Joneses still center their lives around their faith. They attend Bible study groups two evenings a week and Kingdom Hall services on Sunday. But they now have less time for proselytizing. "We're trying to average 10 hours a month," says Mrs. Jones, "but it's difficult. With the baby, most of our work has to be done on weekends."

The Joneses, who are Negroes, exemplify another aspect of the society. The society has traditionally welcomed Negroes into its ranks on a basis of full equality. Some estimates put Negro membership as high as 20 per cent of the total.

Life is not easy for Mr. and Mrs. Jones. Both must work to maintain their three-room apartment. Mrs. Jones was subjected to strong criticism for her refusal to sanction a blood transfusion as she lay near death in 1963. But she clings to her principles.

"Religion," she says, "isn't a thing of convenience to be discarded when it becomes inconvenient. You have to live it every day and every way." ♦

The Mormons

David O. McKay, president of the Mormon Church.

Dedication and Industry

A Native and Controversial American Faith Faces Its Problems—Including Its Negro Policy—Confidently

SALT LAKE CITY.

THE Mormons abandoned polygamy in 1890. Will they soon abandon another historic policy also frowned upon by many of their fellow Christians, the exclusion of Negroes from positions of authority within the church?

No one can say, not even the highest authorities in the Mormon Church. Leaders in this headquarters city of the largest Mormon body, the Church of Jesus Christ of Latter-Day Saints, insist they know of no present intention to remove the anti-Negro bar. Such an action can be taken only by white-haired, nonagenarian David O. McKay, who the Mormons believe receives revelation from God in his capacity as president of the church.

Still, Mormon leaders concede that they have been discussing the Negro question in their highest councils. The issue has political implications; George Romney of Michigan, a devout Mormon, has had to stress repeatedly in his gubernatorial campaigns that he has always worked for equal rights for all races. And many Mormons, exposed at home to the civil-rights issue and abroad to the emergence of African nations, are becoming increasingly troubled by the church's attitude toward Negroes.

Mormons pride themselves on their tolerance toward all men, including Negroes. In fact, they admit Negroes to simple membership in the church.

But to Mormons, equal rights in the civil, nonreligious area is one thing; equality under God is another. Joseph Smith, who founded the church in the early Nineteenth Century, wrote that Negroes are descendants of Cain and that they therefore bear a curse that God placed on Cain's descendants.

"Why are so many of the inhabitants of the earth cursed with a skin of blackness?" asked Brigham Young, second president of the church. He answered his own question: "It comes in consequence of their fathers rejecting the power of the holy priesthood, and the law of God. They will go down to death."

Negroes as a result are not permitted to progress beyond simple membership in the church's priesthood. Since every male Mormon enters the church's priesthood at the age of 12 and serves for the rest of his life (the church has no paid ministry), the prohibition against Negroes restricts them to a kind of second-class status.

It's hardly a surprise, then, that the Mormon church has only a few hundred Negroes on its rolls. And, though Mormon missions seek new members in most parts of the world, its voice is strangely silent in the Negro nations of Africa.

A conscious Mormon effort to give the church an international flavor, encouraged by Mr. McKay, is nourishing sentiment for revision of the Negro policy. "The church is assuming a world-wide image," says one Mormon official.

Salt Lake City is putting more emphasis on local leadership, less on direction from Mormon headquarters. In earlier days the church urged every convert to move to "Zion"—Utah. Now it encourages them to stay at home.

The new emphasis is paying off handsomely. The church's membership has doubled over the past decade and a half; it climbed above 2,000,000 in 1963.

More important, Mormon leaders detect a greater sense of dedication to the church, a growing feeling of spiritual conviction in a faith whose members have never lacked zeal.

The sidewalks in downtown Salt Lake City swarm at noon with bright-faced young men

The famous Salt Lake Temple, heart of the Mormon faith, in Salt Lake City, Utah.

sporting fashionable new suits and ties. They're Mormons in training to serve the church as missionaries at their own expense, here or abroad. "They leave here with missionary fire in their eyes," says an older Mormon. Most of them retain that enthusiasm all their lives.

In a day when it's popular in some circles to say the world has entered a "post-Christian era," participation in church affairs by Mormon members is unusually high. Not long ago, only 19 per cent of the members attended Sunday afternoon or evening "sacrament meetings" (worship services) and only 28 per cent went to Sunday school. Worship attendance now stands at about 40 per cent; Sunday school attendance, at more than 42 per cent.

The practice of tithing, which some Protestant and Roman Catholic clergymen believe is

The Mormon creed is based on writings like these—which represent a fragment of what Joseph Smith maintained that he saw in 1823, when a heavenly being revealed to him sacred writings on long-hidden metal plates. Smith's translation of the plates is known today as *The Book of Mormon.*

out of date, remains strong among Mormons. Officials say an increasing percentage of Mormons are giving the church a full 10 per cent of their income.

From the Mormons' sizable treasury in Salt Lake City comes an average of 50 per cent of the expenses for new Mormon chapels, or churches, around the world. Mormons are building 300 new chapels a year—nearly one every day. The wards, or congregations, hold no mortgage-burning ceremonies; every chapel is fully paid for before it's dedicated and used.

Hugh B. Brown, one of two counselors serving Mr. McKay in the church's three-man "First Presidency," believes that the Mormons' impressive surge in recent years can be traced both to the increased zeal within the membership and to the breaking down of prejudices against the church among non-Mormons. Everywhere the visitor to Salt Lake City turns, it seems he sees the beehive, Mormon symbol of industriousness. It's on the state flag; it's on hotel keys. The dome atop the restored home of Brigham Young has been designed to resemble a beehive.

If a single word could describe the Mormons, it would be "industriousness." A reporter arriving to see Mr. Brown at 7:30 a.m. encounters a prominent business executive leaving after an earlier appointment. President McKay frequently arrives at his office at 6 a.m. and remains until the sun sets.

Except for living allowances, the full-time officers of the church receive no compensation for their efforts. Sometimes they sacrifice lucrative business positions when they are "called" to service for the rest of their lives. The emphasis on the member's obligation to serve filters down through the entire church. Every Mormon receives a "calling," an assignment, that he's expected to fill. Some, for example, serve as "ward teachers," members of a congregation who visit every Mormon family at least once a month.

Paradoxically, the Mormons' deep involvement in church activities has contributed to several unfavorable popular impressions.

It's said, for example, that Mormons are clannish. Mormons don't deny that they may appear so, but they explain that they make no conscious effort to stick together; if they do, they say, it's only natural, for their social as well as their spiritual life revolves around the church. They hardly make lively partygoers among non-Mormons, for most adhere to the church's opposition to smoking and to the drinking of alcoholic beverages.

Many non-Mormons also believe that women occupy a subordinate place in the Mormon scheme of things. Though the percentage of Mormons who practiced polygamy never rose above 3 per cent, the church's one-time sanctioning of more than one wife to a husband wrongly created images of harems not unlike those of, say, Seventeenth Century shieks.

Mormons discourage married women from working for they insist that work not interfere with the rearing of the family. But many Mormon women participate actively in community and cultural groups, from PTA's to garden clubs. Mormons boast that the women of Utah, early leaders of the suffrage movement, were the first to vote in the entire United States (1870).

Mormons stress education. They maintain an extensive system of schools staffed by full-time teachers to supplement the public education of their children with moral and religious instruction. They say that in proportion to membership, more Mormon children in America graduate from college than in any other major religious group. The Mormons' Brigham Young University, in Provo, Utah, is the nation's largest church-related university.

A Teacher Strike

Church officials squirm, then, when reminded that the Mormon-dominated Utah Education Association (UEA) in 1963 threatened to stage what would have been the first statewide teachers' strike in the United States, and the following spring engineered a teachers' walkout of several days' duration. The UEA activities angered most Utah Mormons, some of whom served as substitute teachers to keep the schools open.

A great advocate of education, the poet Ralph Waldo Emerson, once described Mormonism as "the only religion of power and vitality that has made its appearance for the past 1,200 years." The statement could be debated, particularly in the light of developments since Emerson's time; the Christian Science faith, for example, born practically in Emerson's back yard, has grown and flourished since his day.

But it can't be disputed that Mormonism is distinctively American and distinctively different from other religions.

The church was organized in 1830, seven years after the 17-year-old Joseph Smith attested that a heavenly being had appeared before him and told him of sacred writings, hidden in upper New York in a hill called Hill Cumorah. Mormons believe that Smith translated the writings on the metal plates with divine assistance. The writings record the history of the inhabitants of America from about 600 B.C. to 421 A.D. Called *The Book of Mormon* after one of the prophets during this thousand-year period, the writings are considered part of the gospel along with the Old and New Testaments.

Mormons are Christians, but not Protestants. They believe in the Trinity of the Father, the Son, and the Holy Ghost. But unlike Protestants, they "protest" no historic trends in other Christian faiths, nor do they claim that they represent an innovation in religious history.

Instead, they believe their church is a restoration in the "latter days" of the original Gospel of Jesus, which they say had been corrupted for 15 centuries. Mormonism, then, becomes a restoration of the primitive church, with apostles, prophets, evangelists, and teachers.

They see the discovery of America and the development of democracy in the United States as tailored by divine guidance for the church's restoration under the prophet Joseph Smith. At one point, Smith prophesied that the American Constitution would "hang by a thread" and that Mormons would save it.

Liberal to Conservative

Representatives of all shades of political opinion embrace the Mormon faith; Mormons in Congress include both Democrats and Republicans. But the Mormons' best-known political figure is Ezra Taft Benson, President Eisenhower's Secretary of Agriculture. And the political sentiments of Mr. Benson and his son, Reed Benson, have caused a lively and continuing debate among Mormons.

Reed Benson long-time Utah resident, now heads the Washington, D.C. office of the John Birch Society. His father, a lifelong conservative, does not belong to the Society; in fact, his membership in the church's Council of Twelve Apostles prohibits his joining the anti-Communist organization. But the elder Benson has described the John Birch Society as "the most effective non-church organization in our fight against creeping socialism and Godless communism." And he has called Robert Welch, Birch Society founder, "one of the greatest patriots in American history."

In late 1963 the church assigned Ezra Taft

Gov. George Romney of Michigan, a leading Mormon, strives to correct an impression that his church is anti-Negro.

The Mormon Tabernacle Choir performs in its home auditorium. The choir appears from coast to coast and has a world-wide reputation.

The Mormon look of the future. A new temple opens in Oakland, California.

Benson to Europe as president of its European mission. Benson critics gleefully said the church was "shipping out Benson to get rid of him"; admirers applauded his "being sent to the front line," as his mission territory abuts the Iron Curtain. Church officials denied both interpretations. Mr. Benson, who ranks fourth in the traditional line of succession to the Mormon presidency, was simply being sent on a routine church assignment, they said.

Reed Benson's activities did result in a church reprimand. When it became apparent early in 1963 that he was using Mormon chapels and recreation halls to recruit members for the John Birch Society, President McKay forbade the use of church buildings for political meetings of any sort. In letters to inquiring Mormons, Mr. McKay wrote: "The church is not opposing the John Birch Society or any other organization of like nature; however, it is definitely opposed to anyone's using the church for the purpose of increasing membership for private organizations sponsoring these various ideologies."

Are the Bensons the Mormons who Joseph Smith prophesied will save the Constitution "hanging by a thread"? Some Mormons think so.

The Mormons' belief that they are the restoration of the primitive church of the first few centuries after Jesus' time leads them to acceptance of continued revelation from God.

In an address at Pittsburgh Theological Seminary, Mr. Brown of the First Presidency recalled that Dean Inge of the Church of England had said, "Oh, that some man would arise who could authoritatively say to the world, 'Thus Saith the Lord.' "

"We believe that day has come," Mr. Brown said. "We ask, is it possible that religion is the one department of human interest, investigation, and research where progress is impossible? Did Christ intend to leave His church without divine guidance?"

Through Joseph Smith, Mormons believe, God revealed his sanction of polygamy among Mormons of high character. Through Wilford Woodruff half a century later came divine guidance that the practice should be stopped. Congress had outlawed polygamy in 1872, and the Supreme Court had ruled the law constitutional. One article of faith in the church, written by Joseph Smith, reads: "We believe in being subject to kings, presidents, rulers, and magistrates, in obeying, honoring, and sustaining the law."

Mr. Woodruff also predicted, before the turn of the century, that "the day will come when all that (Negro) race will be redeemed and possess all the blessings which we now have." In 1947, before becoming church president, Mr. McKay said: "Sometime in God's eternal plan, the Negro will be given the right to hold the priesthood."

When might this time arrive? Mormons themselves don't know. Says Mr. Brown: "It would be rather presumptuous of any man to anticipate what God may want to do in the future." ♦

Special Background Reports:

The Architects of

"Gloria" by Sister Mary Corita

American Theology

The Power of the Written Word Demonstrated Anew By Men Whose Books Shape Religion Behind the Scenes

IF CLERGYMEN pour the mortar of religious change, the architects of change are religious thinkers. Few of these thinkers become prominent in the public eye, but they exert immense influence on the churches and synagogues of the nation.

The themes Protestant thinkers have expressed in recent years have paralleled the themes of much of the literature and art of the times. Exuberant optimism flourished in both religious thought and the arts early in this century. Religious liberalism, led by the Rev. Harry Emerson Fosdick of the Riverside Church in New York, triumphed over conservatism in the 1920s and carried high the banner of harmonizing the ancient Christian gospel with modern culture.

Then the effects of the Depression rippled through every stratum of society, the League of Nations collapsed, and World War II engulfed the American nation as no war had engulfed it before. Optimism gave way to disillusionment, disillusionment to despair. Persons in the mainstream of Protestant thought turned their energies back toward the Bible in search of the authentic Christian faith, hoping to expound it in its purest form against the challenges of godless cultures.

Liberalism, the emphasis of which started with man—his needs, his morality, his civilization—became passe; the new wave (neo-orthodoxy), which started with God and His "saving act through Christ," took over. Where liberals in their thinking had followed a path from man up to God, neo-orthodox thinkers started with God and His revealing Himself to man. Here they borrowed conservatism's characteristic feature—the Word of God disclosed through the Bible—while striving hard to relate the Word to the scientific age of the Twentieth Century.

In religion as in many other fields, American intellectuals borrowed ideas from their European colleagues. Europe had already suffered vast devastation and despair when the decade of the 1920s opened. And it had already produced a theologian, Karl Barth, who was to speak to the needs of the new age.

Now the acknowledged leader of current Protestant thought, Barth relied heavily on the existentialist philosophy of a Nineteenth Century Dane, Soren Kierkegaard, and a Twentieth Century Spanish Catholic, Miguel de Unamuno. This philosophy countered idealism by portraying human life as estranged from God and founded in frustration, despair, and sin. Rejecting confidence in man's self-sufficiency, Barth stressed his sinful nature and God's gift of salvation to man despite his sins.

But Barth preserved the theologian's prerogative of modifying his thoughts ("Thank God I'm not a Barthian!" he once rejoiced with his customary wit). He later softened the tenor of the "crisis theology" expressed in a 1919 book, *The Epistle to the Romans*. Commenting on the impact the book had made, Barth compared himself to a person who, he said, "ascending the dark staircase of a church tower and trying to steady himself, reached for the banister, but got hold of the bell rope instead. To his horror, he had then to listen to what the great bell had sounded over him and not over him alone."

The giants of contemporary American religious thought, notably Reinhold Niebuhr and

Paul Tillich: He helped transport "crisis theology" to the United States.

Paul Tillich, caught hold of the bell rope too. How this affected them influenced Catholic and Jewish as well as Protestant thinkers, as it has influenced the actions and attitudes of churches and synagogues in the 1960s.

Paul Tillich

The man who, more than any other, brought Continental "crisis theology" to the United States was Paul Tillich, a German-born theologian who taught at Union Theological Seminary in New York from 1933 to 1955. A versatile thinker and prolific writer, Professor Tillich continues to write and lecture as he approaches his 80th year. He completed the third volume of his magnum opus, *Systematic Theology,* in 1963.

Professor Tillich places great importance on his concept of the doctrine of "justification by faith," the paradox that God accepts sinful man as if he were righteous. This enables man to conquer his feelings of pride and guilt and to face the problems of life without trying to explain them away. Man is freed from himself through faith, through submitting to a power greater than his own. He must, in turn, place his ultimate trust in the living God and not in anything erected by human beings, such as his church or his government.

Always concerned with reaching out to people outside the Christian faith, Professor Tillich has had an important, if indirect, influence on the growth of interfaith understanding. He also has tried to relate religious faith to culture and psychology.

Many Protestants, as well as Roman Catholics, however, believe he has cut the heart out of the Christian mind ("I don't think he's really a Christian," charges a critic). They recoil, for example, at his rejection of the bodily resurrection of Jesus. But Professor Tillich is regarded by many as the foremost intellect in the field. Says one opponent: "It takes a lot of doing to pin him to the mat."

The very power of Professor Tillich's mind and the eloquence with which he expresses his thoughts make some persons question whether his influence on religious thought will be permanent or merely transitory. Asks a careful student of his theology: "When he's no longer there to preach the gospel according to Tillich, I really wonder whether it will be carried on."

Reinhold Niebuhr

Few question the lasting influence Reinhold Niebuhr will have upon religious and, for that matter, social and political thought in the United States. His beliefs occupy the center of the theological currents of the mid-Twentieth Century, and his personality dominates the field of religious thought.

Born in 1892 and reared in the conservative Lutheran tradition, he was attracted early to the ethical applications of the Christian gospel. Washed with the religious liberalism and social idealism of the times, he ventured forth from Yale Divinity School in 1915 determined to demonstrate the social lessons of Christianity by ministering to a congregation of factory workers in Detroit.

His 13-year pastorate in Detroit resulted in a sweeping rethinking of his theological ideas. By the time he left to join the faculty of Union Theological Seminary, he had become sharply critical of the liberals' hope of creating a Kingdom of God on earth through the efforts of men.

In a Christian Century article in 1939, Professor Niebuhr said that "there is not a single bit of evidence to prove that good triumphs over evil in this constant development of history." His own experience in Detroit had had a profound impact on his thought: "The simple little moral homilies which were preached in that as in other cities, by myself and others, seemed completely irrelevant to the brutal facts of life in a great industrial center."

Four years after he left Detroit, in 1932, he completed *Moral Man and Immoral Society*. The volume became the first tract for a new theology that dominates Protestant thought today, neo-orthodoxy.

The essence of Professor Niebuhr's theology involves the doctrine of original sin, which he describes not as sin inherited from Adam but as a natural human inclination toward pride and self-interest. Only the grace of God can provide salvation from sin. This salvation, however, doesn't free man completely from the consequences of sin or from the complex decisions he must make. Sometimes, in fact, Christians must choose between two evils rather than between an evil and an absolute good.

Thus in the days just before World War II, as many distinguished Protestant clergymen were preaching pacifism, Reinhold Niebuhr led a group of prominent churchmen in founding the periodical Christianity and Crisis. In its first months, the journal preached that despite many errors in British and American ways, the Axis powers had to be subdued: "The halting of totalitarian aggression is prerequisite to world peace and order."

Professor Niebuhr described his basic theological position most thoroughly in his monumental two-volume effort, *The Nature and Destiny of Man,* published in 1941 and 1943. Since then he has turned increasingly to problems of history. Appointed professor emeritus at Union in 1960, he continues to speak out on social and political issues—Vietnam, for example, and the 1964 Presidential campaign.

Inherent in Professor Niebuhr's actions and

Reinhold Niebuhr: Sometimes the Christian has to choose between two evils.

thought is the view that Jesus' ethic demands a perfection that can't possibly be attained. His conclusion: The Christian must recognize his inadequacy and ask forgiveness, working for reform and trusting that what he does on faith will be significant in the unfolding of God's purpose.

Commented the late Clifton E. Olmstead in *History of Religion in the United States:* "Niebuhr's concept stood between the pessimism of Barthianism, which saw the Kingdom of God only as a future hope, and the unqualified op-

John Bennett: Save liberalism's best.

Martin Marty: Protestants must take "post-imperial" stance.

timism of American liberalism, which confused the Kingdom with human progress."

John C. Bennett

Inevitably, some religious thinkers believed that Professor Niebuhr had gone too far in rejecting religious liberalism. Perhaps the most influential was Dr. John C. Bennett, who became president of Union in 1964 after having served on the faculty there since 1943.

In 1942, Dr. Bennett wrote a chapter in *Liberal Theology: An Appraisal* in which he urged that the best in liberalism be salvaged and united with the best in orthodoxy. This school of thought has become known as neo-liberalism.

Man is a creature of God and is essentially good, neo-liberals say. It's important to emphasize, as liberals do, that man is free and responsible for his actions and thoughts. But the neo-orthodox view that sin exists and corrupts men can't be ignored, contend neo-liberals. A perfect society can never be achieved, although some progress can be made. Men must constantly repent in order to save themselves from the sins of self-righteousness and pride.

Conservatives

While conflicts among mainstream Protestant thinkers were dominating the front lines of religious thought in America, the conservatives began to regroup their forces. By the 1950s, the conservatives were defending their faith on more rational grounds than before without changing their basic position. What's more, they started to display an interest in social ethics quite foreign to fundamentalists of the 1920s and the 1930s.

Two of the most persuasive advocates of conservative theology in American Protestantism are Prof. Edward J. Carnell of Fuller Theological Seminary in California and the Rev. Carl F. H. Henry, editor of the conservative biweekly Christianity Today. The Rev. Dr. Henry, who left a faculty position at Fuller in 1956 to join Christianity Today at the urging of evangelist Billy Graham and other "evangelical conservatives," argues that religion must return to belief in the "fundamentals" of the Bible, such as the actual reality of the virgin birth, the full deity of Christ, and His bodily resurrection. These, he contends, the liberal and neo-orthodox thinkers often deny. He criticizes the church unity movement: "Ecclesiastical elephantiasis is no remedy for the ailments of isolated denominations; mergers tend merely to reproduce illnesses."

The Rev. Dr. Henry's position is rather moderate, however, compared with the position of some conservative thinkers today. A more extreme conservatism, championed by Prof. Cornelius Van Til of Westminster Theological Seminary in Philadelphia, contends that the present denominations have been swallowed up by liberalism and that conservatives should devote their energies to forming new denominations that will be doctrinally "pure," such as

Carl Henry: Mergers reproduce illness.

the Orthodox Presbyterians. The Rev. Dr. Henry doesn't go this far; he says only that denominations must be returned to their old moorings.

A New Generation

New theological currents ran swiftly and deeply in the years between the two world wars. Rarely has history produced a generation of theologians as productive as the generation of Barth, Tillich, Niebuhr, and Bennett.

But these men, who so vastly influenced the clergymen of today, are slowing down. What of the new generation in Protestant theology?

No theologians of comparable stature have yet emerged. Theological fads, like TV Westerns, come and go with astonishing rapidity. Bishop John A. T. Robinson of England scandalized Anglican clerics and titillated American theological students by writing *Honest to God,* a 1963 best-seller in England that popularized and added a new dimension to the "demythologizing" system of the German theologian Rudolf Bultmann. But comparatively liberal religious thinkers in America, such as Prof. Markus Barth of Pittsburgh Theological Seminary, the son of Karl Barth, debunk the tendency to "demythologize"—to strip away the alleged "myths" in the Bible—and argue that the Christian must accept, say, the Resurrection of Jesus as historical fact.

The younger Protestant thinkers thus far have made their richest contributions on cultural issues. Many in the new generation—Prof. Jaroslav Pelikan of Yale Divinity School, Prof. William Hamilton of Colgate Rochester Divinity School, Prof. Franklin Littell of Chicago Theological Seminary—are devoting their major attention to this field. Perhaps the most promising, certainly the most prolific, of these is Prof. Martin E. Marty of the University of Chicago Divinity School.

Professor Marty's output is phenomenal. Just in his mid-30s, he has been pastor of Lutheran churches in the Washington, D.C., and Chicago areas. He serves as associate editor of the liberal Protestant weekly Christian Century, co-authoring in the Century the brightest column in religious journalism, "Penultimate." In the past five years he has written more than a book a year and served as editor or co-author of several more.

In his long essay in *The Outbursts That Await Us,* Professor Marty shows why he is regarded as a prominent apostle of the newly fashionable "post-Protestant" approach. Protestantism can't continue to control American society as it has in the past, Professor Marty argues; recent Supreme Court rulings on prayers and Bible readings in public schools, rulings toward which he is sympathetic, demonstrate this. Protestants must, therefore, take what Professor Marty calls a "post-imperial" stance: They should think carefully about accepting widespread Federal tax exemption for their own church institutions, for example, if they criticize Catholic demands for tax relief or for Federal aid to parochial schools.

Though this course may be hazardous, he contends, Protestantism must take the risk. "Its status may momentarily suffer," he says,

John Courtney Murray: For a dialogue between faiths.

"but it will emerge stronger from the ordeal."

Professor Marty urges all Protestants to look back in American history, to reappraise events from the writing of the Constitution to the waves of immigration. His own appraisal of the Founding Fathers convinces him that they were religious men, but that they could hardly have been expected to foresee the informal tie-in between Protestantism and government in the last century or the conflicting claims of the faiths in this century. Trying to apply what Jefferson, Hamilton, and Madison said about church and state to Twentieth Century conditions, therefore, may prove fruitless in Professor Marty's view.

Catholic Thinkers

"The Catholic Church in America has counted for astonishingly little in the formation of the American intellectual climate," wrote D. W. Brogan in *U.S.A.: An Outline of the Country, Its People and Institutions*. Catholic intellectuals freely admit that the American church still feeds on Europe for its thought.

The reason is a natural one: Intellectual continuity has persevered in Europe, while it was ruptured in the United States. More than 11,000,000 Catholic immigrants spilled into the United States in the 30 years through the 1920s. Many, such as the Irish and the Poles, came from countries with a strong heritage of suppression of original thought. The result: It took the Catholic Church decades to catch its breath, to afford the luxury of developing intellectuals as well as parish priests.

It can afford the luxury now, and dynamic Catholic thinkers have begun to appear. They are not systematic theologians, in the sense that Barth and Tillich are systematic theologians who develop a coherent, comprehensive body of theology; they work within the framework of the Catholic system, which they regard as possessing fully developed principles. Thus it is much more difficult for a Catholic than for a Protestant to build up a stature comparable to Barth's or Tillich's.

Catholic thinkers in the United States tend to specialize in certain well-defined areas. The Rev. Godfrey Diekmann, editor of Worship magazine, has made notable contributions to thought about Catholic liturgy. The Rev. Bruce Vawter of Kenrick Seminary in St. Louis has distinguished himself in Biblical studies. Most influential of all, the Rev. John Courtney Murray of Woodstock College, a Jesuit seminary in Maryland, has written incisively for three decades on various facets of American society.

Father Murray's most important contribution lies in church-state relations. Traditional Catholic doctrines in this area deal with the church in nations ruled by monarchies. Father Murray has taken the various aspects of church-state relations—tax exemption, government aid to church schools, censorship of religious writings, and so on—and tried to relate Catholic doctrines on these topics to democratic nations with many different religious faiths.

Father Murray, in *We Hold These Truths*, sees civic unity in the United States as "a thing of the surface." Beneath the surface are four great movements: Catholicism, Protestantism, Judaism, and secularism. The problem is how to make these movements work harmoniously as an "American society—civil, just, free, peaceful, one."

Father Murray declares that "religious pluralism is against the will of God." Yet, in

Rabbi Heschel: Defender of the Bible.

the next sentence, he adds: "But it is the human condition; it is written into the script of history." With religious unity unlikely, what can be done? "We could limit the warfare" among the faiths, he suggests, "and we could enlarge the dialogue." Then in the pluralistic America of many religious faiths "a unity would be discernible—the unity of an orderly conversation." Father Murray's call for a "dialogue" helped inspire the era of good feeling among the faiths in the United States in the 1960s.

Jewish Theologians

Judaism in America has spawned its share of creative thinkers. Each of the four branches has its towering figure.

In Orthodox Judaism, which preserves the traditions and theology of Jewry in the Old World, that figure is Rabbi Joseph Soloveitchik, a professor at Yeshiva University in New York. In Reform Judaism, the "liberal" branch that has simplified Judaism and adapted it to modern conditions, Rabbi Solomon Freehof of Rodef Shalom Temple in Pittsburgh is the most influential architect of thought. Rabbi Abraham Joshua Heschel, professor of Jewish ethics and mysticism at New York City's Jewish Theological Seminary, is the foremost thinker of Conservative Judaism, which seeks a middle ground between Orthodox and Reform. Finally, Reconstruction Judaism, conceived only in 1935, is dominated by its founder, Rabbi Mordecai M. Kaplan, who retired from the faculty of Jewish Theological Seminary at 82 in 1963. Reconstructionists view Judaism more as a civilization than as a faith, and try to promote Jewish communities that would encourage a sense of Jewishness.

The middle ground in Jewish thought bears an intellectual kinship to the middle ground in Protestant theology. The Polish-born Rabbi Heschel, who earned his doctorate at the University of Berlin in the 1930s before being expelled by the Nazis, has devoted most of his energies since his university days to defending "the intellectual relevance of the Bible."

Philosophy and science, he argues, can't help man solve the ultimate questions of life. "Marx and Freud are interesting," he says—and the voice could be many a Protestant's or Catholic's—"but in extreme situations, such as in dealing with good and evil, do they lead anywhere?" ♦

Special Background Reports:

An Unusual Look

MENTION the name "Martin Luther King, Jr." Into most minds springs the image of an activist, a Negro general who leads his troops onto the civil-rights battlefields.

The image is valid, but so is another image. It is the image of a Christian minister, an image largely overlooked even when the 35-year-old clergyman in late 1964 became the youngest person ever to win the Nobel Peace Prize.

Perhaps, as some say, the Rev. Dr. King perverts the Christian message. Perhaps, as others maintain, he captures its very essence. Whatever the case, he bases his actions on his Christian convictions.

"The essence of the Christian gospel? To me it's very simple," he tells a visitor in his measured, mellifluous tones during a long conversation in a private home in the South. "The essence of the Christian gospel is love."

The word "love" flows freely in his conversation. It's part of the title of his book of sermons, *Strength to Love.* To him the traditional issues of theology—sin and salvation, the divinity of Christ, His virgin birth, His bodily resurrection—are peripheral. Love is central.

By love, he means neither romantic love nor love for friends, but good will and understanding for all men. The Greek New Testament, he notes, uses three words for love: *Eros,* romantic or aesthetic love; *philia,* affection between friends; and *agape,* a redeeming good will that "cleanses" both the person who is loved and the one who loves.

"Agape is the highest form of love," says the Rev. Dr. King, thumbing through his red-letter edition of the New Testament. "It's completely unselfish; it seeks nothing in return." When the Apostle Paul spoke of love in his first letter to the Corinthians, he used the word *agape*: "And now abideth faith, hope, and love, these three; but the greatest of these is love."

"Certainly the supreme example was the experience of Christ on the cross," the Rev. Dr. King goes on. " 'Father, forgive them, for they know not what they do.' This was real redemptive love. Here was a symbol of crime, the cross. Yet redemptive love transformed it into a symbol of salvation."

Other religious beliefs of the Rev. Dr. King bear few marks of the fundamentalist Baptist tradition in which he was raised. With his father, a preacher in the old Baptist tradition, he is co-pastor of Atlanta's Ebenezer Baptist Church. But his sermons contain no "hard" preaching on heaven and hell, no preoccupation with sin and salvation.

He rejects, for example, the idea that men are innate sinners. He defines sin as "the estrangement that always develops when man misuses his freedom and revolts against God." Men inevitably sin, but this doesn't mean they're innately bad. Nor are they innately good. They have potentialities for both bad and good.

What set Jesus apart, he believes, was Jesus' unique goodness. "I don't think anyone else can be Jesus. He was one with God in purpose. He so submitted His will to God's will that God revealed His divine plan to man through Jesus."

In this sense, he says, Jesus was divine. But

at Martin Luther King

Too Often Identified Only With Civil-Rights Drama, He Talks Here of Christianity and Preaching

the Rev. Dr. King rejects the virgin birth of Christ as a literal fact. The early Christians, he says, had noticed the moral uniqueness of Jesus; to make this uniqueness appear plausible, they devised a mythological story of Jesus' biological uniqueness.

The Rev. Dr. King did not originate these ideas, of course. He's more of a clergyman than a creative theologian, more of a messenger of ideas than an originator of them. "Martin King is an excellent preacher, an even better orator," writes Negro author Louis E. Lomax in *The Negro Revolt*. "But as an intellectual, Martin himself would be the first to testify to the narrowness of his training. . . . Seminaries teach men to believe, not to think."

The theology of Martin Luther King thus is a synthesis of thoughts culled from other men's minds. In fact, he describes his "intellectual pilgrimage" precisely as a synthesis.

In his seminary studies at Crozer Theological School in Pennsylvania and at Boston University School of Theology (where he earned his Ph.D.), he was influenced first by religious liberalism, which stresses the social rather than the spiritual concerns of man. Reading philosopher Reinhold Niebuhr, however, he soon concluded that "liberalism is all too sentimental in its analysis of man, and doesn't grapple sufficiently with the problem of evil."

Yet the revolt of Niebuhr's "neo-orthodoxy," he found, went too far in stressing a hidden, unknown God and man's capacity for evil. Today he believes in "neither liberalism nor neo-orthodoxy, but in a synthesis that combines the truth of both and avoids the extremes of both."

Thus, in speaking about Christian love, the Rev. Dr. King acknowledges that it may never be completely fulfilled. "Men have a tragic inclination to yield to selfish impulses. But one always has the capacity to strive for love. It remains the regulating ideal."

He takes this ideal from a literal reading of Christ's words on love. "This is my commandment," John reports Christ as saying, "That ye love one another, as I have loved you." Luke quotes Jesus: "Love your enemies, do good to them which hate you." In Matthew's account of the Sermon on the Mount, Jesus tells His disciples: "Resist not evil: But whosoever shall smite thee on thy right cheek, turn to him the other also."

Fundamentalists tend to take everything in the Bible literally; yet when pressed, many of them write off the phrase "Love your enemies" as unrealistic. The Rev. Dr. King writes off a literal view of the virgin birth; yet he insists that Jesus' words, as reported in the New Testament, be interpreted literally.

In doing so, he has made what many clergymen consider a singular contribution to modern religious thought. Using the words of Christ and the example of Gandhi in India, he was the first—and remains the foremost—to really articulate the concept of nonviolent resistance for Christianity in America.

When the Swedish scholar Gunnar Myrdal in 1942 wrote *An American Dilemma,* still considered by many the definitive work on the American Negro, he did not mention Gandhi, nonviolence, or passive resistance. He committed no oversight. The doctrine of nonviolence was not applied to the Negro movement until 1955, when the Rev. Dr. King, 26 and a year out of seminary, assumed the leadership of the bus boycott in Montgomery, Alabama.

In the young minister's first speech to the

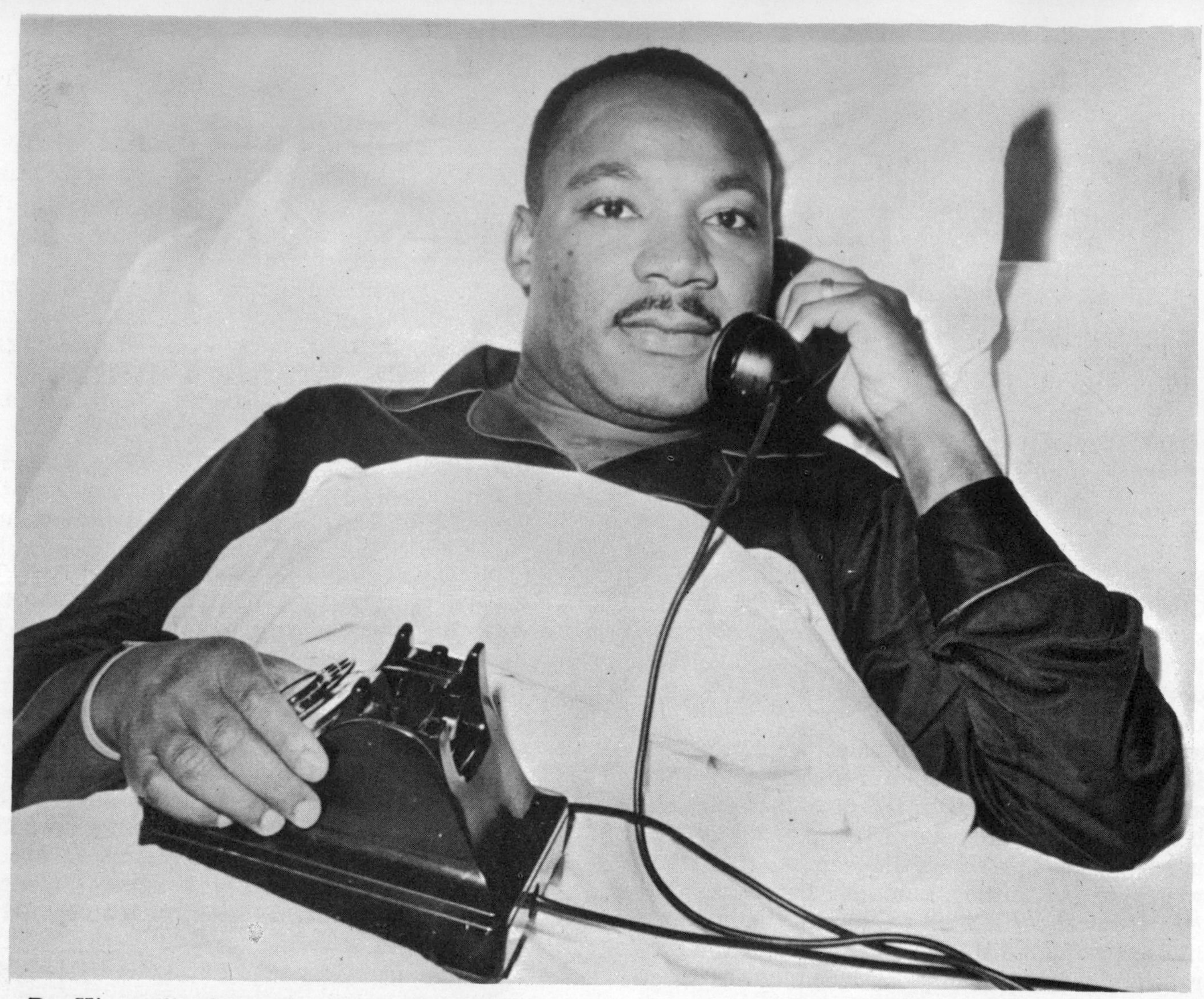

Dr. King talks from his hospital bed shortly after hearing that he had won the Nobel Peace Prize.

Montgomery demonstrators, he tried to combine what he termed "two apparent irreconcilables." He attempted to arouse the demonstrators to action by convincing them their self-respect was at stake; he balanced this with a positive affirmation of the Christian doctrine of love in order to "keep this fervor within controllable and Christian bounds."

Christians must "love" people even if they don't "like" them personally, he insists. "I wouldn't like to have dinner with Sen. (James O.) Eastland (Mississippi Democrat) every night. But I have to love him, like every man, because God loves him."

The Rev. Dr. King has his critics, and they include not merely Southern segregationists and "mild" Christians in the North concerned about property values. Some Christian thinkers, including some Negroes, believe he distorts the Christian gospel.

The Rev. Joseph R. Washington, Jr., chaplain of Dickinson College and a Negro, is one of these critics. In *Black Religion,* he chides the Rev. Dr. King for having borrowed freely from the philosophies of non-Christians: "It is as though Socrates, Thoreau, Hegel, and Jesus were all dumped together into one philosophical bowl like tossed salad," with Gandhi added for flavor.

The Rev. Dr. Washington contends that his fellow graduate of Boston University's School of Theology sprinkled "a dash of love" onto the philosophy of nonviolence merely to prevent bloodshed. "Instead of constituting a positive factor, love was injected as a negative factor." Now, a decade after Montgomery, "the honeymoon with love has given way to a pragmatic emphasis upon justice. The religion of love is no longer at the center of the nonviolent movement. Instead of reconciliation and the Man on the Cross, there is the image of the cup of endurance running over."

In *Letter from Birmingham City Jail,* a 14-page defense of the Negro nonviolent movement, the Rev. Dr. King wrote that "Freedom is never voluntarily given by the oppressor; it must be demanded by the oppressed." His critics argue, however, that demanding "Freedom Now" violates the Apostle Paul's vision of a Christian love that "beareth all things, believeth all things, hopeth all things, endureth all things."

When the Rev. Dr. King and his followers declare "love your enemies," these critics contend, they actually seek something in return—recognition of their equality. Thus it is a selfish love, and not the unselfish love associated with Christ.

Unquestionably many Negroes regard nonviolence more as a tactic than as a guiding principle. The Rev. Dr. King and his closest associates say that they deplore this attitude. "The minute you allow race to become a factor in your relationship with another person," he says, "you've lost the *agape* quality."

As a Christian minister, the Rev. Dr. King follows a two-part formula: First, relentlessly proclaim that love is the essence of the Christian gospel. Second, carry this conviction to the street and store.

The formula has won him countless epithets—and countless accolades. "On the basis of his deep Christian commitment and courage," says Methodist Bishop John Wesley Lord of Washington, D.C., the Rev. Dr. King is nothing less than the "moral leader of the nation."

The Rev. Dr. King, as is natural, takes a more modest view. The day he received the Nobel Peace Prize, he denied that the award had any political implications. "I am a minister of the gospel," he said, "not a political leader."

The comment illuminated a facet of the man rarely discussed. It recalled what he had said as he told a visitor goodby in the sanctity of a private home: "I'm glad to see that someone recognizes I'm a preacher." ♦

The King family in a rare—and unposed—group photograph. In rear, Mrs. King, Sr., with grandson Dexter; Mrs. King, Jr., with baby Bernice; Yolanda and Martin Luther III with their father; in front, Martin Luther King, Sr.

Religion and Race

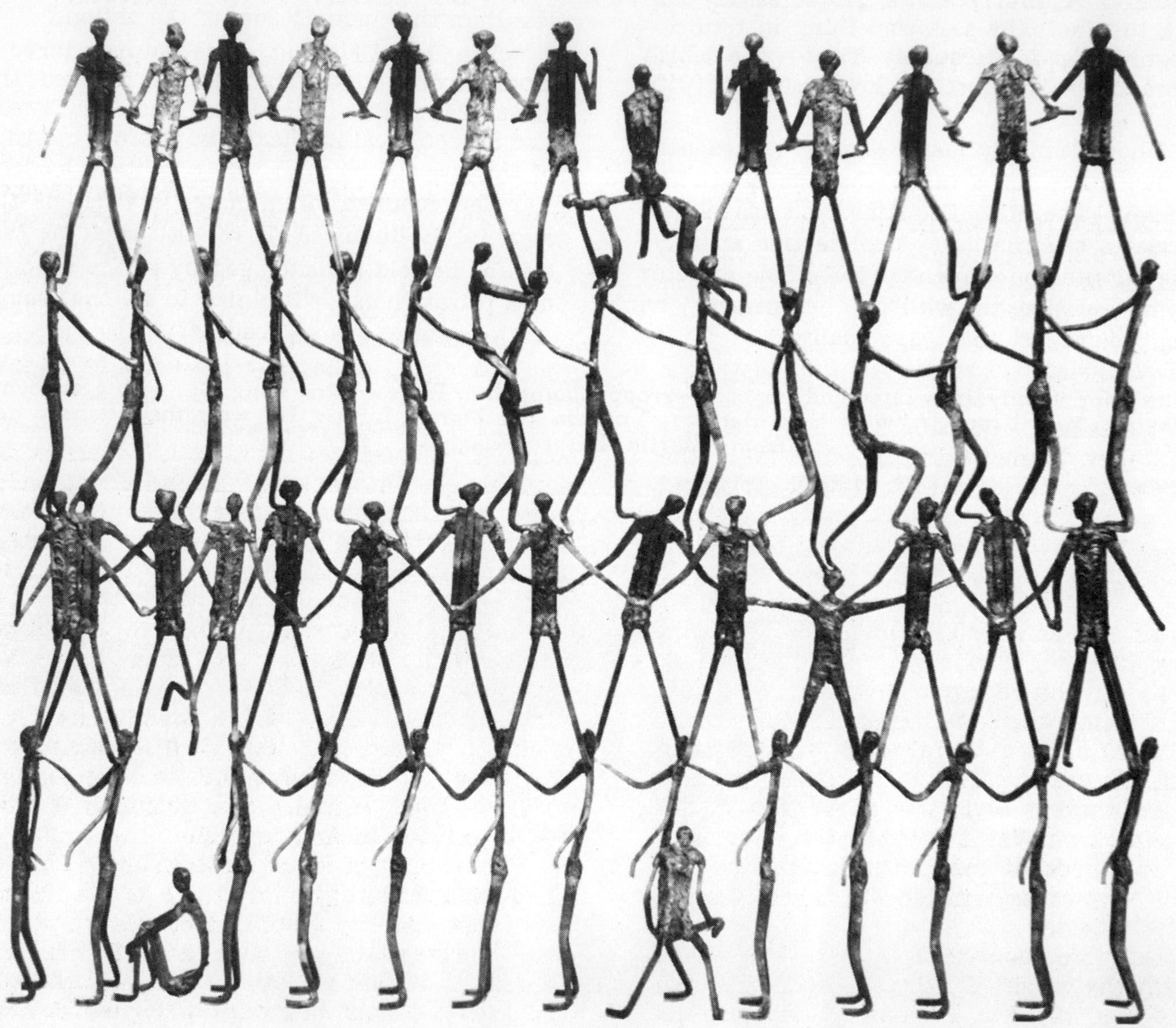

—"Fabric of Human Involvement" by Clark Fitzgerald

The Challenge of Civil Rights

The Churches Commit Themselves Heavily to Equal Rights, Then Meet Their Critics—In Pew and Press

NEW YORK CITY.

AMERICA'S religious leaders, who admit that for years they preached a lot but did too little in the Negroes' struggle for equal rights, have moved from the pulpit into the street.

"We suddenly faced the fact that the people who were oppressed were saying, 'We don't want to hear another word from you, buddy,'" says the Rt. Rev. Daniel Corrigan, director of the home department of the Protestant Episcopal Church.

What the Negroes sought from white churchmen was action, tangible evidence that the white church was willing to share in their trials as well as their triumphs. Now they are getting it.

Several white clergymen were arrested during a demonstration at a segregated amusement park near Baltimore in July 1963. The following month ministers, priests, and rabbis streamed into the nation's capital to participate in the huge March on Washington. In the summer of 1964, hundreds of clergymen traveled to the South to protest segregation and to help Negroes register to vote.

These are momentous moves. They have brought the weight of religious leadership into the Negroes' struggle. Perhaps this involvement helps head off violence and points the way to reconciliation; perhaps, as some argue, it only makes reconciliation more difficult. But though the short-term costs are high and the sacrifices great, many Christian thinkers believe this new commitment will inspire a spiritual rebirth within the church.

"This is a fundamental issue of human rights," declares the Rev. Robert W. Spike, the boyish-looking leader of the civil-rights troops of the National Council of Churches. "The very integrity of the Christian gospel is at stake."

If the integrity of the gospel is at stake, wonder many laymen, why have the churches done so little until now? And are the churches right in doing what they have finally begun to do?

The issues can be debated for hours. They are being debated now, in fact, in thousands of churches across the land. In many churches there are lighter collection plates and less crowded pews since the debate began; in many others there is a vitality, a sense of commitment, that has been absent until now.

But the facts cannot be debated. The facts tell a dramatic story. They show that the churches moved in mid-1963 with a swiftness and decisiveness they had not displayed for decades. They show that since then the churches have preserved this momentum. In doing so, the churches have written a new definition of the role of religion in American life.

The church, of course, never has been totally aloof from the struggle for justice for the Negro and other minority groups. Amid the havoc of the Reconstruction days after the Civil War, the American Missionary Association established 536 schools for the newly freed Negroes. A few of those schools still survive; they produced some of today's most educated Negro leaders.

More recently, city clergymen have struggled to overcome prejudice and poverty hand in hand. Many of them have worked actively to eliminate anti-Negro housing covenants and discriminatory practices in government, business, and labor. As early as 1942 the Congregationalists (now part of the United Church of

Moments of anger, violence, and destruction on city streets have convinced many churchmen they must move quickly to help where they can.

Christ) created a race relations department that, among other things, identified specific racial problems in several Northern cities and conducted a survey that led directly to desegregation aboard railroad coaches.

Yet by the time 1963 arrived, the initiative for racial change had passed out of the hands of the whites. The Negro, impatient with the white, had already taken the lead.

In January 1963 the three major faiths sent delegates to Chicago for what was billed as the first national interfaith conference on any topic in the nation's history. The conference, timed to coincide with the 100th anniversary of the Emancipation Proclamation, dealt with a problem few were then predicting would preoccupy the nation in 1963: The unequal status of the races.

Many clergymen credit this National Conference on Religion and Race with first alerting them to the importance of the racial issue. The Rev. Galen R. Weaver, a United Church of Christ executive working in the area of race relations, explains why:

"It was a pretty sobering thought that 100 years after the Emancipation Proclamation, Negroes could not share equally in jobs, housing, public accommodations, and education. Most sobering of all was to recognize that many of the churches and their institutions still were showing evidences of segregation."

Then came racial violence in Birmingham. Soon white churchmen were reading the eloquent "Letter from Birmingham City Jail," by the Rev. Martin Luther King, Jr. In the letter, which was a response to an appeal to "the principles of law and order and common sense" by eight white Alabama clergymen, the Negro leader explained why he, as a Christian clergyman, was so deeply involved in civil-rights activity and his disappointment with the white moderate and the church.

"I have almost reached the regrettable conclusion," wrote the Rev. Dr. King, "that the Negroes' great stumbling block in the stride toward freedom is not the White Citizens' 'Counciler' or the Ku Klux Klanner, but the white moderate who is more devoted to 'order' than to justice. . . ."

Secure Behind Windows

Within the church, said the Rev. Dr. King, some Southern clergymen had directly opposed the Negro cause; "all too many others have been more cautious than courageous and have remained silent behind the anesthetizing security of stained glass windows."

Many churches, he added, had demonstrated they had committed themselves "to a completely other-worldly religion which made a strange distinction between body and soul, the sacred and the secular. . . . But the judgment of God is upon the church as never before. If the church of today does not recapture the sacrificial spirit of the early church, it will lose its authentic ring, forfeit the loyalty of millions, and be dismissed as an irrelevant social club with no meaning for the Twentieth Century."

The letter electrified the religious community in the North. It was reprinted widely; the American Friends Service Committee, for example, distributed thousands of copies of its 14-page reprint, and Christian Century also reprinted the letter in full.

"Letter From Birmingham City Jail," more than anything else, created the climate for action among Northern churchmen. But it remained for an unpublicized meeting in Harlem the day after Memorial Day to provide the actual jolt that brought action.

Negro author James Baldwin, singer Harry Belafonte, and other leading Negroes had emerged disillusioned from talks with Attorney General Robert Kennedy a few days earlier. The Rev. Jon L. Regier of the National Council of Churches, learning of their disillusionment, then invited Mr. Baldwin and other Negro thinkers to exchange views with the leaders of several of the large Protestant denominations. The Harlem meetings that resulted, recalls the Rev. Dr. Regier, gave the Protestant leaders "the firm conviction that they must act."

A week later the general board of the National Council of Churches adopted an extraordinary statement. It called upon the church "to confess her sin of omission and delay, and to move forward to witness to her essential belief that every child of God is a brother to every other." The National Council, which represents 31 Protestant and Orthodox denominations with a total of 40,000,000 members, pledged that its leaders would "engage personally in negotiations, demonstrations, and other direct action."

Episcopalians already had their marching orders. So did the Presbyterians. Other mainstream Protestant denominations began to fall into line.

The Synagogue Council of America urged rabbis to enter the struggle. The voice of Roman Catholicism, silent nationally from day to day because each bishop is sovereign in his own diocese, spoke strongly in pastoral letters from bishops to their communicants in every region of the nation.

The Gwynn Oak Incident

On the Fourth of July, prestigious clergymen of the Catholic, Protestant, and Jewish faiths marched shoulder-to-shoulder with Negroes protesting racial segregation at the Gwynn Oak Amusement Park in Maryland. Clergymen of lesser prominence had engaged in demonstrations before in scattered cities throughout the South. But the arrest in a border state of men of the stature of the Rev. Eugene Carson Blake, the highest official in the United Presbyterian Church, dramatized the depth of the churches' new commitment and their determination to fight segregation everywhere, not just in the South.

Gwynn Oak became the symbol of the new movement. It showed, said the Rev. Michael Allen, an Episcopal priest from New York City, shortly after he was arrested there, that "the white middle class is finally becoming aware of the importance of this battle. The church cannot pretend to lead that battle. We're too late for that. All we can do is serve it."

Since Gwynn Oak, they have served it in many ways. They helped stage the March on Washington on August 28, 1963. They organized the most intensive interfaith lobby in history for passage of the Civil Rights Act. Through the Commission on Religion and Race of the National Council of Churches and similar commissions in several denominations, they posted

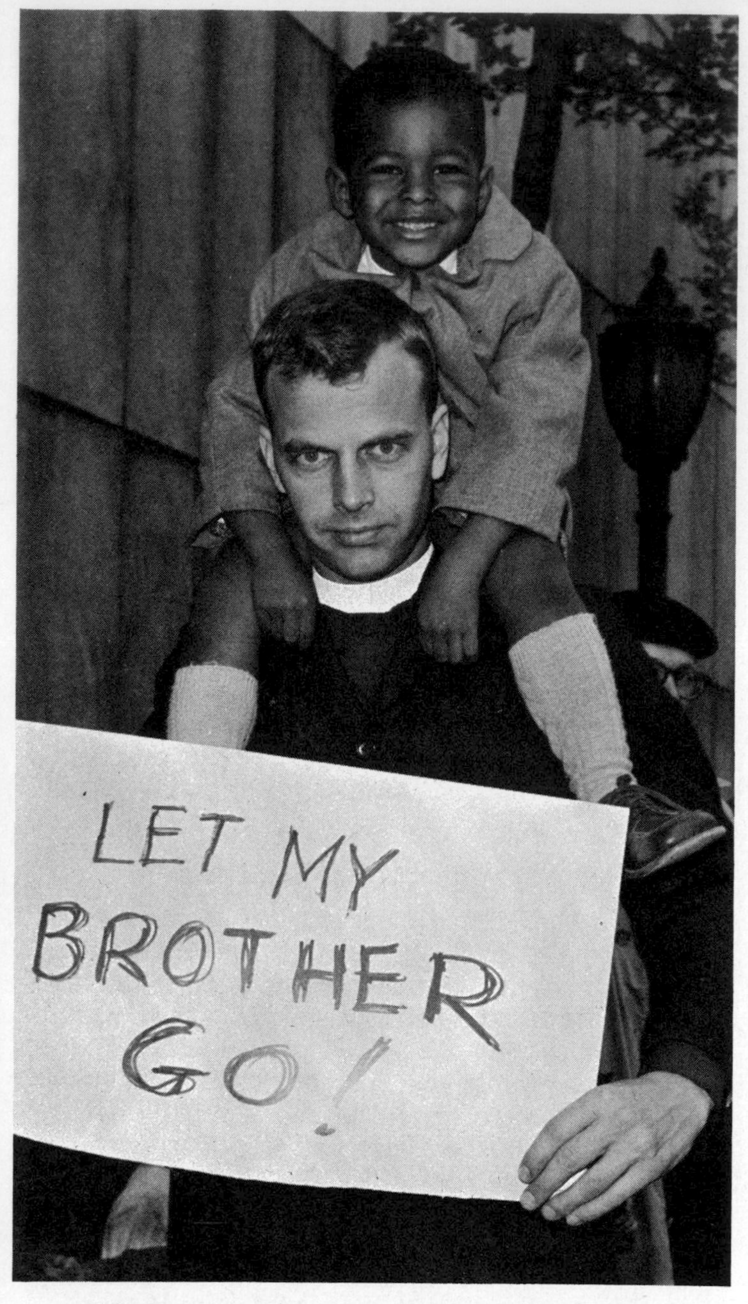

Signs and young ministers like these are a part of many civil-rights demonstrations.

thousands of dollars of bail money for jailed demonstrators and funneled funds to ministers who had lost their pulpits because of outspoken stands on civil rights.

At the beginning of the summer of 1964, the National Council of Churches operated an orientation school for student volunteers in the Mississippi Summer Project conducted by civil-rights organizations in Mississippi. One of the three youths murdered—near Philadelphia, Mississippi, in late June—had been a trainee at the school less than a month before.

In the summer and fall of 1964, the churches in California spoke frequently and strongly against repeal of California's fair-housing law. The heads of all eight Catholic dioceses in California issued a statement asserting that the God-given equality of men does not permit discrimination on a racial basis. The major faiths cooperated more closely on the fair-housing campaign than they had on any previous ballot issue in California.

In Mississippi more than 40 Negro churches were bombed during the summer and fall of 1964; out of the ashes came interfaith cooperation unprecedented for Mississippi. Clergymen of many faiths—Southern Baptists and Roman Catholics, Disciples of Christ and Jews, Episcopalians and Negro Methodists—formed a committee to raise money for the rebuilding of the charred churches. "It's like two men in a foxhole who had never known each other," said one Mississippi Baptist clergyman. "When they suddenly face their common enemy, a comradeship develops."

The Freeze-Out

As they attacked what they called "the sin without," the injustices in society, churchmen also attacked "the sin within," discriminatory practices within the church. Often, they knew, an invisible eye separates Negroes from whites at the church door; often chilly indifference or antipathy freezes Negroes from membership lists.

Many church-operated hospitals, orphanages, and homes still reject Negroes; denominations such as the 2,000,000-member United Church of Christ have moved to cut off their funds unless they desegregate. Many church staffs still hire only white persons; the National Council of Churches has ordered staff executives to hire Negroes until their staff balance reaches the same ratio as Negro membership in the National Council.

Sunday School materials have encouraged Christian brotherhood but have been written as if they were to be used only by whites; churches have begun revising them. Seminaries, though generally open to all, have sought students from predominantly white colleges; they are now going to Negro colleges to recruit Negro candidates for the ministry.

Churches even have started to insist that their agencies revise purchasing policies to ensure they buy only from non-discriminatory employers. In September 1964 the National Catholic Conference on Interracial Justice

(NCCIJ), acknowledging the economic power of the Catholic Church, asked all Catholic bishops to institute a fair employment purchasing program. Either purchasing policies are used "to maintain the status quo in the employment field—and thereby perpetuate racial and religious discrimination," reasoned the NCCIJ, "or they are used to end discrimination in an affirmative way." The NCCIJ at the same time established a compliance program to aid the bishops willing to cooperate; under the program the NCCIJ is setting up training institutes for diocesan compliance agents and machinery to provide these experts with technical help later.

The larger effort of the churches on race, however, involves society as a whole—and the whole of society. This takes the form of an effort to make civil rights meaningful to every citizen. "We're aiming first at the full recognition of the human dignity of every person," says the Rev. John F. Cronin of the National Catholic Welfare Conference. "We all tend to think of Negroes in stereotypes, not to know them as individuals."

Under the leadership of Father Cronin and his counterparts from the Protestant and Jewish faiths, the churches are promoting interracial visits to white and Negro homes and biracial work in local communities to combat job discrimination, reduce high school dropouts, and train the illiterate.

At Both Ends of the Hose

To dramatize the importance of civil rights, many clergymen have indicated their willingness to place themselves in picket lines and, if need be, at the receiving end of fire hoses. "But we have to work at the other end, too," says the Rev. H. B. Sissel, a United Presbyterian official in Washington, D.C. "We have to help cut off the water."

This task exists in its most compelling form in the cities and towns with racial strife. "The white policeman in Alabama who kicked Nellie Ponder until she bled is a member of the church, too," observes the Rev. Dr. Regier. "We dare not ignore the person who believes that segregation is the way of the Lord."

That means they cannot ignore some of their colleagues. A few clergymen continue to believe fervently in segregation. When President Kennedy invited 243 clergymen to the White House in June 1963 to discuss the racial problem, a minister from a small fundamentalist

One of the best-known and most effective city youth projects.

denomination delivered an impassioned speech, flavored with Biblical quotes, in which he said God had placed his curse on the Negro.

Church leaders know that their new approach will disturb many and alienate some. "When our general board acted," says the Rev. Dr. Regier of the National Council of Churches, "it saw that it could cost us heavily in financial support and result in divisiveness within churches."

Cost the churches it has.

A few churches in the South have withdrawn from their parent denominations in protest over their new racial stance. Many more have cut off the proportion of their contributions to their parent denomination that is supposed to go to the National Council of Churches.

Church institutions such as hospitals and universities have been hurt financially. Some 100 Methodist churches in South Carolina, for example, withdrew financial support from Wofford College, a Methodist school, after it opened its doors to Negroes. In a lighter vein, the editor of a Methodist publication chuckles that he has received a few requests from readers to cancel their subscriptions and return their money. The joke is on the irate readers. They haven't paid a cent; it's free.

Finances have suffered in individual churches all over the country. Building drives in some churches have been slowed. Nearly every minister or priest can think of at least one family that has reduced its giving because of the racial issue. In one congregation in a Chicago suburb, a financial boycott by part of the congregation resulted in a 25 per cent decline in the church's income.

A Decline in Suburbia

Attendance has dwindled here and there. An extreme case: An Episcopalian priest stood between demonstrators and the home of a Negro who had just moved into a previously all-white neighborhood in suburban Philadelphia. The following Sunday, attendance in his 800-member church plunged from several hundred to 40.

A few officers have resigned dramatically. A leader in a Presbyterian church near Washington, D.C., pulled out two months before new elections were to be held. He protested the racial stand the Presbyterians have been taking nationally and in his own church.

Ministers have been forced out. More than 60 Methodist clergymen have left Mississippi since the start of 1963, nearly all over the civil-rights issue. Many more ministers continue to hang on in churches torn with internal strife. A letter urging people in a large Northern metropolitan area to participate in the March on Washington, for example, asked them to contact a Presbyterian minister who was vice chairman of a religious interracial council. The minister received more than 100 unfavorable letters, many anonymous and some vicious. Several officers in his church resigned, and his choir director and organist left. The minister is still in his pulpit. But, in the words of one of his colleagues, "He won't be getting a raise for quite a while."

A Tucson minister, who is proud that some of his members have helped to picket a segregated restaurant, found more support in his congregation. After he took part in the March on Washington, his church officers published a statement in the Sunday worship bulletin commending him for his participation. Though he heard "a lot of growling," he estimates that only a dozen or so of his 2,000 members left the church in protest.

Church conflicts, naturally enough, have tended to break out most sharply in areas where there is community conflict. When Mrs. C. Gustav Bernstrom brought out some writing paper and envelopes at a women's meeting one night at St. Paul's Lutheran Church in Rensselaer, New York, and urged her friends to write their congressmen about civil-rights legislation, she heard no dissent. The town of 10,000 has few Negroes; no eyebrows have been raised in her church when an occasional Negro child has joined the church.

Abuse by Phone

But a minister near the racially disturbed town of Folcroft, Pennsylvania, found to his dismay that a different sentiment prevailed in his church. After he allowed his church to be used for a meeting called to issue a statement deploring violence in Folcroft, he and his family received a torrent of abusive telephone calls and indecent letters. No crusader or zealot in the racial cause, he had tried only to help restore peace in a Philadelphia suburb being approached by Negro enclaves.

Reactions within local congregations to the harder line on Negro rights have been as pronounced in the North as in the South. In good part this is because the groups that have taken the toughest stance—the Roman Catholic Church and such Protestant denominations as the Episcopalians, the United Presbyterians, and the Congregationalists (United Church of Christ)—have comparatively few churches in the South; the Southern Baptists, with more than 10,000,000 members, do not belong to the National Council of Churches.

Another pattern: Dissent over the racial issue flares up more readily in Protestant congregations than Catholic. The reason is partly theological, partly practical.

"Our great accomplishment in this area

in recent years has been identifying segregation as a moral problem," says the Very Rev. Daniel M. Cantwell, chaplain of the Catholic Interracial Council of Chicago. "I've heard it thousands of times: 'That's your opinion, Father.' They don't say this any longer. The bishops have spoken."

The bishops spoke in their annual statement in 1958 and again in 1963, declaring in effect that a person who advocates segregation is committing a sin. Many Protestant denominations have said much the same thing, but their words carry less authority among individual members.

Catholic priests need not fear the consequences if they speak out in accordance with the voice of the bishops. Unlike most Protestant ministers, who must answer to their congregations, priests are assigned to their parish by their superiors. A Mississippi priest fighting a quiet war against segregation in Mississippi describes the freedom this gives him: "I'm training a Negro boy now to be an altar boy," he says. "I'm not telling my parishioners about it, I'm just going to present them with it. And they'll accept it."

Southern Protestant ministers cannot be quite so bold if they want to stay where they are. Moreover, many Southern ministers—though they sympathize with the ultimate objectives of their Northern brethren—believe that militant tactics are misguided. "We can move slowly and try to carry all that we can with us," wrote the Rev. Robert Collie of Kentwood, Louisiana, in the New York Times Magazine, "or we can move swiftly and leave tens of thousands behind."

Resentment creeps into the attitude of many Southern Protestant ministers. "Sometimes," wrote the Rev. Mr. Collie, "when some group comes into the South and does something dramatic and all I can do is try to handle sullen relationships, I feel like the 'dogface' looking at the 'flyboys' going over to their hour of danger and then home to a soft bed while he has to settle back in his foxhole."

Fears of a "Communist plot" in the civil-rights movement influence many ministers and laymen. Rigid opponents of the church's stand

Even the nuns are ready to demonstrate. Here they picket the all-white policy of a fashionable Catholic women's club in Chicago in 1963.

in congregations from Maryland to California, from Ohio to Alabama, say they are convinced that a Communist conspiracy has infiltrated the movement.

"One of our members is absolutely convinced that Martin Luther King is a Communist," says the Rev. Lorton Heusel, pastor of a Religious Society of Friends (Quaker) congregation in Wilmington, Ohio. "You can't dissuade him; he won't read any material that shows otherwise."

Mr. Heusel's congregation displays the entire spectrum of sentiment on the church's civil-rights stand; a tiny minority advocate sit-ins and breaking the law if necessary. Most, however, believe that the civil-rights push has gained too much momentum.

Progress in Ohio

Wilmington lies only 70 miles from the Ohio River and Kentucky, and much of its heritage is Southern. But it is Ohio nonetheless. And progress has been made in recent years in accepting the Negro on equal terms.

The Presbyterian church in Wilmington has absorbed Negro Presbyterians moving in from different communities without incident. Several Negro students at Wilmington College worship at Quaker services. Mr. Heusel has exchanged pulpits with a Negro preacher in the community; only one person complained to Mr. Heusel. And employers in his congregation now "accept that fact that if a man is qualified for a job, it shouldn't matter whether he's white, black, or blue. Ten or 15 years ago they didn't feel this way."

Despite all of the opposition, the churches' march into the racial wars has made a difference. It has influenced the tenor and direction of the Negroes' civil-rights struggle. But even more, it has injected a new atmosphere into the great majority of white churches.

When national church leaders are arrested in demonstrations, as many have been, the man in the pew may question the propriety of their breaking the law. But he also listens to the minister or priest who argues that "unjust" laws must succumb if they clash with "higher" moral laws.

When denominations lobby in Congress for passage of such laws as the Civil Rights Act, as many do, the man in the pew may question the wisdom of the church in involving itself in political matters. But he also listens to the churchman who argues that justice delayed for the lack of a law is justice denied.

"For the longest time," says the Rev. Donald G. Huston, minister of the First Presbyterian Church of Gladwyne, Pennsylvania, "people in labor, government, and other pursuits were saying the church is irrelevant to the world. They began to light fires under the ministers.

"About the time the ministers got the message, the Negro struggle came along. Then labor and government and the others said, 'By God, we don't want the church to be that relevant!' "

One wealthy family in Gladwyne stepped up its annual pledge from $500 to $5,000; it had finally been convinced, it indicated, that the church was worth supporting. Another churchman reports a different reason why some have been increasing their contributions: "A lot of people are pledging more to wash away their guilt feelings on the race thing. I know. I did."

The crusading minister of an Eastern church reports that in less than four years, his membership figure has risen 50 per cent and his budget 100 per cent despite vocal opposition to his racial stand. The going got harder for him when he carried the civil-rights case to state officials not long ago. "Three of my officers hit the roof, and at their next meeting they thought up a program to keep me busy."

A Selection Process

But he, for one, is convinced that the church will emerge from the current turmoil the stronger for the experience. "We're separating the sheep from the goats," he says. "We're going to lose the nominal church people. But we'll gain the devoted church statesmen."

A feeling thus pervades church leadership that the church, in losing its life, will find it—that the racial upheaval may prove the instrument of a genuine spiritual renaissance in the churches of America.

"Religious institutions are undergoing their most drastic test in the history of America," asserts the Rev. Dr. Weaver of the United Church of Christ. "If the church doesn't come clean on this, if it puts revenues and popularity above its mission as the redeeming institution in society, then God will have to find other instruments to do His will." ♦

—Delmar Lipp

Side by side during the Washington, D.C., march.

Church "Lobbies"

WASHINGTON, D.C.

CALL religious lobbying on Capitol Hill "improper," or call it "courageous." It goes on—and it's growing.

Church groups applied the weight that tipped the balance for passage of the Civil Rights Act of 1964, and religious pressure killed the Becker Amendment on school prayers. Priests, ministers, and rabbis whose faces are familiar in the halls of Congress are serving on the advisory committee of the Community Relations Service, which is working behind the scenes for compliance with the Civil Rights Act, and some have joined Walter Reuther's citizens committee on poverty.

The church, in coming months, will beam its voice onto a stronger frequency on such issues as poverty, immigration, and disarmament. All the while the drumfire will persist on civil rights.

The churches, by every account, played a decisive role in the civil-rights struggle in Congress. Hubert Humphrey, Democratic floor manager for the bill in the Senate, termed them "the most important force at work" on behalf of the measure. The leader of the Southern forces, Georgia's Richard B. Russell, blamed the bill's passage on pressure from President Johnson and many of the nation's clergy.

"This is the second time in my lifetime an effort has been made by the clergy to make a moral question of a political issue," recalled Senator Russell minutes before the Senate voted to shut off debate. "The other was Prohibition. We know something of the results of that."

A moral issue the clergy unquestionably sought to make it. And the emphasis on the "moral," as opposed to the "political," is one of the elements that distinguishes the "new look" of church lobbying in Washington.

"You can always fight 'politics,'" asserts a young lobbyist of the cloth who, like many of his associates, earned his first battle stars in the civil-rights campaign. "But it's difficult to fight 'morality.'"

The theme is being repeated on poverty legislation. "Modern technology is increasingly bringing within man's possibilities the elimination of poverty," declares the National Council of Churches (NCC), whose member churches comprise two-thirds of American Protestantism. "Poverty is therefore ethically intolerable. The persistence of poverty has become a matter for which men are morally responsible."

Catholics and Jews also are stressing the "moral" aspect of the poverty problem. In their common approach, the three faiths demonstrate another element of the new look in church lobbying.

The old-time superficial "brotherhood" has vanished, victim of a new era of candid discussion among the faiths. Confesses one Protestant: "Before, when we faced an issue, we used to ask, 'Where are the Catholics?' Then we'd take the opposite position."

Now Washington spokesmen for the three faiths wrestle with the issues and disagree when they must. But hard reasoning on the Civil Rights Act resulted in the unprecedented joint testimony before Congress by national leaders of all three faiths in July 1963. And frank conversations now undergird the churches' growing interest in speaking out on such broad issues as poverty and peace.

No longer, in fact, do churches lobby large-

The Strong Arm of Persuasion

The Clergy and Their Representatives Are a Force To Reckon With on Capitol Hill: How They Do It

ly to protect their own interests—as on Social Security for the clergy, for example. No longer do they speak incessantly on issues dear to their own theology—alcohol, say, or gambling—and remain silent on larger concerns.

But the new look applies not merely to church offices in the shadow of the Capitol. It applies to church conventions in Denver and Des Moines. It applies to pastors and their congregations in Hackensack and Sacramento. "We don't get the question, 'What are you doing lobbying?' any more," declares James Hamilton, young civil-rights strategist for the National Council of Churches in Washington. "Instead they're asking, 'What more can we do?' "

Church lobbying has many shades, many forms. It can be as direct as a straight pitch to a congressman in the privacy of his office or as subtle as a bishop's impromptu comment to the press hundreds of miles away. Its practitioners may openly acknowledge they're trying to influence votes, or they may speak in euphemisms about "keeping our people back home informed."

Drop into the second-floor offices of the Friends Committee on National Legislation (FCNL) at 2nd and C Streets, N.E., in the Capitol Hill section. There's no effort there to disguise activities with euphemisms, no uneasiness over the job they're doing. Declares the Friends' E. Raymond Wilson, dean of Washington's church lobbyists: "Lobbying is as American as hamburgers or the Fourth of July."

Mr. Wilson deplores what he believes is the prevalent public view "of a partially eclipsed God who can shed His light on missionary activities in Cambodia and the Congo, but not on Congress. Not that church bodies speak with the full wisdom of God, but members of Congress do need the warmth of religious fellowship."

Congress, it's evident from a huge wall chart in FCNL offices, feels the warmth of Quaker fellowship. The chart shows every member of Congress, the dates Quakers visited them or their assistants in the past year or two, and the subjects discussed. FCNL staff members or volunteers held more than 600 "interviews" with congressmen in 1963 and even more in 1964.

Mr. Wilson helped form the FCNL in November 1943, when the pacifist Friends were especially concerned about protecting the interests of conscientious objectors in the draft. The FCNL, Mr. Wilson proudly recalls, was "the first full-time legislative staff of a religious denomination to work on the three jobs of lobbying: Sending out information to its members and bringing them to Washington; getting out in the field to discuss the issues; lobbying in the narrow sense—interviewing members of Congress intensively and testifying before legislative committees."

Of the more than 1,000 lobbyists registered under the Lobbying Act of 1946, fewer than 10 are connected with religious groups; 3 of these are staff members of the FCNL. The Unitarians are the only other denomination with a registered lobbyist. The Woman's Christian Temperance Union (WCTU) is an example of a nonsectarian but religion-oriented organization that has a registered lobbyist who speaks on a wide range of subjects—alcoholism, narcotics, obscenity, even school prayers. Another registered lobbyist, the Christian Amendment Movement, works in just one field of interest; it

—Larry Stevens

That omniscient Quaker chart, showing every congressman and when visited, studied by E. Raymond Wilson, dean of the church lobbyists.

sponsors a proposed constitutional amendment, perennially introduced in Congress and perennially pigeonholed, that would commit America to "the authority and law of Jesus Christ."

Most churchmen on Capitol Hill don't register as lobbyists because, they contend, they're not lobbyists in the usual sense. They distinguish between lobbying for one's own interests—the type pursued by labor unions, companies, and trade associations—and lobbying for what they construe as the interests of society.

"We're not concerned about partisan benefits that may come to the church as an institution," explains the Rev. A. Dudley Ward, general secretary of the Methodist Board of Christian Social Concerns. "Furthermore, the members of Congress have a right to expect the persons who are supposed to represent the moral consensus of the nation—or the lack of moral consensus—to speak out."

On balance, Washington churchmen speak very little to congressmen themselves and far more to their members back home. "I'm ashamed to admit this," confides one Protestant lobbyist, "but I didn't see a single senator or congressman during the whole civil-rights thing."

The Rev. H. B. Sissel, Washington spokesman for the United Presbyterians, made a "deliberate and calculated" decision not to visit congressmen himself. Mr. Sissel doubts that the church lobbyist can be effective: "He has no votes, no money, no technical information to offer." What's more, Mr. Sissel believes, the lobbyist can spend his time more productively enlisting support among people who do have influence on congressmen—their constituents.

Church offices have mushroomed in Washington in postwar years; more than a dozen groups maintain full-time representatives in the city and others, such as the Episcopalians, have men who visit the Capitol regularly from other cities. But the greatest growth has occurred not in personnel, but in publications.

From the Baptist Joint Committee on Public Affairs stream "position papers" on almost every nuance of the continuing church-state debate. From the imposing 10-story headquarters of the National Catholic Welfare Conference (NCWC), the nerve center of Catholicism in the United States, pour influential statements on social welfare, education, peace, and family life.

"Education" Works

Inevitably, these "education" efforts have an impact on Congress. A NCWC priest once told of a congressman who was disturbed because he had learned too late the NCWC position on the Taft-Hartley Act; due to the poor timing, the congressman said, he had voted the "wrong" way. Many Catholic legislators suffered similar distress when they supported the proposed school-prayer amendment, only to have the NCWC come out against it.

To see how one Washington church "lobby" mobilizes its resources in the context of the new look, trace the activities of the Washington office of the National Council of Churches on behalf of the Civil Rights Act. The action began in June 1963, when the general board of the NCC created a Commission on Religion and Race.

The commission received a three-part mandate from the general board: Urge denominations to desegregate their own institutions, help churches aid in the desegregation of communities, and work for "meaningful" civil-rights legislation. Jim Hamilton, a husky 1956 graduate of George Washington Law School and a 5½-year veteran of the Washington staff, was drafted to work full-time on civil rights.

NCC strategists quickly reached four crucial decisions:

First, cooperate with the Leadership Conference on Civil Rights, a loose confederation of about 80 organizations ranging from fraternal societies to labor unions.

Second, work informally with Washington "lobbies" of individual denominations, issuing statements on a tri-faith basis where possible.

Third, formulate tri-faith testimony for early delivery before Congress, and follow up with visits to key legislators by the religious leaders testifying.

Fourth, concentrate "field work" on the Midwest and Rocky Mountain regions, where labor unions and other traditional supporters of strong civil-rights legislation were weak.

The Midwestern and Mountain states, the NCC knew, had sent a number of congressmen to the House who were uncommitted on civil rights; they possessed a huge block of uncommitted votes in the Senate. And so, less than a month after the March on Washington in late August 1963, the suspenseful campaign for support—support where it counted—began.

To Lincoln, Nebraska, for a two-day meeting, the NCC brought 150 top church leaders from 13 states. The purpose: To help them understand, in Mr. Hamilton's words, "the dimensions of their involvement in the civil-rights legislative fight," and to prod them into planning how to enlist support in their home states. Similar one-day meetings were held in succeeding weeks in Denver, Indianapolis, and several smaller cities.

Through Middle West

In October, four-man teams roved Ohio, Illinois, Iowa, Nebraska, South Dakota—five states that held critical votes in the House. On each team were a minister (to speak of the religious motivation for concern over civil-rights legislation), a Negro youth (to say, Mr. Hamilton explains, "I've been through it—and it's hell"), a legislative expert (to describe the bill), and a contact man from the state council of churches.

The teams toured the breakfast and luncheon circuit, encouraging clergymen and laymen to return to their churches and enlist others in telephone and telegram appeals to their congressmen, or even to organize delegations to visit their congressmen in Washington. Where they could, the teams called on other faiths for help; a rabbi participated in Sioux City, Iowa, a priest in Dubuque.

All the while, the NCC was pumping out fact sheets on the bill as it progressed through the House. The periodic reports went to about 5,200 church leaders.

In Washington, Mr. Hamilton was joining leadership conference delegations visiting key congressmen on the House Judiciary subcommittee—George Meader of Michigan, Clark MacGregor of Minnesota, Charles Mathias of Maryland. Twice while the bill was in the House, the three faiths sent joint telegrams (on public accommodations and on fair employment) signed by prominent national spokesmen.

The House passed the bill in February 1964; every Illinois congressman voted for it, and so did two of Nebraska's three congressmen. Within days Iowa-bred Jim Hamilton was back in the hustings, this time in the Great Plains. The Rev. Jay Moore, from the Commission on Religion and Race, visited the Mountain States region.

This time they met with smaller groups —groups of 20 or so. They recorded tapes to circulate among the churches. And they began to spot indications that their earlier work was paying off.

In Sioux Falls, South Dakota, a power executive told Mr. Hamilton he had spoken with Sen. Karl E. Mundt there the previous week end and would see him again in Washington that week. When Mr. Hamilton visited Nebraska "to tell them to tighten up" on Sen. Roman L. Hruska and Sen. Carl T. Curtis, a state council of churches leader told him they had already been buttonholed. Newspaper ads signed by churchmen began to appear in influential newspapers—in Sen. Bourke B. Hickenlooper's home town of Cedar Rapids, Iowa, for example.

The last push began on April 28, 1964, when 6,300 churchmen around the nation jammed Georgetown University's McDonough Auditor-

A delegation from the United Church of Christ visited Senator Humphrey in 1964, when the Civil Rights Bill was still pending—and made their views known.

ium in Washington for the National Inter-Religious Convocation on Civil Rights. The next day, daily services sponsored by the Commission on Religion and Race ("a counterpoint to the Senate filibuster") began at a Lutheran church on Capitol Hill; the services continued, with attendance as high as 270 and as low as 2, until the bill passed. At the Lincoln Memorial, theological students representing more than 100 seminaries—Protestant, Catholic, and Jewish—opened a 24-hour vigil for civil-rights legislation.

"Yes, I know, I know . . . the seminaries," interrupted a senator when one seminary student started to explain why he was visiting the senator's office.

On May 18, the day after the 10th anniversary of the Supreme Court decision on school desegregation, 260 churchmen from 43 states assembled at the Lutheran church, marched to the Supreme Court for a brief prayer, and then visited their congressmen. Soon afterward, three NCC men, including Mr. Hamilton, struck out for the Great Plains to urge churchmen to make a last-minute pitch.

The harvest was plentiful. Voting for cloture were both senators from Iowa, both from Nebraska, both from Kansas, both from South Dakota. Many factors influenced votes in both houses of Congress, but for some congressmen, religious pressure was the decisive one. Grumbled a Kansas conservative in the House just before the vote: "I'd like to vote against it, but I can't. The church groups are on my tail."

"Who knows what influence we had, or why?" muses a contemplative Mr. Hamilton as he gazes at a wall map of congressional districts. "We only know this: It wasn't just the church operating as a church. It was the church operating in lay fields, involving the business community, reaching into the power structure."

It was, in short, the classic political pattern. In one city, it was a huddle with the Red Feather man who knows the community power structure; a pitch to a Methodist minister followed, and the minister in turn contacted the

The National Council of Churches, not without its critics, takes a stand.

president of the largest bank in the state, who promised to contact a senator. In other cities, other persons were involved, but the pattern was the same.

"We kept churning," says Mr. Hamilton. "We kept saying, 'We gotta do something this week, next week. We gotta keep the boiler going.'" The Catholics, he says, were more conservative in their approach, "perhaps more wise."

The Catholics relied on a network of more than 55 Catholic interracial councils to build grass-roots support for the bill. Only in May 1964 did they organize a major Midwest conference sweeping across state lines and pulling in delegates from 50 dioceses. In Washington, NCWC priests refrained from extensive visits to legislators. "We had the feeling you could overdo the Roman collar around Capitol Hill," says one NCWC priest.

By the Hundreds

Some Protestant denominations felt no such restraint. More than once the Episcopalians brought several score churchmen to the Capitol; they used the "blanket" approach, reporting one time they saw 400 of the 435 House members. A United Church of Christ "Witness in Washington" in March attracted more than 100 people from 22 key states who fanned out to see their senators. More than one denomination paid the travel expenses of some of their volunteer churchmen.

If the church lobbies harvested votes, they harvested criticism, too. Charging that the NCC was "engaging in political activity of a lobbying nature" in violation of its tax-exempt status, Sen. Strom Thurmond of South Carolina in March demanded an Internal Revenue Service inquiry.

The controversy hinges on one word in the Internal Revenue Code. Religious organizations qualify for tax exemption if no "substantial" part of its activities involve propaganda or efforts to influence legislation. What is "substantial"?

The only guideline is a 1955 case in which a circuit court indicated that if "less than 5 per cent of time and effort" of the organization were devoted to "political" activities, these activities would not be considered "substantial." The NCC points out that less than 1 per cent of its budget goes to its Commission on Religion and Race, and only a part of this sum went to support of the Civil Rights Act.

Jim Hamilton: The voice of the National Council of Churches on the Civil Rights Bill.

Scores of Southern churches associated with the NCC have been withholding their payments in protest over NCC activities on civil rights. A Thurmond aide echoes their sentiments: "We stand against everything the National Council stands for, except preaching the gospel—and they don't do much of that."

The "revolt" probably won't spread much beyond the South and Southwest, but it expresses a consequence of a second criticism against church lobbying: What right do churches have to spend money from the collection plates for purposes individual members oppose?

The Friends Committee on National Legislation, the most aggressive lobby on the Hill, avoids this criticism as neatly as it avoids the first. As a registered lobbyist, it claims no tax exemption. And as a group independent from the Religious Society of Friends, receiving financial support from separate sources, it spends no loose bills dropped into collection plates.

"The FCNL speaks for itself and for like-minded Friends," it declares in its testimony and in its newsletter. "No organization can speak officially for the Religious Society of Friends." Many church lobbies make similar disclaimers, and some—the Committee for Racial Justice Now of the United Church of Christ, for example—collect their funds from special offerings.

A fear the churches will muddy still further the murky waters of church-state relationships disturbs some critics of church lobbying. "Keep your church out of politics," Senator Thurmond warned a group of Methodist lawyers in North Carolina. "But you—you as individual Christians—should work to use your influence politically."

Counters America magazine, a voice of liberal Catholicism: "Separation of church and state has never been interpreted to mean the insulation of lawmaking from the moral demands of religious faith."

Finally, critics wonder where the churches will draw the line between proper and improper concerns. The church-inspired Anti-Saloon League, during its heyday in the first two decades of the Twentieth Century, unashamedly delivered and withheld votes on the basis of a single criterion: How the candidate voted on temperance. Complained one writer in 1919: "The average member of Congress is more afraid of the Anti-Saloon League than he is even of the President of the United States."

The Friends' Mr. Wilson and his more timid associates in other denominations seek no return to the days of the Anti-Saloon League. Mr. Wilson argues that it's improper for churches to endorse political parties or candidates, or to permit political meetings to be held on their grounds.

But Mr. Wilson rebukes his colleagues for a lobbying stance he believes is still too meek. "The churches haven't been doing 10 per cent of what they should be doing on social action," he complains. Seven representative Protestant denominations, he calculates, spend from 4 cents to 19 cents per member each year—"the cost of an ice cream cone or a Coca-Cola"—on social action.

Rumblings on Capitol Hill indicate Mr. Wilson may be swimming against the tide. Some churchmen, like some legislators, are uncomfortable about any consistent church alliance with labor. They warn, too, that anti-poverty programs, for example, are complex packages of legislation, with any number of church-state traps that can divide opinion sharply among the faiths. "Civil rights had the virtue of being a completely unambiguous issue in terms of Christian implications," says Dr. Lewis I. Maddocks of the United Church of Christ.

But the central question remains: What is the proper role of the church on Capitol Hill? "The answer has been rewritten this past year," said the NCC's Mr. Hamilton as he relaxed in his office a few days after Congress passed the Civil Rights Act. "I hope it has been rewritten unalterably."

Later in the year Mr. Hamilton and his associates at the National Council of Churches set to work at another rewriting task. For the simple statement of purpose of the NCC's Washington office, written in the early 1950s, still contained these words: "The Washington Office as such is not to engage in efforts to influence legislation." ◆

The Churches And Goldwater

WASHINGTON, D.C.

CLERGYMEN have preached politics in Presidential campaigns since pro-Federalist ministers in state churches in New England derided Thomas Jefferson in election day sermons. Seldom, however, were churchmen's attacks as widespread or as shrill as they were in 1964 against Barry Goldwater.

"The churches were more deeply immersed in the 1964 Presidential campaign than in any campaign since 1864," declares Dr. Franklin H. Littell, professor of church history at Chicago Theological Seminary and a prominent authority on politics in the pulpit.

The churches, of course, have displayed a new militancy in many political and social areas in recent years. On the streets and in legislative forums, they have plunged deeply into the thickets of civil rights, poverty, the United Nations, and countless other controversial issues.

But the new militancy cannot alone explain the churches' offensive against Barry Goldwater. The churches disagreed with the Republican nominee on most issues, yes, but disagreement over issues could not have produced the firepower apparent in the anti-Goldwater barrage.

The churches saw in Barry Goldwater a threat—a threat to the kind of America they espoused, a threat to the kind of religion they preached. Significantly, only a few churchmen made a point of endorsing President Johnson; the churches' message for the most part was not pro-Johnson, but anti-Goldwater.

The churches considered Barry Goldwater a threat partly because he failed to disavow right-wing supporters. They did not regard the nominee himself as dictatorial, but they feared that some of his more vocal backers would deny to others the very freedoms they claimed to defend. Over and over the clergy—especially Jews and Protestants—reminded their people that the Protestant church in Germany had largely remained silent while Hitler was winning power and later while he was eliminating millions of Jews. Prominent churchmen—Bishop Reuben H. Mueller, president of the National Council of Churches; Methodist Bishops Lloyd C. Wicke of New York and A. Raymond Grant of Portland, Oregon; Dr. Lewis W. Jones, president of the National Conference of Christians and Jews, and others—helped form the Council for Civic Responsibility in mid-campaign to try to combat what they called the "ominous increase" of the dissemination of "radical, reactionary propaganda."

Too, in many churchmen's eyes, Barry Goldwater presented a threat to a compassionate America, an America that protects the underdog and helps its own poor and the poor of other lands. Never mind that Mr. Goldwater insisted that his philosophy would help the poor and the underdog more in the long run; the churches demanded evidence, immediate evidence.

Finally, Mr. Goldwater challenged the prevalent attitude among church leaders toward religion itself in the American system. "Is this the time in our nation's history for the Federal Government to ban Almightly God from our school rooms?" he asked on a nationwide telecast two weeks before the election; "I trust not." When he ticked off organizations that support a prayer amendment, however, he could mention only two with any influence in religious circles, the National Conference of Catholic Youth and the National Association of Evangelicals. The overwhelming majority of religious groups supported the Supreme

Thunder From the Pulpit

Churchmen Speak Out With Frankness on Politics, Battering the Man From Arizona in the Process

—"Swords Into Ploughshares" by Moissaye Marans

Court decision on prayer in the public schools, arguing that in an America of many faiths the home and the church, not the classrooms, are the proper places for religious indoctrination.

Did the political endorsements by churchmen make any difference? Perhaps not a great deal. Indeed, most visible evidence—members' resignations, angry protests in pastors' studies—suggests that the endorsements boomeranged. As the Very Rev. George G. Higgins, director of the social action department of the National Catholic Welfare Conference, wrote in his syndicated column, the Yardstick, Americans "resent clerical support of, or opposition to, candidates for political office."

Remember, however, that the clergyman in the pulpit has a captive audience. Unlike the political columnist in the newspapers, who must compete with sports and sin and subway crowds, the man in the black robe can command undivided attention in a quiet, thoughtful atmosphere.

Remember, too, that the judgment of churchmen in most parts of the nation was nearly unanimous. Dissent—support for Mr. Goldwater—was rare. Surely this judgment influenced to some degree the vast number of citizens who belong to churches or synagogues.

No denominations as a whole denounced Mr. Goldwater's candidacy. But more than 725 Episcopal bishops, clergymen, and laymen signed a statement that accused the Republican nominee of "transparent exploitation of racism." The Chicago district of the predominantly Negro A. M. E. Zion Church criticized Mr. Goldwater and urged its pastors to conduct "voter education" drives for support of President Johnson. And Methodist boards of Christian social concerns for the Detroit and

A devoted Episcopalian, shown here with Mrs. Goldwater, the Republican did not escape criticism even from his own Church.

Newark, New Jersey, conferences (groups of churches) stirred controversy by terming Mr. Goldwater's positions inconsistent with Christian ideals.

"If we are to judge Senator Goldwater by his voting record and his public utterances, whether on race relations, foreign relations, care of the old and sick, on maintenance of genuine economic health, or on preservation of world peace," declared the Newark Methodist body, "his positions have been irreconcilable to the Christian ideals we have sought to translate into political reality." The statement was the first on Presidential candidates in the 107-year history of the Newark Conference.

A number of religious publications that rarely endorse candidates seized the anti-Goldwater banner. The Witness and the Churchman, magazines published by members of his own Episcopal denomination, opposed him for the Presidency; never before, proclaimed the Witness, had a national party nominated a candidate "so openly contemptuous of all the church has been saying and teaching in the last 30 years or so."

A United Church of Christ biweekly, United Church Herald, declared its "forthright opposition to Barry Goldwater," though denomination officials stressed that the magazine could not speak for the church as a whole. The American Lutheran chose a more indirect approach; some candidates, it said, "make subtle appeals to man's innate prejudice—especially prejudice against the Negro. That is an issue no Christian can ignore."

Prestige on the Line

Two prestigious Protestant journals that cross denominational lines, Christian Century and Christianity and Crisis, attacked Mr. Goldwater vigorously. "Goldwater? No!" proclaimed Christian Century two weeks before the Republican convention opened. A week later the weekly published comments on Mr. Goldwater by seven specialists in Christian ethics; most agreed, said Christian Century somberly, that "at this point in history an ideology other than that he espouses must guide the nation if it is to avoid disaster." During the campaign most of the Century's issues carried anti-Goldwater editorials, terming his "chief weaknesses" his "penchant for the stock answer and the hair-trigger action"; only one editorial ("Johnson? Yes!") emphasized the magazine's positive support of President Johnson. In the previous 60 years Christian Century had supported just three Presidential candidates: The Republicans' Hoover in 1932, the Democrats' Roosevelt in 1936, and the Republicans' Willkie in 1940.

Christianity and Crisis has a mere 12,000 subscribers compared with the Century's 37,000. But it packs immense influence in Protestantism, for its editorial board includes such prominent theologians as Reinhold Niebuhr, John C. Bennett, Henry P. Van Dusen, and Robert McAfee Brown. For the first time in 25 years, it decided to use its influence in a Presidential campaign. A vote for Mr. Goldwater, it asserted in a 12-page edition devoted exclusively to an analysis of his views, would be a vote for "irresponsibility, recklessness and reaction."

Unbalanced Criticism

For pure vitriol, nothing quite approached the condemnation of the Republican candidate in Ramparts, a monthly edited by Catholic laymen in California. Mr. Goldwater, declared Ramparts, "is Dr. Strangelove incarnate; he is possessed, paranoidal, utterly evil, and close to suicidal."

Ramparts' editors did not represent a consensus of American Catholics. Catholic priests and laymen's organizations generally cultivated neutrality more than their Protestant and Jewish counterparts. Christian Century's liberal Catholic counterpart, the weekly America, for example, pointedly refused to endorse either nominee.

Most rabbis who spoke in the pulpit spoke against Mr. Goldwater. Rabbi Joachim Prinz, the influential president of the American Jewish Congress, told his congregation that a "Jewish vote for Goldwater is a vote for Jewish suicide." The Republican candidate, he said, "is not a man that hates. He is a decent, honest, articulate, religious, and most dangerous man. He is surrounded by every hate group in the United States, every anti-Semite in America. . . ."

Most mainstream Protestant ministers apparently favored President Johnson; perhaps one-fourth in the nation's metropolitan areas worked anti-Goldwater references into their sermons. Few, however, were quite so outspoken—

Dean Sayre: He didn't like either Johnson or Goldwater and said so.

or created quite so intense a reaction—as the Rev. William Sydnor, rector of an Episcopal church in Alexandria, Virginia, where George Washington served as vestryman and where Robert E. Lee was confirmed. "When one listens to or reads Senator Goldwater," declared the Rev. Mr. Sydnor, "one finds that respect for God's law is shockingly absent and adherence to God's law is ignored with conscienceless abandon." Some of the Rev. Mr. Sydnor's parishioners found his comments shockingly off target; half a dozen rose and left the church as he spoke, and several others asked him at the church door to drop them from the communicants' list.

A Negro clergyman dropped an equally explosive bomb—and soon found himself in the middle of the fallout. The Rev. O. J. Hayman, a Maryland leader of the African Methodist Episcopal Church, first endorsed Mr. Goldwater, saying he had "done more for civil rights and the cause of the Negro than President Johnson ever did." President Johnson, he added, "with the exception of the politically hot civil-rights bill, has always been a segregationist. I don't believe this leopard can change spots." The denomination's Ministers Alliance of Baltimore and Vicinity, by its own description, promptly "reeled with shock." Within a week, the Rev. Dr. Hayman did, too; he reversed his position and endorsed President Johnson because of "the excitement generated among the Negro community" and "for the sake of my people."

Less publicized than endorsements but far more frequent were pulpit allusions to moral decay in America, with cynicism in both parties offered as evidence. The Very Rev. Francis B. Sayre, Jr., dean of Washington Cathedral in the nation's capital, captured headlines when he called Mr. Goldwater "a man of dangerous ignorance and devastating uncertainty" and President Johnson "a man whose public house is splendid in its every appearance, but whose private lack of ethics must inevitably introduce termites at the very foundation." Obscured was a larger theme of his sermon: "Few eyes are lifted in this nation to a nobler purpose than selfish gain."

Preach to the Heart

Clerical sentiment for Mr. Goldwater ran deepest in Southern Baptist and Church of Christ churches in the South and Southwest. Except for politically oriented evangelists such as the Rev. Billy James Hargis, however, Southern ministers preaching politics in the pulpit were as rare as Negro politicians endorsing Mr. Goldwater. "We just preach the gospel in the pulpit," said one Arkansas Baptist. "We figure if we can get people's hearts right, they're going to vote right."

Many Southern preachers didn't figure this way in 1960, when the Southern Baptist Convention and a majority of state Baptist conventions declared that Catholic beliefs on church-state issues disqualified any Catholic (read "John F. Kennedy") from the Presidency. And in 1928, when the Catholic and anti-Prohibitionist Al Smith ran for President, not only did many Southern ministers preach and campaign against the Democratic candidate (openly on Prohibition, more subtly on anti-papism) but some actually managed state-wide party campaigns for Herbert Hoover, the Republican nominee.

"There wasn't a single figure in the South —a governor, a senator, anyone—who had the political influence (Methodist) Bishop (James M.) Cannon had," says Dr. Kenneth K. Bailey, professor of history at Texas Western College and author of *Southern White Protestantism*. "And Bishop Cannon used his influence."

"Vote as you pray," urged a church-sponsored advertisement in the Memphis Commercial Appeal on the eve of the 1928 election. A Methodist minister gleefully told the El Paso Times that 18 of the 20 newspapers published by Southern Baptists and Southern Methodists "are openly and boldly for decency, morality, and good government in this crisis," and that "the other two are certainly not supporting Al Smith." Both the Southern Baptists and the Southern Methodists resolved as denominations to oppose any candidates not positively committed to Prohibition.

Protestant ministers in the North and West decried Al Smith's candidacy too, but the voice of the church proved a major influence only in the South.

Not so in 1864. Throughout the Union during the Civil War election, ministers committed themselves as deeply to Abraham Lincoln as to any candidate before or since. Abolitionist preachers—Congregationalists, Methodists, Baptists—campaigned openly for the President on the stump as well as in the pulpit.

The intertwining of politics and religion, it's often overlooked, was very much a part of Nineteenth Century America; the Know-Nothing Party of the 1840s and 1850s, which loomed as the party of opposition to the Democrats until it split over slavery in 1855, was a party of anti-Catholic and anti-foreigner Protestants based largely on religion.

Southern ministers as well as Northern, then, theological conservatives as well as theological liberals, have used their energies on the political stump. The results have been mixed.

Clergymen unquestionably helped elect their men in 1928 and 1864. But a Presbyterian minister, the Rev. Samuel D. Burchard, probably cost James G. Blaine the electoral votes of New York and thus the Presidency in 1884. A few days before the election, in speaking for a group of ministers meeting with Blaine, he associated Blaine's opponent, Grover Cleveland, with "rum, Romanism, and rebellion." The phrase infuriated Roman Catholics and sent them to the polls in large numbers to vote for Cleveland.

Little wonder that Blaine himself later wrote a friend that he had lost the Presidency because "the Lord sent upon us an ass in the shape of a preacher." ♦

The Evangelicals

Tired of the Social Gospel, They Urge Ministry To Emphasize Men's Souls, Not Stomachs

NEW YORK CITY.

THE TODD-AO screen at the Billy Graham Pavilion at the World's Fair surveyed the heavens, the giant California redwoods, the ruins of ancient Greece and Rome. Finally it narrowed in on Billy Graham himself.

"You must turn to Christ by simple faith and accept Him as your Lord and Savior." A pause. "Notice again, I said 'by faith.' "

The pitch, a very old one in Christianity, has been out of fashion in mainstream Protestant churches through much of this century. Now, however, in several major denominations deeply involved in social issues, some ministers and laymen are organizing movements advocating a revival of what they call "evangelical," or "conservative," Christianity. These "evangelicals"—and many Christians who consider themselves "evangelical" or "conservative" do not agree with them—insist that the churches are devoting too much attention to improving men's material condition on earth and not enough to saving men's souls.

Southern Presbyterian "evangelicals," chafing over what one describes as "moral and ecclesiastical irresponsibility" displayed by their church, organized a movement called "Concerned Presbyterians" in late 1964. The organization has opened an office in Miami and established a network of contact men in each of the 16 synods (regions) of the Presbyterian Church in the U.S. (Southern Presbyterians).

A similar movement soon will be announced in the United Presbyterian Church, the northern branch of Presbyterianism. Evangelicals—largely East Coast laymen—are drafting a long statement protesting their church's leadership in the civil-rights struggle, the Protestant unity movement, and other ventures.

The Protestant Episcopal Church also is feeling the fervor of the evangelical conservatives. The Rev. Peter C. Moore, a New York City priest who serves unofficially as American secretary of the three-year-old Evangelical Fellowship in the world-wide Anglican Communion, describes the Episcopalian movement as "just rumblings at the moment." But the Rev. Philip E. Hughes, a Church of England priest now serving as visiting professor at Georgia's Columbia Theological Seminary, plans to rally Episcopalian evangelicals in America at a conference in June 1965.

The new conservatives engage in none of the Communist-baiting tactics or "down-with-Darwin" campaigns that are popularly associated with the stereotype, if not always the actual embodiment, of religious fundamentalists today. In the religious spectrum they lie between rigid fundamentalism and the comparatively liberal doctrines espoused by most "mainline" Protestant leaders.

Unlike some "mainline" leaders, they defend the virgin birth of Christ, His full deity, and His physical resurrection, and say that theologians who question these doctrines dilute the message of the scriptures. They don't deny that Christians should concern themselves with social matters, but they deplore the popular tendency to place social concerns ahead of evangelistic work.

"The liberals are swatting at the branches of the trees when they ought to be getting down to the roots," says the Rev. G. Aiken Taylor, editor of the conservative Presbyterian Journal.

Echoes Dr. Stuart Barton Babbage of Columbia Seminary: "If the root of faith is severed, the fruit of morality will shrivel and die."

To discover why evangelicals are uniting

A Turn to the Right

within various denominations to protect the "root of faith," it is useful to trace the origins of Concerned Presbyterians.

An informal fellowship of conservatives has existed among Southern Presbyterians for years. In fact the Southern Presbyterians' support of not one but three semi-official church magazines—one liberal, one middle-of-the-road, one conservative (Presbyterian Journal)—encourages perhaps more open discussion among factions than in any other Protestant denomination.

Late in 1963, a group of ministers and laymen in the liberal factions formed a Fellowship of Concern. They urged, among other things, a deeper Southern Presbyterian commitment to civil-rights legislation and to union with other denominations.

The general assembly of the church in April 1964 took important steps toward integration of all-Negro presbyteries (groups of churches) into all-white presbyteries and toward forbidding the exclusion of persons from worship or membership because of their race. It refused demands to pull out of the National Council of Churches, under attack for its civil-rights actions and its ecumenical flavor, and indicated a candid desire to merge with the United Presbyterians in the North.

Soundly defeated, the evangelicals quickly regrouped their forces. They discussed the idea of forming Concerned Presbyterians at an executive committee meeting of the Presbyterian Journal's board a month after the general assembly. At the annual "Journal Day" observance in August 1964 in Weaverville, North Carolina, about 500 Presbyterians from throughout the South endorsed plans for the movement. The next month representatives from almost every synod met in Atlanta to formally establish the organization.

Prefer Laymen

Founders of Concerned Presbyterians hope it will develop principally as a laymen's movement. "Ministers are subject to reprisal as laymen are not," says the Rev. Dr. Taylor. Miami real-estate man Kenneth S. Keyes is chairman of Concerned Presbyterians, and Roy LeCraw, a former mayor of Atlanta, co-chairman.

Concerned Presbyterians knows it may attract segregationists interested in the movement for the wrong reason. "We regard racism as a distortion of the gospel," declares the Rev. Dr. Taylor. "But you can't always take responsibility for your friends."

Some Concerned Presbyterians concede that the hardening of battle lines may someday lead to a split of the church. The movement's leaders, however, disclaim any intent to break away. Declares Dr. L. Nelson Bell, associate editor of Presbyterian Journal and the father-in-law of Billy Graham: "We are here to call our church back to those things on which she was founded and on which she alone can be great."

An evangelical resurgence is nothing new, of course. Historian James H. Nichols has used the phrase "evangelical undertow," a phrase in common usage now, to describe trends apparent in pre-Reformation days.

The Days of Faction

Earlier this century, however, an evangelical movement within a denomination usually led to a split at the drop of a doctrinal dispute. The Orthodox Presbyterians broke from the Northern Presbyterians in 1936 over what they considered "modernistic" tendencies in the parent body; similar convictions drove the Conservative Baptists out of the American (Northern) Baptist denomination in the mid-1940s. Other evangelical groups have dropped out of denominations when the parent body has merged with another; witness Boston's historic Park Street Church, which refused to join other Congregationalist churches in the new United Church of Christ several years ago.

The evangelical movement now tries to work within the existing denominations. The most enduring example is the conservative wing of President Johnson's denomination, the Disciples of Christ. For two decades the wing has remained within the Disciples while operating independently outside it, in league with additional churches, as the North American Christian Convention. Its membership and missionary work have grown remarkably fast; it now embraces more than half of the 2,000,000-member constituency of the Disciples of Christ. But insiders believe it won't remain submerged forever; the determination of Disciples leaders to participate in the unity movement, they say, probably will force a split by 1970.

Evangelical sentiment defies measurement. Almost every Protestant congregation contains

—Eve Arnold-Magnum

Evangelist Oral Roberts proclaims the "Roots of Faith" to a spellbound audience.

Prof. Edward J. Carnell of Fuller Theological Seminary: A leading evangelical thinker.

G. Aiken Taylor, editor of the Presbyterian Journal: "Swatting at the branches. . . ."

evangelical conservatives. Rumblings toward the right, however, may not always be motivated by evangelical theology. Example: Have certain Methodist congregations in Alabama and Mississippi withdrawn from the Methodist Church in recent months because of evangelical concerns or because they believe God has ordained racial segregation? "In religion, as in politics, it's hard to judge in the South how much is conservatism and how much is race," says the Rev. Carl F. H. Henry, editor of Christianity Today, the most influential organ of evangelical thought.

Dean Jerald Brauer of the liberal-oriented University of Chicago Divinity School contends that persuasive spokesmen for the evangelicals create an impression of strength, but that the movement's influence has been diminishing.

But the Rev. Dr. Henry believes evangelical sentiment has increased since an Opinion Research Corp. poll several years ago showed that 35 per cent of all Protestant clergymen were fundamentalist, 39 per cent conservative (evangelical), and a mere 26 per cent neo-orthodox or liberal. And the Rev. John C. Bennett, president of the most formidable fortress of liberal theology in America, Union Theological Seminary here, detects "a new ferment of activity on the part of some conservatives who have gained respectability."

The steady growth of the National Association of Evangelicals (NAE), which speaks for 43 denominations and has a constituency of 2,000,000 persons, offers some evidence of evangelical vitality. Even some churches within "mainstream" Protestantism, such as First Presbyterian in Schenectady, New York, First Baptist (American Baptist) in San Francisco, and Park Avenue Methodist in Minneapolis, belong to the NAE individually while retaining their status in their parent denomination.

The enduring appeal of the Rev. Billy Graham also testifies to the strength of the evangelical movement and to its inroads into mainstream Protestantism. Methodist Bishop Gerald Kennedy served as chairman of the Los Angeles Crusade in 1963; Episcopalian, Methodist, and Congregationalist (United Church of Christ) churchmen participated in the planning for the Boston Crusade in 1964.

The brilliance of some evangelical theologians, such as Prof. Edward J. Carnell of Fuller Theological Seminary in California, has helped the movement attain respectability even in the eyes of some theological liberals. The more responsible evangelicals, like the more responsible advocates of the social gospel, have learned to wield the weapons of scholarship instead of invective. On such critical issues as the mission of the church and the origins of the Bible, they display positive initiative instead of negative response.

"The Church's mission in the world is spiritual," proclaims the Rev. Dr. Henry in his book, *Aspects of Christian Social Ethics*. "Its influence on the political order, therefore, must be registered indirectly, as a by-product of spiritual concerns." Evangelicals such as the leaders of Concerned Presbyterians believe that the business of the church is to preach the gospel and lead people to a spiritual rebirth; through changed lives, they contend, persons "saved by Christ" will help improve the world.

"Too many seem to regard getting arrested in racial demonstrations as a mark of sanctity, a ticket to heaven," says one evangelical. Conservative Presbyterians like to quote the Westminster Confession of Faith, a major doctrinal standard of Presbyterianism: "Synods and councils are to handle or conclude nothing but that which is ecclesiastical: And are not to intermeddle with civil affairs which concern the commonwealth unless by way of humble petition in cases extraordinary. . . ."

Evangelicals are equally zealous in defending the "integrity" of the Bible. They consider the Bible the revelation of God's Word, and thus infallible. Unlike some fundamentalists, however, they vigorously insist that the Bible be quoted in context.

Critics of the evangelicals complain that they misinterpret the message of the gospel. "The gospel *is* social," cries a Texas Episcopalian. "That's what it's all about."

The Rev. Dr. Bennett contends that evangelicals have a static rather than a dynamic view of the Christian faith. "The scriptures must be interpreted in relation to the problems of our time," he argues. "The conservatives freeze the process of interpretation at the Seventeenth or Eighteenth Century."

Finally, some critics believe that evangelicals oversimplify complex relationships. "You have to look at the whole man," says the Rev. Eugene Carson Blake, stated clerk of the United Presbyterian Church and a prime target of the newly vocal evangelicals within the "mainline" denominations. "There's an ancient heresy that thinks of Christianity as having to do with spirits but not with men. The problem of the churches is to ensure that the spiritual controls the material, not rejects it."

Like their critics, Concerned Presbyterians and their fellow evangelicals worry about hunger abroad in the world. But the hunger they emphasize is spiritual, not physical—a longing for spiritual belief and commitment. The Christian's first task, these emerging voices urge the leaders of Protestantism, must be to satisfy this kind of hunger. ◆

Billy Graham

LOS ANGELES.

HE was young, tall, and handsome. His long, blond hair tumbled across his face as he paced across the creaky stage. He jerked the cord of a lapel microphone from beneath his feet, coiling it behind him, and jabbed a bony, manicured finger toward his congregation.

"One of these days," he cried hoarsely, "the wrath of God is going to be poured out. Some of these people who laugh at prayer and revival meetings will change their minds. Brother, this old tent won't hold all the people who'll be trying to get in."

The year was 1949, the preacher just another evangelist. His name: Billy Graham.

Fourteen years later, the Rev. Billy Graham returned to Los Angeles. The 5,000-voice choir for the 1963 Crusade would have had trouble squeezing into his 1949 "Canvas Cathedral." Not even the Los Angeles Coliseum could hold the crowd for the final service; the Coliseum's turnstiles clicked 134,600 times, and another 20,000 late-comers had to stand outside to listen to the Rev. Mr. Graham's 23-minute sermon.

Los Angeles. Boston. Houston. Berlin. Wherever he goes, he's a "sin-smashing success," in the florid phrase of an early Graham press agent.

The age of revivals, the theologians had said after World War II, was past. "We are tired of religious revivals as we have known them in the last half-century," declared the Rev. Willard L. Sperry, dean of Harvard Divinity School, in 1946. "Among all but the most backward churches it is now agreed that education is the best way of interesting our people in religion."

Even the fundamentalists of "the most backward churches," in Dean Sperry's words, agreed sadly that revivalism was indeed on the wane. Since the death of Billy Sunday, who quit a brilliant baseball career "to hit home runs for Jesus" in the early part of the century, no evangelist had stirred the souls of millions.

But when Billy Graham appeared on the scene, something happened. The crowds came, and the repenting sinners surged down the sawdust aisles in increasing numbers. One of the first was Stuart Hamblen, owner of a racing stable and a popular radio personality in Los Angeles. Another was Louis Zamperini, a star in the 1932 Olympics and a concentration camp hero of World War II. Still another was Jim Vaus, an electronics genius who handled wiretapping chores for Los Angeles mobster Mickey Cohen.

The Rev. Mr. Graham, a Southern Baptist minister, was speaking for the fundamentalists in this era, and he addressed himself to them, too. His manner was that of the itinerant Southern evangelist; he was God's flashily dressed prophet of doom. He copied many of Sunday's methods and seemed flattered by comparison to the Chicago ball player. Sunday had been "A Gymnast for Jesus"; Billy Graham became the "Gabriel in Gabardine," and often as not it was bright green gabardine set off by an orange tie, white shoes, and a cowboy hat. More conventional clergymen and citizens were offended—

Back to the Bible

The Rev. Mr. Graham Has Come a Long Way Since The Early Days, but the Message Has Changed Little

and Billy Graham became a controversial preacher.

But like the nation that has become his parish, Billy Graham has changed. So have most of his critics, and some of his friends, too.

If he is still a Gabriel in gabardine (and a Crusade staff member winces at the recollection of the phrase), the gabardine is likely to be dark blue and is sure to be impeccably tailored. His tie is probably dark and muted. The stock publicity shot is a portrait by Bachrach, the photographer of Presidents, and in it the Rev. Mr. Graham's wavy hair, much darker than in 1949, is carefully combed.

His delivery is slower, markedly unlike the Walter Winchell staccato he used to use that was sometimes hard to understand. His sermons show more preparation.

The Rev. Mr. Graham still has his critics, though his success has reduced the shrillness of their criticisms. Many liberal churchmen still complain that his call for sinners to make "Decisions for Christ" encourages snap decisions on far-reaching matters of faith.

There is also the carping that his converts "don't last." Some don't, of course, but many do. Stuart Hamblen now writes revival-type songs (*This Old House, It Is No Secret*) and devotes his full time to religious work. Jim Vaus works in a mission for youngsters in New York slums, and Lou Zamperini operates a camp for wayward boys in California.

The Rev. Mr. Graham sometimes answers this criticism with Billy Sunday's famous retort. When a critic scoffed that his revivals did no lasting good, Sunday snapped: "Neither does a bath, but it does you good." The Rev. Mr. Graham further cites his own example: "There were 400 who accepted Christ in Charlotte, North Carolina, the same night I did nearly 30 years ago. I know of five ministers who came from that group. I know many outstanding businessmen who stood there that night and they still are living Christian lives."

Besides the Rev. Mr. Graham, one of the five ministers is Grady Wilson. The Rev. Mr. Wilson has been with Billy Graham for more than 15 years and is perhaps his closest associate. Another close associate is Cliff Barrows, his song leader, of whom the Rev. Mr. Graham once said: "He is the closest thing to the indispensable man."

The fact that most liberal churchmen support Graham crusades in their home cities seems to imply they're willing to waive their theological objections. But to many fundamentalists, this implies that it is the Rev. Mr. Graham who has compromised with an old enemy.

His descriptions of hell seem less vivid than they once did, and it is certainly true that he hobnobs with champions of the social gospel. Yet most of his fundamentalist critics concede that Mr. Graham still preaches the crucial "five points of fundamentalism": The literal infallibility of the Bible as the inspired word of God, the virgin birth of Jesus Christ, the substitutionary atonement (that Christ died to redeem any who claim Him as their substitute), the bodily resurrection of Christ, and the bodily second coming of Christ.

This is the key to the Graham success, says the Rev. Eugene Crow, director of evangelism for the Southern California Baptist Convention. "He isn't really a great preacher," the Rev. Dr. Crow contends. "But he preaches the classic

Billy in 1949. The flashily dressed prophet of doom.

formulation of the Gospel, the real essentials of the Christian faith."

Some critics deplore the Rev. Mr. Graham's references to visits with world leaders as egotistical name-dropping ("When I met Winston Churchill, he said to me, 'Young man, do you see any hope for the world?,'" he once told a Crusade congregation). And some churchmen argue that his stand on civil rights is a fuzzy one.

On the eve of the March on Washington in 1963, he told a Los Angeles congregation that he was concerned that some clergymen had made the race issue their gospel. "This is not the Gospel," he declared. "The Gospel is the good news that Jesus Christ died for our sins, and that he arose from the dead, and that God is willing to forgive our sins and give us new life and peace and joy." Forced integration, he said, "will never work. You cannot make races love each other by law alone, or accept each other at the point of a bayonet."

"Let's Do Something"

Yet he enraged his Southern followers in 1957 when he insisted that the Rev. Martin Luther King sit beside him on the platform at his New York Crusade. A South Carolina governor several years ago denounced him as a "well-known advocate of integration." He has Negro ministers on his staff and insists his audiences be integrated; his 1964 Easter Sunday sermon in Birmingham before the largest integrated crowd in Alabama's history was a major achievement in Birmingham's progress toward improved race relations. A week later he told the National Association of Evangelicals: "We evangelicals should have been leading the way to racial justice, but we failed. Let's confess it, let's admit it, and let's do something about it."

Whispers persist that he might some day enter politics. He likes to associate with political figures; he played golf frequently with former Vice President Richard M. Nixon and the late President John F. Kennedy. But when the whispers became louder as the 1964 Presidential primaries were beginning to warm up, he silenced them quickly: "God has given me a higher calling—winning souls to Christ. I have no intention of going into politics now or later."

The Rev. Mr. Graham insists he is a political neutral. He once told a British press conference that he was not "anti-socialist, anti-liberal,

Billy in the 1950s. A dark suit for a Wall Street audience.

or anti-conservative. I am completely neutral." Yet he often criticized President Harry S Truman and went out of his way to praise former President Dwight Eisenhower. He once ridiculed the United Nations, and although he had visited President Kennedy in the White House, he told his Los Angeles audience one night that "so-called Christian America . . . someday will stand condemned before the bar of God's justice for our indifference to the suffering of others," making it clear that he was talking about U.S. and British policy toward those suffering under Fidel Castro.

If this is neutrality, a Pasadena pastor said tartly, "you sure can't call it nonpartisan neutrality." Still, the Pasadena pastor's church participated in the 1963 Crusade, and, he said, "We'll be in the next Crusade, too."

At Los Angeles, the Graham staff and the local churches introduced a "follow-up" technique designed to broaden the impact of the Crusade. Two weeks after the Crusade ended,

Today the evangelist is a frequent visitor to the White House. Here he breakfasts with President Johnson.

more than 7,500 two-man teams called on persons who had attended the Coliseum Crusade but had not stepped forward to make their "decisions for Christ." During the four-day "visitation evangelism" stage, the teams called on about 150,000 persons.

The "team concept," which has worked so well in many ways for the Rev. Mr. Graham, was borrowed from Billy Sunday. The Graham inquiry rooms, in which those who "go forward" can talk to trained counselors about becoming Christians, were first used by Dwight L. Moody in 1875. The invitation to "come forward," which many liturgical clergymen find distasteful, was used by Charles G. Finney in his revivals of 1835.

But the Graham team has perfected the techniques to an effectiveness that the others could hardly have imagined. He has added radio and television, and his magazine, Decision, first published in 1960, has a paid circulation of 2,500,000.

Nothing is left to chance. The Rev. Mr. Graham works out of his home in Montreat, North Carolina. But the men who fan out from the Minneapolis headquarters know exactly what each team member is expected to do.

Some Graham followers are fretting now that his organization is getting top-heavy. The Minneapolis office has grown from one room and

The message must be carried everywhere—into taverns as well as pews. Here in Boston, Billy Graham does just that.

one secretary in 1950 to a complete office building and 400 employes. Billy Graham is the No. 1 customer of the U.S. post office in Minneapolis.

Many of these letters are invitations to lead revivals, but the popular evangelist is cutting down on the number of his personal appearances. Television gives him extensive exposure; television audiences in 42 states watched films of the crusader's most exciting five nights in Los Angeles. And he is devoting increasing time to other fields not normally cultivated by evangelists.

One field that particularly appeals to him is the ministry to students. "Five years ago an evangelist wouldn't have gone to a university," says a Graham associate. "And if he had, he would have been jeered out of the hall." Now the Rev. Mr. Graham appears at week-long seminars at such academic centers as Harvard, Massachusetts Institute of Technology, and the University of Michigan.

As long as his health is good—and at times it isn't—Billy Graham seems sure to roll on for years. He gets to the people. However he does it, he moves the masses.

His success puzzles the evangelist himself. Someone once asked him, "Why Billy Graham?" He smiled. "I don't know," he replied. "That's the first thing I'm going to ask God when I get to heaven." ♦

The Pentecostals

A moment of rapture. . . .

Speaking in Other Tongues

In Moments of Rapture, Some Pentecostals Break Into Languages That Puzzle Linguists, Churchmen

NEW YORK CITY.

THE voice delivering the prayer in the blue-carpeted ballroom of the Statler-Hilton trailed off amid a crescendo of sound in the audience. Suddenly a female voice pierced the ecstatic mumbling and silenced it.

"Ramiya rabelata . . . rabak saka chuka. . . ." Fluent, beautiful, the strange syllables flowed forth for a full minute. Then, silence. In a moment a stumpy, dark-complexioned man two rows from the stage extended his arms to interpret. "I am the Lord thy God!" he shouted in a high-pitched monotone. "I have created heaven and earth! . . ."

The occasion was a convention of the Full Gospel Business Men's Fellowship International; the participants, practitioners of the fast-growing phenomenon of speaking in tongues.

Persons who "speak in tongues"—that is, utter sounds the meaning of which they do not understand—contend that the experience gives them an unusual closeness to God. The zeal of Full Gospel members who swarmed over the Statler-Hilton—old-line Pentecostals and "Spirit-filled" members of mainstream Protestant churches—testified to the strength of a movement that is receiving careful attention from many Protestant and Catholic leaders.

The Pentecostal movement, says the Rev. Henry P. Van Dusen, retired president of Union Theological Seminary in New York, is nothing less than "a revolution comparable in importance to the establishment of the original apostolic church and to the Protestant reformation."

Speaking in tongues, widely publicized in 1960 when first reported among Episcopalians, has now quietly infiltrated every major Protestant denomination. Once the province largely of the unlettered and the unsophisticated, it now flourishes also among the debonair and the highly educated.

Catherine Marshall LeSourd, author of the best-seller, *A Man Called Peter,* about her late husband, the Rev. Peter Marshall, has spoken in tongues "in a limited way" in private devotions. McCandlish Phillips, reporter for the New York Times and a member of the fashionable Broadway Presbyterian Church, speaks in tongues now and then. Colleen Townsend, a former Hollywood starlet now married to a Presbyterian minister in California, has spoken in tongues.

The Pentecostal experience has come to 600 members of a huge Presbyterian church in Hollywood, California, and to a few members of an Episcopalian church in Alice, Texas. It has appeared in a Methodist church in rural Beach, North Dakota, and in a Baptist church in Baltimore's inner city.

The Episcopal Church has appointed a committee of bishops to study the phenomenon; in Europe, two Anglican bishops have offered surreptitiously to help finance the movement. The Rev. Jolly Harper, Methodist district superintendent in Shreveport, Louisiana, with 50 ministers under his supervision, tells of "a great gladness in my heart" when he first spoke in tongues. And the Rev. Francis E. Whiting, an official of the Michigan Baptist Convention, defends divinely inspired experiences such as speaking in tongues by warning that the choice is Pentecost or holocaust.

The strength of the movement in mainline churches is hard to assess, for publicity often exposes laymen to ridicule and ministers to censure. One denomination, for example, refused to ordain a candidate for the ministry in 1960

The exuberance of the Pentecostals shows itself in many ways. When the temperature soared to 107 degrees in El Paso, Texas, the First Assembly of God Church used the weather as a prop for its daily message to passers-by.

when it learned he had spoken in tongues. Five Methodist ministers in a single conference, a region in an East Coast state, have engaged in the practice but refuse to acknowledge it publicly.

The most precise estimates possible indicate that more than 250 of the 5,000 American Lutheran churches have groups that speak in tongues, at least occasionally. Some 3,000 Episcopalians in the Los Angeles area alone are reported active in the movement.

Professional research on glossolalia, or speaking in tongues, has been almost nonexistent until quite recently. Now the Lutheran Medical Center in Brooklyn has a team—a psychiatrist, a clinical psychologist, and a linguist—conducting a study of glossolalia under a grant from the U.S. Department of Health, Education, and Welfare. And since the spring of 1963 Prof. Stanley C. Plog of UCLA has been conducting a cultural and psychological survey of glossolalia, searching especially for what attracts people to the movement, what they believe they have been lacking in their religious lives, and what they are discovering.

With interest increasing among mainstream Protestants, two large publishers came out with books on the practice in 1964. Doubleday published *Tongue Speaking*, a sympathetic book by an Episcopal priest who had not spoken in tongues, the Rev. Morton T. Kelsey of Monrovia, California. Then McGraw-Hill published *They Speak With Other Tongues*, by John Sherrill, an Episcopal layman and the son of a former Southern Presbyterian moderator. In the book Mr. Sherrill, senior editor of Guideposts magazine, relates how he began speaking in tongues.

Why do Christians speak in tongues? Is there any Biblical basis for the practice?

What the Bible Says

The Rev. Mr. Kelsey finds seven direct references in the New Testament to speaking in tongues, plus eight descriptions in which glossolalia is apparently referred to.

The central New Testament event involving speaking in tongues is recorded in Acts 2. Here the Bible tells of the Day of Pentecost and the first outpouring of the Holy Spirit on the new church, during which the early Christians "were all filled with the Holy Spirit and began to talk in other tongues."

The Apostle Paul devoted an entire chapter, the 14th chapter of his first letter to the Corinthians, to the subject of speaking in tongues. His purpose was to place the practice in its proper perspective. "Put love first," he wrote. "Do not forbid ecstatic utterance, but let all be done decently and in order."

Tongue speaking apparently occurred regularly in the early church. Wrote St. Augustine, who lived in the Fourth Century: "We still do what the apostles did when they laid hands on the Samaritans and called down the Holy Spirit on them by the laying on of hands. It is expected that converts should speak with new tongues."

The practice has continued in the Eastern Orthodox Church without attracting much attention; it is, after all, no more mystical than other practices in the Eastern tradition. In the West, however, it soon became associated more with demons than with angels. This became the official position of the Roman Catholic Church, expressed in the Catholic book of public services, the *Rituale Romanum*.

The Historical Record

Down through history speaking in tongues has been quite common at the beginning of great religious revivals. Early Quakers spoke in tongues. So did early Mormons until their leaders discouraged the practice "because it has brought ridicule and disrespect from the ungodly"; many elders of the church spoke in tongues at the dedication of the Mormon Temple in Salt Lake City.

Isolated instances of tongue speaking were reported in Rhode Island, Arkansas, and even among Presbyterians in Kara Kala, Armenia, during the Nineteenth Century. But only when a one-eyed, sloppily-dressed evangelist named William J. Seymour started speaking fluently in strange tongues in an old Los Angeles livery stable in 1906 did the movement begin to catch fire.

The committed and the curious came from all over the nation to receive the "baptism of the Holy Spirit" as evidenced by speaking in tongues. The message they carried back home produced the old-line Pentecostal churches, whose aggressive evangelism has resulted in a membership today of 2,000,000. From the Pentecostal Fire-Baptized Holiness Church, with 574 members at the latest count, to the Assemblies of God, with over 500,000, some 26 denominations consider themselves Pentecostal churches.

Few denominations have made a more spectacular statistical record than the Assemblies of God. Their membership has increased tenfold since 1925. From their modern headquarters in Springfield, Missouri, they support more than 800 foreign missionaries—half the number sponsored by the Foreign Missions Board of the missionary-minded Southern Baptists, who have a membership 20 times as large.

Until 1960, enthusiasm for speaking in tongues was confined almost exclusively to the Pentecostal churches, even though scattered ministers and laymen in the historic Protestant churches had experienced the phenomenon in private prayer. Then the Rev. Dennis Bennett, rector of a large Episcopal church in Van Nuys, California, found inner refreshment by speaking in tongues, and the refreshment proved contagious. Conflict rent his church, and he resigned amid wide publicity. The spark within mainstream Protestantism turned to fire.

Mainstream Protestants who spoke in tongues formed the Blessed Trinity Society, with headquarters in Van Nuys, to spread word of the charismatic revival. Under Mrs. Jean Stone, wife of a Lockheed Aircraft executive, the society began publishing a slick-paper quarterly called Trinity, aimed at the sophisticated.

Mainline Speakers

Many mainline Protestants have begun speaking in tongues while participating in prayer groups. Mrs. Stone estimates that some 75 prayer groups with "Spirit-filled" members are meeting weekly in the San Fernando Valley; in one of the largest, 10 or 20 persons speak in tongues for the first time each week.

Tongues have erupted in student fellowship groups on many campuses—Yale, Princeton, UCLA, Stanford, Massachusetts Institute of Technology, and others. And Full Gospel Business Men's Fellowship, formed by Pentecostals in the early 1950s, has tailored its appeal increasingly to members of mainline churches.

The new tongue speakers differ in several ways from the old-line Pentecostals. They have no interest in splitting off to form new churches, but try instead to make tongue speaking an added dimension of the Christian experience in mainstream churches. They place more emphasis on the use of tongues as a form of private prayer, less on dramatic displays in public. They usually show little emotion when they speak in tongues; although they appear to be in a trance, they rarely shake, weep, moan, or roll on the floor as many Pentecostals do—a practice that inspired the derisive term "Holy Roller."

Many Pentecostals tend to regard speaking in tongues as the only conclusive evidence that a person has been filled with the Holy Spirit, and thus as the chief means of salvation. The new practitioners stress that the Apostle Paul considered tongues only one of many gifts of the Spirit (others include faith, healing, and miracles).

"Some people approach tongues as if it will solve all their problems," says Catherine Marshall LeSourd. "But it's not a panacea. They 'receive' and they still have problems. They still lose their tempers, and their egos are still all over the place."

Closer to the Core

Mrs. LeSourd, a close friend of the Sherrills, says that the experience took Mr. Sherrill "from the historic Christ to the contemporary Christ," from a rational view of Jesus to an intimate awareness of him as a person. "Whenever you have an experience like that," she says, "it's pure gold. You must keep a spiritual experience in perspective, but if it's truly Christ-centered, you're on safe ground."

What's it like to speak in tongues?

Ask George Muffly, a sales engineer who lives in Akron, Ohio. Mr. Muffly, an active Congregationalist, learned about the Full Gospel convention while in New York on a business trip; intrigued by the little he had read about tongue speaking, he dropped in one night at the Statler-Hilton. Two hours later, in a plush room off the main ballroom, Mr. Muffly began speaking in a strange tongue as a "charismatic counselor" stood over him.

"It seems a certain amount of joy and peace comes over you," Mr. Muffly told a visitor of whom he had been totally oblivious moments before. "There's something to it, all right. I want to keep on coming."

People can first experience tongues while others hover over them, as perhaps 15 people did that night in the anteroom, or they can burst out in tongues initially when they are

At a recent Pentecostal meeting in New York's Statler-Hilton, dozens found themselves speaking in tongues.

completely alone. Dr. Robert Frost of Baylor University Medical School first spoke in tongues as he was opening a can of soup for his children's lunch. M. G. Robertson, son of Sen. A. Willis Robertson of Virginia, says he began speaking in tongues while he and his wife prayed at the bedside of their sick boy.

"When you're speaking in tongues in private prayer," says Mrs. Stone of Trinity magazine, "you're praying up to God. When you speak in tongues in public, it's usually God speaking down to His people." In public, someone always interprets what the tongue speaker has said.

The tongue a person speaks can be a distinct foreign language he contends he does not know, such as Hebrew or Japanese, or it can be a stream of apparent words that linguists cannot recognize.

It is not gibberish. John Sherrill once slipped two samples of gibberish among religiously inspired tongues onto tapes that linguists were studying, and the linguists instantly recognized the gibberish as different from the tongues.

A high proportion of the tongues are known languages the linguists can recognize. Linguists have not determined whether tongue speakers always speak in a certain language or sometimes create their own, for they note that there are some 2,800 known languages and dialects spoken in the world. Linguists are working, too, to discover whether persons who speak in common languages such as Japanese have had any contact with these languages in their past.

A person's first experience of speaking in tongues almost invariably gives him a spiritual lift. A dentist in West Hartford, Connecticut, described the experience as like a jolt of electricity—painless but stimulating. Mr. Sherrill recalls he was "bathed in, surrounded by, washed through with love." A highly educated Scottish Jew once wrote that it "lifted me into a higher realm and gave me a sense of the nearness of God."

To Heal the Sick

Tongue speakers often use the phenomenon in connection with physical healing. One morning, after a worship service at the Statler-Hilton, a "charismatic counselor" prayed over a 71-year-old woman from Minot, North Dakota, asking that her arthritis go away; she burst into tongues, leaped up, and ran across the room. "I haven't been able to run for 20 years!" she exclaimed.

A moment later a Baptist minister, who had been talking calmly with a visitor, went forward for healing himself. "Lord God," prayed the counselor, "I want you to curse that cyst on the left side of this man's back and burn it out." A torrent of peculiar words poured from the Baptist minister's mouth. Then he rose, brushed past the visitor without a glance, and paced alone at the back of the room for perhaps five minutes. "Praise Lord Jesus," he murmured repeatedly. "Bless Lord Jesus."

Speaking in tongues unquestionably gives people an evangelical fervor. "What does it do for you?" asked a Methodist businessman from Pitman, New Jersey, as he grabbed the lapel of his questioner's coat in the busy lobby of the Statler-Hilton. "Man, it makes you a better Christian." Trinity magazine's Mrs. Stone estimates she has helped convert 10,000 persons to Christ; before she spoke in tongues, she had helped convert none.

Catholics who encounter tongue speakers, wrote the Rev. Daniel J. O'Hanlon, a Jesuit, in America magazine, "will find much to admire and possibly even a few things to imitate." He listed the tongue speakers' emphasis upon an "intimately united community" and the simplicity of their faith as two especially appealing characteristics.

Tongue speaking can have negative aspects. It sometimes causes serious conflict within congregations. It has attracted some "gift seekers" interested only in an emotional "jag" and not in the religious commitment that is supposed to follow. Tongues can stunt religious and psychological growth if not kept in perspective. And if a person tries but fails to experience tongues, psychological damage can result. Finally, the very enthusiasm—the "holy boldness"—of tongue speakers has a way of making others feel like second-class Christians. "Better felt than tell't," admonished a Full Gospel official as he tried to persuade an acquaintance to try speaking in tongues.

Varied Reactions

Reactions among leaders of mainline denominations have ranged from shock to forbearance. The Rt. Rev. James A. Pike, Episcopal bishop of California, advised his clergy not to participate in services promoting tongues and directed that they "exert no pressure in any form" to induce tongue speaking in any person. The practice, he declared, is "heresy in embryo."

In the summer of 1964 the American Lutheran Church dismissed an evangelist for promoting glossolalia. Paraphrasing Paul, the Rev. Fredrik A. Schiotz, American Lutheran president, said: "I would rather speak five words with my understanding that I may instruct others also than 10,000 words in a tongue." The Rev. Dr. Schiotz sees the movement as "a reaction against the tendency to over-intellectualize the Christian faith."

But the Rev. John A. Mackay, retired president of Princeton Theological Seminary, has been deeply impressed by the vitality of the charismatic revival. "If it's a choice between the uncouth life of the Pentecostals and the esthetic death of the older churches," he says, "I for one choose the uncouth life." ♦

'There Appeared to Them Tongues'

Acts 2:

WHILE the day of Pentecost was running its course they were all together in one place, when suddenly there came from the sky a noise like that of a strong driving wind, which filled the whole house where they were sitting. And there appeared to them tongues like flames of fire, dispersed among them and resting on each one. And they were all filled with the Holy Spirit and began to talk in other tongues, as the Spirit gave them power of utterance.

Now there were living in Jerusalem devout Jews drawn from every nation under heaven; and at this sound the crowd gathered, all bewildered because each one heard the apostles talking in his own language. They were amazed and in their astonishment exclaimed, 'Why, they are all Galileans, are they not, these men who are speaking? How is it then that we hear them, each of us in his own native language? . . .' And they were all amazed and perplexed, saying to one another, 'What can this mean?' Others said contemptuously, 'They have been drinking!'

But Peter stood up with the Eleven, raised his voice, and addressed them: '. . . These men are not drunk, as you imagine; for it is only nine in the morning. No, this is what the prophet spoke of: "God says, 'This will happen in the last days: I will pour out upon everyone a portion of my spirit; and your sons and daughters shall prophesy; your young men shall see visions, and your old men shall dream dreams. . . . And then, everyone who invokes the name of the Lord shall be saved. . . .'"

I Corinthians 13:

I MAY speak in tongues of men or of angels, but if I am without love, I am a sounding gong or a clanging cymbal. . . .

I Corinthians 14:

PUT love first; but there are other gifts of the Spirit at which you should aim also, and above all prophecy. When a man is using the language of ecstasy he is talking with God, not with men, for no man understands him; he is no doubt inspired, but he speaks mysteries. . . . The language of ecstasy is good for the speaker himself, but it is prophecy that builds up a Christian community. . . . The prophet is worth more than the man of ecstatic speech—unless indeed he can explain its meaning, and so help to build up the community. . . .

I say, then, that the man who falls into ecstatic utterance should pray for the ability to interpret. . . . Thank God, I am more gifted in ecstatic utterance than any of you, but in the congregation I would rather speak five intelligible words, for the benefit of others as well as myself, than thousands of words in the language of ecstasy. . . .

In short, my friends, be eager to prophesy; do not forbid ecstatic utterance; but let all be done decently and in order.

Fargo-Moorhead

A New Kind of Layman—Educated, Active, Quick to Command, Eager for the Spiritual Life—Emerges

FARGO, N.D.

CHRISTIAN laymen act less like "God's chosen people" than like "God's frozen people," charge two British theologians in a recent book. But "God's frozen people" are beginning to thaw out. In many faiths and in many ways, laymen are assuming a role unprecedented since the earliest Christian communities of the First Century A.D.

"Cell" groups for prayer and Bible study are multiplying, and retreat centers and evening "schools of theology" prosper as prodders of the Christian conscience. Laymen such as William Stringfellow, a New York attorney, are writing books on theology. Some churches—Presbyterians in Tiburon, California, and Unitarians in Pittsburgh, for example—are giving laymen equal time in "talk-back" sessions after ministers' sermons.

In the fall of 1964 the lay renaissance took on a further dimension. Churchmen in Fargo, North Dakota-Moorhead, Minnesota, a metropolitan area of 100,000 persons, held an intensive "Faith in Life" program designed to instill a sense of Christian responsibility in the entire populace of this Red River Valley center. American Lutheran Church professionals who engineered the seven-day project plan to conduct a similar program in the Duluth area in 1965 and possibly in Minneapolis-St. Paul in 1966.

"Fargo-Moorhead is the first serious effort in America to apply saturation evangelism to an entire community," says Dr. Franklin H. Littell, professor of church history at Chicago Theological Seminary. "Most denominational boards of evangelism still talk as if we were in the 1850s, when only 16 per cent of the people were church members. The problem now is that 96 per cent of us claim at least some affiliation with a church; what we've got to do is evangelize the 'Christians.' "

Christian leaders have complained for years about "jellyfish" Christianity in America, a Christianity motivated more by a desire to join than by a compulsion to serve. Postwar Europe, they say, has empty churches but full personal commitment, while the United States has full churches but empty commitment.

The road to commitment, critics contend, is to enlist laymen to take their Christian faith into the office, the town hall, the bowling alley—to get them "off the seats and into the streets," in the words of a pastor in Brookings, South Dakota, where "Faith in Life" was introduced on a more modest scale in 1963. Christians should desert churches during the week, in effect, but interest housewives and their husbands in thinking about faith and ethics in the home and on the job.

"Being a lay person in the world is just as much a divine calling as being a priest," says the Rev. Victor Klostermann of the University of Vienna, an expert at the Vatican Ecumenical Council.

The laymen's renaissance in Protestantism has been going on quietly for two decades or more. In Catholicism a similar renaissance has been dramatized by the unprecedented interest in laymen at the Vatican Council.

"Now is the hour of the laity," declared Pope Paul VI in 1963 as he admitted laymen to a church council for the first time. The Catholic bishops' decision in 1963 to permit the use of local languages in the Mass was designated largely to give worship added meaning to Catholic laymen. At the Vatican Council session

The Lay Renaissance

A new kind of layman. . . .

in 1964, the bishops considered how the Catholic layman's knowledge and talents can be put to use in the parish and diocese and how he can express his faith in his daily life.

The new interest in laymen among Protestants and Catholics arises partly from the growing sophistication of laymen and partly from a re-examination by Christian scholars of what "the church" means.

In the Tenth Century, say, or even in the Eighteenth, most laymen were not equipped with the knowledge they needed to handle church responsibilities. "Now we have the kind of laymen who are not prepared to be silent, docile, and obedient," comments Professor Littell of Chicago. "We can either resent it or accept it."

In earlier days, and even in some parishes today, Christians have tended to think of "the church" as a building, or perhaps as the ordained priesthood. During the Reformation four centuries ago, Martin Luther spoke of the "priesthood of all believers"; the Apostle Peter had written to "strangers scattered throughout Pontus, Galatia, Cappadocia, Asia, and Bithynia," the Bible relates, that "ye are a chosen generation, a royal priesthood. . . ." Yet many people today, bemoans the Rev. John Oliver Nelson, a Protestant prophet of the laymen's movement, "still think the only way to be a Christian is to be a minister."

Among Catholics

Two decades or so ago, laymen began to stir. Since World War II, and especially since the opening of the Vatican Council in 1962, Catholic organizations for periodic prayer and religious study among laymen—the Christian Family Movement, the Holy Name Society for parish men, sodalities (fellowships) for women in the parish—have gained momentum. Opus Dei (God's Work), a Catholic laymen's society in which the members take specific vows, spread to the United States from Spain in 1949; it now has several thousand laymen in the East and Midwest working quietly but intensively "to spread the life of evangelic perfection among all classes of civil society, especially among intellectuals," in the words of the Vatican.

In the late 1940s several Protestant denominations, inspired by the example of the National Council of Presbyterian Men, formed huge fellowships of Christian laymen. Nondenominational fellowships began to spring up, too. The Laymen's Movement for a Christian World (LMCW), for example, helped popularize Laymen's Sunday throughout Protestant churches. The International Christian Leadership (ICL) has sponsored thousands of prayer breakfasts for government and community leaders; it was at the ICL's Presidential prayer breakfast in Feburary 1964 that President Johnson made his ill-fated proposal for a "memorial to God" in Washington, D.C., prompting wags to ask, "Is God dead?"

The huge fellowships unquestionably have had some effect. One executive, inspired by a national fellowship assembly, left a high company position to work full-time in Christian education. But theologians warn of the superficiality of many fellowship programs and of their anti-clerical, anti-theological inclinations. "The watchword seems to be, 'the more people we get together—and the more often we get together—the happier we will be,'" says the Rev. Dr. Nelson.

The First Retreat

In 1942 a group of Protestants led by the Rev. Dr. Nelson founded the first of a new wave of laymen's retreat centers, Kirkridge, in the Pocono Mountains of eastern Pennsylvania. Kirkridge tries to bring together what the Rev. Dr. Nelson terms the churches' "social radicals and devotional radicals"—"those who picket and those who pray." Topics for week-end retreats at Kirkridge range from liturgy to theology to race relations. One retreat in the fall of 1964, on "Confronting the Feminine Mystique," brought women from as far as Vermont and Virginia; another, a "Retreat for Square-peg Seminarians," attracted seminary students who plan unconventional ministries.

Laymen's retreat centers for Protestants flourish now at Parishfield, Michigan; Rye, New York; Richmond, Indiana, and elsewhere. A new center is beginning full-scale operations in Kerrville, Texas. But the most dramatic activity in the retreat movement is occurring among Roman Catholics in the form of *Cursillos de Christiandad* ("Little Courses in Christianity").

The first *cursillo* was held in the United States in 1957, in Spanish, eight years after the *cursillo* movement was inaugurated in Spain. Not until 1961 was the first *cursillo*

The appeal of a quiet, meditative sojourn in the woods is luring more and more Protestants and Catholics to the lay retreat centers.

held in English. Over the next three years *cursillos* were held in more than 25 states, attracting more than 30,000 Catholics for the three days of prayer, song, personal testimony, and discussion. A follow-up phase involving periodic meetings, absent in most Protestant retreat programs, has proved one of the strengths of the *cursillos*.

Most Protestant retreats, like the Catholic *cursillos*, aim not at supplanting existing church work, but at infusing new life into it. "Laymen go on retreats to fulfill personal needs," says the Rev. Dr. Nelson, who left the Yale Divinity School faculty in 1964 after 14 years to assume full-time direction over the Kirkridge center. "Laymen have a heightened sense of spiritual need today just because there is a heightened sense of everything in our society." He walked to a huge picture window in his home overlooking the Delaware Water Gap and looked out at the brilliant colors of autumn. "But they go for another reason too. They go in search of a specific idea of what it means to be a Christian back home."

Back home—in Rahway, New Jersey; in Ozona, Texas; in Anderson, South Carolina, and in hundreds of areas—churches and seminaries have started laymen's "schools of theology." They offer several weeks of evening courses in

The busy "Faith in Life" week at Fargo-Moorhead: Left, folk singers parody suburban churches. Below, participants consult a bulletin board for their next step.

"Church History," say, or "Introduction to Isaiah," or perhaps "The Church and the Racial Problem."

Valuable as these are, however, Professor Littell and many of his fellow theologians warn that laymen's "schools of theology" run the risk of training Christians to be church school superintendents instead of committed laymen in the community. If they do produce only church administrators or, equally damaging, if they produce Christian dilettantes who delight in reciting Barth and Bonhoeffer, the fault lies partly with clergymen and partly with the seminaries that train them, Professor Littell contends.

"A new kind of layman requires a new kind of pastor," he argues. The layman who works quietly among his fellow plumbers or his fellow engineers in Phoenix, like the laymen who worked together in "Faith in Life" in Fargo, needs a pastor sympathetic to the new emphasis on working in the world.

Not to Convert

The pathfinders in Fargo-Moorhead expected no sudden new era. "If anybody thinks we're going to convert Fargo, he's crazy," said Mr. Stringfellow, one of some 40 Christian leaders imported for the week. "But maybe somewhere, somehow, we'll make a connection with just one person. If we do, that's enough to justify it all."

"Faith in Life" quite clearly made some connections, though no one could measure how numerous or how deep they were. A pair of folk singers jolted television audiences with incisive commentaries on churches and society. For example, a parody of *A Mighty Fortress Is Our God,* about a suburban church, ran:

"But what if one should come?
Be he drunk or pimp or bum,
In our new church so meek
He'll never last a week;
We'll build ourselves a fortress."

A missionary from Japan used the subtle approach instead of the shock approach when he spoke to a high-school language club. Dressed in Japanese lounging wear and wooden *geta* (shoes), he clomped across the ill-lit stage looking like comedian Art Carney. For half an hour he enthralled his audience with comments on Japanese culture. Then he brought out his clarinet and the hint of a message. "The first time I went to Japan I carried a weapon of war; the second time I took this weapon of peace." And he told of a familiar tune he discovered the Japanese knew. Never mentioning its title, he swung into a lilting *What a Friend We Have in Jesus.*

"Faith in Life" strategists tried to blanket the community. An insert in the local newspaper announced the week's events seven days before they began. On the eve of the week, the four local television channels ran 28 "spot" announcements about the project. Churches handed out "Faith in Life" buttons on the first day. As the week progressed, Arnold Mickelson, a local layman, monitored the 45 or 50 events each day from a command post in the Town House Motel. The Rev. Loren Halvorson, an American Lutheran Church official and the prime mover behind "Faith in Life," briefed the visiting participants when they arrived and sought their comments before they left.

From Washington, D.C., came Sen. Eugene McCarthy of Minnesota, an active Catholic layman. From Los Angeles came the Rev. A. R. Gornitzka, a Lutheran pastor who in 1963 began a special ministry to company executives and entertainment stars. Ted Cobb, an Urban League official, came from Flint, Michigan, and the 1964 mother of the year, Mrs. Lawrence Stavig, from Sioux Falls, South Dakota.

TV Galore

"Faith in Life" used 60 hours of television time. Panels discussed "Mothers and Their Children" and "The Aging" during the day and occupations (farmers, civil servants, salesmen, working women) in the early evening. Late shows were pre-empted for panels on "Church and State" and "Husbands and Wives." In downtown movie theaters, popular movies that raise religious or moral questions—*Becket, Splendor in the Grass, Black Like Me*—attracted large audiences; panelists debated the issues between showings.

Panelists and speakers shunned platitudes and waded into the controversial. Prof. Leroy Augenstein, a Michigan State biophysicist, made about 10 appearances one day in high school classes, at local clubs, and on panels. "Scientists are approaching the day when they can predict the probability that a child born to parents who have already had an abnormal child will be normal," he declared. "We should begin asking some questions. Does an unconceived child have any rights? Should we leave the decision on conception in these families to the parents, realizing some parents are irresponsible?"

On a television panel one night a local Lutheran pastor noted that the Bible declares that a man who lusts after a woman commits adultery. "We'd better get straight on this," he said. "Is merely looking lusting?"

Local participants did not always find it easy to mix it up on specifics. A television panel on farm prices disappointed one "Faith in Life" leader; he complained that the panelists, who represented three competing farm groups, displayed "tunnel vision" on television, refusing to stray from the party line of their respective organizations. Private "summit conferences" in homes for local leaders in specific vocational areas such as medicine and the military also tended to drag, although visiting "resource leaders" succeeded in planting enough interest in a few of the groups to have them express a desire to continue meeting.

Keep It Local

"Faith in Life" planners deliberately played up local issues where they could. To illustrate violence for a television show, they dug up newsreel footage not on Harlem riots but on National Farmers Organization disputes.

They deliberately played down denominational roles. Lutherans, Catholics, and Episcopalians worked on the project with equal fervor. Churches put up half of the $20,000 required for the week; local businessmen supplied the rest.

Perhaps most important, "Faith in Life" leaders worked through the community structure instead of the church structure. To reach the students in the community, they went to student body presidents instead of church group officers. To reach the men, they avoided men's fellowship meetings in the churches and took "Faith in Life" instead to Kiwanis, Rotary, and Lions.

"We intentionally didn't tell the local clergy much about it till a month before," says one planner. The leaders feared they would be burdened by what one calls the "institutional freight" of the church. They concluded, too. that only a dramatic departure from normal church operations would entice laymen on the fringes to listen.

Predictably, some clergymen resented being by-passed.

"I bugged a Lutheran pastor for days trying to get him to get a labor leader for a panel," says the Rev. Mr. Halvorson of Minneapolis. "I never got anywhere. Finally I asked a Catholic layman and he came up with a great one—an active Lutheran—in 20 minutes."

A more formidable problem was how to get across an abstract idea to a large community in little time. Cracked a volunteer for duty with a mobile unit downtown: "What do I do? Smile and look like I've got faith in life?"

Some Fargo-Moorhead citizens proved totally immune to "Faith in Life." An elderly parking-lot attendant, asked if he had come in contact with it, replied, "faith in what?" Of 10 families surveyed at random by telephone during a Wednesday afternoon television show on "The Role of Women," 4 had not heard of "Faith in Life." Of the 6 who had heard of the project, 4 had watched at least 1 television show, though only 1 was tuned in at the time.

Communication, Yes

The "Faith in Life" message got through to some people more clearly than they themselves realized. An apprentice barber at the Graver Hotel said he was "puzzled about what it's all about." Pressed to define his impression, he said in a moment what speakers were spending hours saying: "The idea, I guess, is to get people involved in things as Christians."

Central ideas eluded even some who had worked for weeks on "Faith in Life." A steering-committee member nudged an out-of-town visitor and nodded disparagingly toward a couple moving through the Town House lobby toward the bar. "There's one at the other end of the stick. Owns a night club and a liquor store." But weren't these the very people "Faith in Life" hoped to reach? "Some guys you just can't reach." The message of "Faith in Life" apparently didn't reach this planner.

Daily devotions challenged the team to think of the community. "Lord of the ticker tape and typewriter, who dwellest in the midst of locker rooms as well as in the forest green; God of the hammering factory, and of discarded products where junk dealers dwell," read the litany one morning, "help us to hear the footsteps walking not alone in the cool of the evening, but on the hot, crowded pavement; where limbs are tired and lives are raw with anger and tension."

An unconventional litany for an unconventional venture. But then the idea behind the entire laymen's renaissance, in a sense, is unconventional. It doesn't come through to some churchmen.

Not long ago a Protestant bishop transferred an energetic minister whose laymen's renewal work made the bishop uncomfortable. "This business of lay training is all right," explained the bishop, "but it interferes with the work of the church."

To John Cogley, a prominent Catholic layman, such a vision of the church—whether Protestant or Catholic—is centuries out of date. Mr. Cogley once composed this little poem, published in America magazine:

WHO IS THE CHURCH?
"Who?
You." ♦

"Faith in Life" meets the people.

New Hampshire

RANDOLPH, N.H.

THE latest international flare-up, so many thousands of miles away, seems so near as the lonely driver guns his car up the bumpy gravel road to the top of Pine Mountain. Anxiously, he flicks his radio dial to the noon news.

Then suddenly, he comes upon a different world. A world of apparent isolation. A world of peace. In a green frame Appalachian Mountain lodge, three Protestant monks and their dozen guests are eating in a silence broken only by a record of a Corelli chorale.

Roman Catholic and Eastern Orthodox monks have eaten in silence and lived in isolation for centuries; the monks of the Middle Ages contributed much to Western culture. In recent years, some Catholic-oriented Anglicans (Episcopalians) and Lutherans have turned to monasticism.

Yet the three monks who spent the summer of 1964 on Pine Mountain differ from most monks. Members of the pioneering Taize monastic community in France, they come from a segment of the Protestant tradition—the segment in the majority in the United States—that has long looked upon monastic life as foreign.

Taize monks take the traditional vows of chastity, poverty, and obedience. Unlike most monks, however, they seek not to escape from the daily rigors of life, but to better prepare themselves to serve it. They seek not to purify a single faith but to foster unity among the many faiths.

Taize may establish a permanent monastic community in the United States. "We aren't so presumptuous as to say we have any 'solutions' for American Protestantism," declared Brother

Protestant Monks

On an Isolated Mountaintop, Dedicated Pioneers Lay The Seeds of a Quiet Revolution in Protestant Life

Pascal, a 23-year-old native of Los Gatos, California, one of two Americans in the 65-member community in France. "We don't say every Christian must do this. But we do say that without this particular form of Christian life, the church would lack something—that the Protestant Church lacked something when it had no monastic community."

The weeks at Pine Mountain gave Taize a first-hand familiarity with American religion. "They've got to learn something about the American church, and the American church has got to learn something about them," said the Rev. Douglas Horton, a former dean of Harvard Divinity School and the organizer of about 200 churchmen who have developed the Pine Mountain property for religious retreats. "What they're trying to do this year is simply to get acquainted."

They've gotten acquainted with remarkable ease. Clergymen and laymen, Protestant and Catholic, journeyed here from all over the East to stay for as brief a time as a day and as long as two weeks.

"My people would be shocked if they knew what I'm doing here," confessed one Protestant clergyman here. "Meditating on a rock, attending a Catholic Mass recited by a visiting priest, consulting a Protestant monk every day for spiritual guidance. They just wouldn't understand."

Worship with this tiny community-in-flux for a couple of days. Eat with the three "brothers" and their visitors in silence. Walk with them beneath the birches discussing Tillich and tithing, psalms and secularism.

The white robes and solemn atmosphere at the three or four worship services each day won't surprise you, but the informality at other times will. So will the healthy humor of the brothers and their guests.

Around the conference table Brother Anthony, a young Dutchman with a degree in psychology, struggled to teach the visitors the Taize way of intoning psalms. Frustrated by the monotone of a Catholic priest, he stopped suddenly. "Not so much—how do you say it—broadcasting in Russia." Another priest supplied the word Brother Anthony wanted: "Jamming." The group laughed, the priest caught on, and ecumenical relations suffered no damage.

Images linger. There is the image of a Presbyterian minister, the hood of his white jacket flung over his head and making him look every bit the monk, walking among the trees reading a red-covered religious book. There is the image of an Episcopal priest from New Jersey wondering aloud at the conference table what makes some people seem holy. There is the image of a college youth who will go to Taize next month for a year, perhaps for his life, unsuccessfully groping for words to explain his statement that "Taize has much that American Protestantism doesn't have."

For those with unusual will power, there is the image of a dozen awakened men rolling sleepily out of their bunks to attend a midnight worship service in the lodge's tiny plywood-paneled chapel.

Others, finally, retain the image of a Catholic priest silently climbing to nature's chapel by dawn's light to recite a Mass celebrating the Feast of the Transfiguration. Splotches of sunshine painted the Presidential Range as the priest recited *"Mea culpa, mea culpa, mea maxima culpa.*" Behind him, beneath a 10-foot wooden cross, a bearded theological student in V-necked sweater and hiking boots—his face the silhouette of one of Christ's disciples—followed the Mass in an English translation.

Pine Mountain, at least for a while, will have no great impact upon American religion. The acquaintance was too short, the conditions too improvised.

Still, many local churches will feel the influence of Pine Mountain. A United Church of Christ minister from northern Vermont, enchanted by the beauty of psalm singing, planned to ask his choir director to develop the art in his church. He was impressed, too, by the repetition of a prayer using the phrase "co-heirs" of Christ, a new concept to him; he was impressed, in fact, simply by the open attitude of the Taize monks: "It's healthy that they don't feel their worship is a jewel they can't share."

A priest thought the people of his parish would benefit from a portion of the worship service he observed, a chain of handshakes during which every member of the congregation receives the blessing "peace be with you" from another member, answers "and with your spirit," and in turn blesses another member with the words "peace be with you." The priest was distressed that members in one neighborhood in

The monks of Taize, the French community that has inspired the American movement.

his parish worship God together, yet live from day to day in such tension that the neighborhood is known as "Battle Row."

In the 25 years since a young theological student, Roger Schutz, founded Taize near the heart of the Western monasticism of the Middle Ages, Taize has acted as the leaven in the bread of many a new religious development. It has sent monks to work—and minister—as bricklayers in Algiers, as dock workers in Marseilles, as factory workers in Coventry, England. It has developed liturgies that have influenced the worship of many faiths. Out of retreats at Taize have come "households of unity"—couples who pledge to pray at least three minutes each day, to work for true unity in marriage, and to refuse to accumulate material wealth.

Taize the Nucleus

Thousands of pilgrims of different faiths visit Taize each year. Taize occupies a unique place in the ecumenical movement; active from the start in interfaith ventures, its two observers invited to the Vatican Council were the only observers who did not represent denominations. Implores the Rule of Taize: "Be a ferment of unity."

Behind the wrought-iron motif that crowns the gate of the monastery at Taize, the Protestant monks spend hours each day in private meditation and community worship living the "interior life" they believe Western rationalism too often excludes. They spend hours more working in the community's printing plant, on its farm co-operative, and in similar enterprises. The community accepts no gifts, existing on receipts from its business ventures.

Brother Pascal, the intense, young Californian, specializes in making stained glass windows. Why did he join the Taize community three years ago? He answered slowly, deliberately. "To me it represents very closely the life Our Lord lived with His disciples."

Brother Pascal is still a novice; like the other American at Taize, a young man from Wisconsin who entered the community in 1963, he has not taken his final vows. Yet here on his native soil he spoke as a foreigner: "We want to learn more about you."

Enthusiastic though the response was to the Taize community on Pine Mountain, not every visitor believed a multi-faith Protestant monastery would succeed in the United States.

The Rev. Douglas Horton: "If a man lives in a group. . . ."

Holt Quinlan, a Harvard divinity student, was one who had some doubts.

"It's very foreign to the American situation," he said. "I admire their spiritual depth, but I think I share the common Protestant bias that looks upon monasticism as unnatural." He measured his words carefully. "This monastic life: Either the sacrifice is too much or maybe it doesn't seem necessary to us to accomplish what we see as a Christian life."

Still, the Rev. David C. Young, a Presbyterian who serves two churches in southern New York, sees great value in a monastic community. He found that his five days at Pine Mountain strengthened his personal faith and gave him a deeper appreciation for the spirituality of other faiths. To him, Taize represents "a Christian parable."

The Rev. Dr. Horton believes that a monastic community can demonstrate a Christian society as no individual can. "A single missionary can preach until he's red in the face," said the eminent United Church of Christ minister. "But if a man lives in a group and develops a kind of creative mutuality, you have something you not only can talk about but can actually see."

This is the parable of Taize. This is the parable of Pine Mountain. ◆

Las Vegas

Fremont Street in Las Vegas: "Casino center" of the world.

Religion in the Casino

Protestants and Catholics Both Try to Meet the Needs Of the Gamblers, Entertainers, and Tourists in Vegas

LAS VEGAS.

QUIETLY, cautiously, the National Council of Churches (NCC) is experimenting with a new form of the Christian ministry—a ministry to the world of fun and leisure. Its first testing grounds are the gambling casinos and plush "showrooms" of this "fun capital of the world."

With the Las Vegas venture already showing signs of paying spiritual dividends, a similar ministry will begin soon—perhaps in 1965—in Miami Beach. Others may follow in such vacation spots as Honolulu, Phoenix, and the Virgin Islands.

"The church has got to devise ways to follow the people, to minister to them where they work and play," says the Rev. Truman B. Douglass, a high executive of the United Church of Christ. "The Las Vegas experiment is one way we think should be tried."

To help the church confront the challenges of the leisure boom, the NCC in late 1963 expanded its "Department of a Christian Ministry in the National Parks" to a "Department of a Christian Ministry with People in Leisure—Recreation." The department will continue its work in the national parks, which it began in 1952. It also will reach out in other ways to people on the move—and to people who serve them.

"We used to make the mistake of thinking only of tourists at resort areas," confesses the Rev. Warren Ost, head of the leisure-time ministry for the NCC. "Now there's a growing movement toward a year-round ministry. It's just as important to minister to the resort community as it is to the tourists who visit it."

Dr. Ost's department supports a year-round chaplaincy at Mt. Hood, the Oregon ski resort, and helps the Colorado Council of Churches maintain a full-time minister at a ski area in the Rockies. It assists the Protestant Episcopal Church in operating coffee houses in Colorado's Estes Park and in Jackson, Wyoming, near Grand Teton National Park. It sponsors a minister with a house trailer who serves trailer camps near Lake Mead in southern Nevada. And it has gone to work in earnest in Las Vegas.

In 1962 the NCC tapped 27-year-old Richard Mawson, a student at Union Theological Seminary in New York, as the first pioneer in the Las Vegas experiment. Mr. Mawson worked for a year on Las Vegas' glittering, seven-mile-long Strip, then returned to Union for his last year of seminary work. Edward Ellis, a student at Boston University's School of Theology, spelled him for a year. Now the Rev. Mr. Mawson, ordained in the interlude, has settled permanently in Las Vegas.

Precise in speech, his hair prematurely gray, "Rick" Mawson lounges in his study and talks about what he did his first year in Nevada's booming city of pleasure. On the bookshelf behind him, *Scarne's Complete Guide to Gambling* competes with *The Acts of the Apostles*—silent evidence of his conviction that the Christian minister must know the world in which he works.

"I got to know the prostitutes, the gamblers, the stagehands by their first names," he says. "I didn't exactly identify with their world; I tried to remain apart in a way. But I accepted with them their guilt for it. Eventually, I earned the right to be heard."

Not that he spoke on a soapbox. "Often I wouldn't mention God, Christ, the church, or the

Where fortunes—and, say the churches, souls—are tried.

Bible for days, even for weeks, to the people I was working with," he notes.

Instead, he tried to "witness" to Christianity, to demonstrate its precepts without fanfare. Working as a night clerk at a luxury hotel on the Strip, he would wave away the $5 or $10 "tokes" (tips) commonly offered to "buy" good rooms when rooms are scarce ("To me, that's a bribe"). "At first," he recalls, "the other employes laughed. Then they started talking about it, questioning it."

Mr. Mawson mingled with showgirls as they awaited their cues backstage, with chefs and waiters working in the kitchen, with bellboys waiting to lug suitcases and golf bags. He compiled a notebook with the names of more than 200 people, and with details about significant events in their lives. And in strategic spots around the hotel—on the switchboard, for example—he distributed little white cards saying "I care," with his name and phone number printed on them.

One evening a secretary in the hotel asked him to talk with a friend of hers, a divorcee whose daughter had suffered an attack of diabetes she feared would prove fatal. He helped reassure her that night and, in the days that followed, listened to her problems. Later she asked, "Why are you interested in me?" Replied the theological student: "Because Someone was interested in me." She asked more questions, told several friends of her experience, then asked him to form a Bible study group.

He conducted the Bible study sessions for seven months. "That group was really the only concrete thing I had to show after a year's work on the Strip," he says.

Mr. Mawson encountered surprisingly little hositility. "We knew he was a seminary student," says one employe of the hotel where he worked. "We accepted him for what he was. His being here did some real good."

He did encounter some resistance, significantly, from the ministers of the Protestant churches in Las Vegas. The NCC's failure to explain its program to the local ministers in advance was partly responsible. So was the ministers' defensive reaction, a trait common to most long-time residents of Las Vegas: "Vegas may be sinful, but so is every Hometown, U.S.A."

The Gap Narrows

The resistance is dwindling. The local ministers and the Rev. Mr. Mawson understand each other better now. And the Rev. Mr. Mawson is drawing on local churches in his ministry by holding seminars for church members who work on the Strip to suggest ways they themselves can witness to Christianity.

Still, a deep difference of approach to the Christian ministry separates the Rev. Mr. Mawson from his fellow ministers in Las Vegas. The experimental ministry, at least as he practices it, takes the Gospel to the people. The churches in the city invite the people to come to them and rarely act until they do.

Says one clergyman: "Some of us said, 'What's the point of Mawson's coming? We expect the laymen in our church who work on the Strip to be working actively. We expect them to ask the people they work with to go down to the church for this meeting or that activity.' "

"This meeting or that activity." The phrase is revealing. For it places the emphasis on social activities rather than spiritual growth, on the organization rather than the message.

"Too often we wait until a person is ready to jump off a cliff before we offer him help," grumbles an advocate of the experimental approach.

Rick Mawson: The National Council of Churches' man in Las Vegas.

How did the local churches minister to people on the Strip before the Rev. Mr. Mawson arrived? A local pastor, asked to give two illustrations, betrays their passive approach. In one case a middle-aged man, a Las Vegas resident who belongs to no church, came to the pastor's office "contemplating suicide" after losing a $30,000 inheritance in gambling.

In the second instance, a tourist from San Francisco who had lost all his cash in the casinos stopped in at the church just before an evening worship service. "We gave him gas money he needed in order to drive home in his Thunderbird," says the pastor. "I'm afraid we'll never see him again."

On another count, the NCC effort may be more vulnerable. Why did it first send students instead of ordained ministers into the land of legalized gambling and nude shows?

The Rev. Dr. Ost admits that lack of funds was one reason. "But students are more flexible —more willing to take risks," he says. "Besides, we believe it's helpful for Rick and others like him to mature in the field in which they're going to work, not outside it." The NCC, standing by this conviction, expects to send additional seminary "interns" to Las Vegas to work as Rick Mawson and Ed Ellis did.

Most local ministers believe this is naive. Contends the Rev. Robert M. Brashares of the First Methodist Church here: "You need a pro in that job—a person with a wide range of experiences, both in parish churches and also perhaps in experimental ministries. You need a man who knows who he is and what he's doing, not a young fellow who's still trying to find out."

The Roman Catholic Church had such a priest ministering to the Strip several years ago. Seeing the need for a 4:30 a.m. Mass for showpeople in a city where the casinos and many entertainment lounges are open around the clock, the Rev. Richard A. Crowley began holding services in the auditorium of the popular Stardust Hotel on the Strip. Three years later, diocesan officials transferred the Mass, which had been attracting about 300 people every Sunday morning, to a church several blocks from the Strip.

The official reason: The auditorium lacked the dignity of a church. Unquestionably it did, and a widespread public misconception that the Mass was being held in the room used for a nude extravangaza didn't help. But rumors persist, too, that some disagreement arose between Father Crowley and his fellow priests in town over methods, just as was the case among the Protestant clergy. Whatever the true reasons, Father Crowley was transferred to Illinois. A lavish going-away party, featuring an unprecedented five-and-one-half-hour program with top entertainers, testified to his popularity on the Strip.

In late 1963 the Catholic Church moved back to the Strip, this time in a church of its own. Aided by a donation of land by the Desert Inn and the Stardust and by pledges from seven hotels totaling $160,000, the diocese built St. Viator Guardian Angel Shrine.

In a way, the shrine represents a middle ground between the National Council of Churches' experimental approach and the traditional approach of the local clergy. "You have to bring God and Christ to the marketplace," says the Rev. Patrick J. Toomey, priest of the new shrine. But Father Toomey makes no scouting excursions into the casinos themselves. "We've made ourselves available," he says. "Being where we are, we'll have no shortage of work."

No clergymen working on the Strip have starry-eyed visions of "wiping out sin" on the Strip in a year, or even a lifetime. "I won't be able to move mountains," admitted Ed Ellis shortly after he began his work there. "But I hope that through contact with me, a few people—bellboys, gamblers, yes, call girls, too—will stop and take a good look at the lives they're living."

Says the Rev. Everett C. Parker of the United Church of Christ, a prime pusher of the new ministry to people involved in today's fast-paced world of leisure: "We don't claim we'll go out and convert all these show people and gamblers. But they're people, aren't they? Must we ignore them?" ♦

The "middle way" between tradition and experiment: St. Viator, the new Catholic shrine reared amidst night clubs and casinos.

—Las Vegas News Bureau

Detroit

–Charles Harbutt

Into the World of Work

Imaginative Clergymen Take Religion to the Factory; In the Motor City, the Production Line Is a Parish

DETROIT.

SINCE 1956 a coterie of Protestant clergymen in Detroit has made its parish the production line and the executive suite.

An unusual locale for religion? Not really. The men behind the Detroit Industrial Mission (DIM) believe no chasm should exist between worship and work. They prod men who spend half of their waking hours in factories to think of religion not as an isolated Sunday morning exercise, but as an ever-present influence in their lives.

Similar industrial missions have gone to work since 1961 in Boston, Chicago, Cincinnati, Indianapolis, and Flint, Michigan. In September 1964, a DIM-encouraged clergyman took the industrial mission concept to the campus, working among the faculty and students at Harvard Business School and Massachusetts Institute of Technology.

Unlike most religious excursions into the world of work, the Detroit Industrial Mission and its offshoots in other cities seek neither to convert nor to convince. On a representative day, the Rev. Scott I. Paradise might huddle with production workers at Whitehead & Kales' heavy steel-fabricating plant to talk about profit-sharing plans. Another minister will discuss union elections, job security, or politics with hourly rated workers on Chrysler's Highland Park plant floor during the lunch break or shift breaks. Perhaps the Rev. Hugh C. White, Jr., executive director of DIM, will have lunch with lawyers in the Detroit Bar Association who specialize in collective bargaining, with officials of the United Auto Workers' giant Local 174, or with engineers at Ford Division-Truck Engineering. A sample topic for a meeting with engineers: Industry's impact upon management men and their families.

"We have in America an industrial society dominated by great corporations," says the Rt. Rev. Richard S. Emrich, Episcopal bishop of the diocese of Michigan and a founder of DIM. "Yet the church has no relevance to the great industrial society." The result, says Bishop Emrich, is that "the tremendous insights of our spiritual heritage are not applied to industry."

DIM staff members argue that a man's work, not his home, exercises the dominant influence on industrial society. Where a man lives, how he votes, whether he goes to a cocktail lounge in the evening or drinks beer at home, all depend largely upon his job. If he works the evening shift, he may rarely see his children. If his company moves its management men around, he and his family may have just settled in one community when they have to move on to the next.

"Yet the church follows the families to the residential areas and ignores the businesses," complains the Rev. Jesse Christman, one of two ordained ministers who joined DIM in 1962 after three and one-half years on the Cadillac assembly line. Neither he nor his associates at DIM want the church to curtail its efforts in the community parish. But they contend that every major decision in life, in industry as in the home, involves a moral decision. Thus they believe the church must work from an industrial mission base as well as the parish base if it's to become more than a week-end diversion.

Hugh White, a stocky, engaging Episcopal minister, first began thinking of the need for industrial mission work in his first pastorate, in Ypsilanti, Michigan, shortly after World War II.

The Rev. Hugh White, a prime shaper of the Detroit Industrial Mission, on the job with a plant manager.

In three years, the war transformed Ypsilanti from a quiet college town of 11,000 to a busy little Detroit of 45,000. He saw Ypsilanti change from a town of people with deep roots in their community to a city of migrants with roots only in industry.

Although his parish membership jumped from 160 families to 400 families, he found his church becoming more and more detached from the real needs of its people. To correct this, he sought out doctors in hospital lounges and wash-up rooms instead of waiting for them to come to church. He lunched with lawyers and business leaders to talk about their professional problems, and he paid periodic visits to factories.

He began to read about the worker-priest movement in postwar France, in which about 100 Catholic priests lived the lives of workers full-time, and about an industrial mission that had been started in 1944 in the steel city of Sheffield, England. And he started wondering whether the United States needed industrial missions of its own.

A three-year study he made on "Christianity and Industrial Life," while on the staff at Parishfield Community, an Episcopal lay training center in Michigan, convinced him that it did. With the encouragement and financial help of Bishop Emrich, who paid his salary out of his own pocket for the first three months, the Rev. Mr. White opened the Detroit Industrial Mission in the fall of 1956.

DIM now has six full-time clergymen, and they meet regularly with men in about 30 office, industrial plant, and union locations. But the Rev. Mr. White's staff at the outset consisted only of one layman and a secretary. He spent his first year or so doing just one thing—making contacts in industry to gain a measure of trust.

"When you approach people in industry," says the clergyman, "they think one of three things: You're coming for money, you're coming to get them to go to church, or you're

The Rev. Scott Paradise leads a lunchroom discussion. Subjects range from union posts to Cuba.

coming to get them to do something special for the church." The idea that a clergyman might be interested in doing something to help them with their problems strikes them at first as absurd, he says.

A year after DIM began, the Rev. Mr. Paradise, a veteran of three years at the Sheffield mission, joined the staff. DIM began setting up regular meetings in workers' homes, in cafeterias, on the production floor—anywhere the men could talk freely and informally.

"We make it clear at the start that we're not a Bible study group and that we're not going to go off in a corner of the shop and pray," says a staff member. They find that employes —whether hourly rated, managerial, or executive—start out calling them "Reverend" but soon switch to first names.

When they ask for permission to talk to men, company officials tend to shy off at first, while union leaders usually assent right away. Executives fear that letting one group in may spawn a host of competing missions. They suspect the "mission" will try to proselyte indifferent Christians or nonbelievers. They worry that discussions may question their management decisions or sharpen workers' grievances against them. Some even question the mission's impartiality: "How can you run with both the foxes and the hounds?"

Once their activities are sanctioned and the men's confidence is gained, generating enthusiasm for the meetings presents few problems. No groups, once on a regular schedule, have disbanded because of a lack of interest. Several meet on week-end evenings and even hold occasional week-end retreats.

Scheduling is important. Hourly rated workers, accustomed to living from week to week, from pay check to pay check, tend to think the mission's staff member has forgotten them if he doesn't come around at least every other week. Middle-management personnel prefer meetings once a month. The Rev. Mr. White meets with high-level executives, who tend to travel only in their own circle, no more than four or five times a year.

Sprinkling Vance Packard-like sociological insights through his conversation, the articulate DIM director notes that it's important, too, to choose different types of topics and to take a different approach when mission members deal with various levels of employes.

With hourly rated men, they pick topics up-to-the-week in timeliness, and they direct their questions and comments in a provocative tone. Among managers, they suggest subjects broader in scope and rarely lead the discussion, letting the men work it out themselves. Executives talk over the deeper significance of their long-range decisions. But in their discussions, because they're accustomed to making decisions based on prepared staff studies, they flounder unless the clergyman takes an active role.

Though the clergymen prod and provoke, they themselves avoid making positive judgments. Their object instead is to urge the men to take a position on the political and economic issues they face. "The weakness of the church today is that it fosters neutrality," says the Rev. Mr. White. "Really, it should give men the spirit to be partisan."

Nondenominational

The staff rigorously tries to avoid taking a denominational approach to its work, fearing this would damage its effectiveness. It works with Jews, with Roman Catholics, with Protestants, with atheists. On its staff are ministers ordained by the Protestant Episcopal Church, the United Presbyterian Church, and the United Church of Christ, and it is supported financially by all three of these denominations. Its board of directors, headed by Dean Francis B. Sayre, Jr., of the Protestant Episcopal Cathedral in Washington, D.C., includes a Roman Catholic layman.

To foster further explorations in the industrial mission field, the men behind DIM and its fellow missions formed a national commission in 1963. The commission promotes the industrial mission concept among companies, unions, and the churches, and raises funds for the movement's development. It hopes to establish a research center for the industrial ministry on a campus with a strong business or industrial school.

Industrial missions constantly engage in what they call a "feed-back" to the church, a sharing with the church of what they learn about men in industry. One of their most disheartening discoveries is that many churches don't know where most of their members work.

The Way God Works

By occupying guest pulpits, speaking to church groups, and writing of their experiences in church journals, industrial mission men believe they can make a theological contribution. "Our work forces us to speak with pertinence, clarity, and timeliness about the way in which God is at work in our world today," says the Rev. Mr. White.

This, in turn, may help the church to discover new avenues for conveying its message. Some local churches with a large proportion of scientists, for example, have recently begun to sponsor regular discussions on science and religion.

The Rev. Mr. White envisions a day in the next few decades when every major metropolitan center will have what he calls an "expert industrial mission." As he sees it, these would be missions versed in a body of literature as yet unwritten. They would be missions helping industrial man define where he is going and how he is getting there. ♦

Dean Francis B. Sayre, Jr., a director of the Detroit Mission, meets one of its parishioners close up.

Daytona Beach

Billy Wade, Chicago Bear quarterback, stars for the Christian Caravan as well.

Athletes and Rock 'n Roll

While Students Frolic, a Christian Caravan Tours The Beach, Bringing the Message of Good Friday

DAYTONA BEACH, FLA.

THREE brawny youths in bathing suits and college sweatshirts stood guzzling their beer amid a quiet crowd on the Florida sand. Lazily they watched an artist on a truck chalk a crown of thorns, then a suggestion of a face. Suddenly, one understood.

"Oh, my God," he muttered. "It's J. C."

"J. C." it was. Jesus Christ. Jesus Christ during Holy Week. Jesus Christ among carousing collegians, where antics during spring vacation weeks in 1964, as in earlier years, were raising many an eyebrow.

A few collegians on the fringes drifted away, oaths on their lips or looks of disgust on their faces. Many more stayed, their attention aroused by the jazz of pianist "Knocky" Parker, the weightlifting of Olympic strongman Paul Anderson, or the fame of Chicago Bear quarterback Bill Wade. They were watching the All-American Caravan, a group of 25 Christians—athletes, musicians, show-business personalities, and the artist—that practice an unusual form of evangelism.

As it had the year before, the Caravan drove up and down the sand at Daytona Beach entertaining thousands of college students on spring vacation. And, ever so subtly, the members of the Caravan reminded the students of the week's religious significance and told them of their own Christian faith.

"We're trying to let them know the church cares," said the Rev. Ed Beck, 6'7" captain of Kentucky's 1958 national collegiate basketball champions and organizer of the Caravan. "We like to believe that if they were home, they would be attending Holy Week services. They can't be in church here, so we're taking the 'church' to them."

The Christian strategists at Daytona Beach faced a wide range of problems. The beach stretches for nine miles; motel promotion ads shrewdly sent to fraternity and sorority houses throughout the South, East, and Midwest had reaped a harvest, by conservative estimate, of 50,000 students.

Beer flowed freely on the beach at Daytona. Students proudly sported large blue-and white buttons proclaiming "I like Busch Bavarian," and black Corvettes wheeled along the beach with empty Schlitz cans—13, by one count—stacked on their antennas. Though most students remained coherent, if not completely sober, an occasional crowd-pleaser cavorted uninhibited with his beer mug (and sometimes a Confederate flag) raised on high.

Infiltrating beer parties to hand out Christian literature, All-American planners agreed, would kill off any chance they might have of making an impact on the students. The Rev. William J. Peckham, like Ed Beck a member of the Methodist General Board of Evangelism, squinted in the sun one day and held up the booklet *One Way for Modern Man,* a modern translation of the Gospel of John. "The American Bible Society just shipped us 28 cases of these, but we can't use them on the beach," he moaned. "It's a great translation, with powerful, contemporary pictures, but it would just get tossed away." Two evenings later, 1,000 of the booklets were picked up by students as they left a Caravan show in a Daytona Beach auditorium.

The Caravan team traveled the beach for 2 or 3 hours each afternoon, stopping for 30 minutes or so at heavily populated spots. A brief jazz concert attracted hundreds, sometimes more than a thousand, to the two trucks in the Caravan. Weightlifter Anderson showed his physical prowess by lifting a table of eight husky collegians, then invited aspiring musclemen to work with him later in the afternoon. Artist Howard Ellis, head of the Methodist Department of Youth Evangelism, drew chalk pictures of Christ; sometimes he added a few words on the Holy Week theme. Pro athletes, their names and teams stamped on their blue "Caravan" sweatshirts, mingled with the crowd to establish personal rapport, then climbed to the platform to suggest why they were there. Sample: "Most of you didn't come here to be preached to, and we didn't come here to preach to you. We're here because it's Holy Week to us."

End of sermon. In a few cases, end of sympathy and back to the blanket on the sand for the collegians. But for the most part the occasional references to Christianity inspired no mass exodus, only surprise and embarrassed discomfort.

"I didn't come down here for religion," said a University of Michigan coed. "But it sinks in more than we let on."

Please, No Regimentation

Some students considered the Christian "pitch" an intrusion on their one week away from the pressures of college. "Everything is regimented at school," grumbled a Purdue engineering student. "We're here to forget everything that's regimented. And then this cat pulls up and draws a picture of Christ."

A more philosophical type complained that the athletes were cheapening religion. "It's just like one of these guys going on the tube and proclaiming he uses Rise shaving cream or Dial soap," he said. "The scene just doesn't seem right."

At nearly every stop, a heckler or two mocked the religious emphasis. Most used actions rather than words, flouting their beer cans and cavorting in exotic sun hats and sweatshirts that read "Olympic Drinking Champion," or "Help Stamp Out Virginity." One afternoon several Jewish collegians chanted "Passover! Passover!," drawing attention to the fact that the week had religious significance for Jews as well as Christians.

Surprisingly few collegians displayed open disgust for the Caravan. Most pawed the sand with their feet when they heard the words "Jesus" or "God," and waited in boredom—feigned or real—until trumpeter "Doc" Evans or banjo artist Marvin Montgomery gave them what they wanted to hear. Only once—when the emcee at an evening show in the huge Coquina Bandshell told the audience he was concluding the show by bringing on an athlete to "speak of his faith"—did masses of students flee the scene.

But there was a mass mocking of the Caravan on Friday—Good Friday—which the evangelists had been counting on as the climax of their campaign. Thundershowers had driven the collegians from the beach on Thursday afternoon, and drizzly weather that evening and Friday morning kept them in their motel rooms. Many, with nothing else to do, took on an extra load of beer.

Grotesque Parody

Friday noon, as the weather improved, a crowd of them gathered on the beach in front of a hotel. Suddenly one youth climbed to the top of a parked car, stretched out his arms in the form of a cross, and shouted, "I am Jesus Christ!" His buddies caught on quickly. Three or four jumped onto the car, kneeled at his feet, and pretended they were rolling dice. From the crowd came the roar: "Crucify him! Crucify him!"

The vivid mockery jarred Caravan members. But they recovered quickly. All week they had recharged their faith each morning in devotionals by the pool side of the Copacabana Motel, dismissing the distractions as unimportant. The Rev. Mr. Beck later found it ironic significance that the Good Friday episode had occurred at the same time of day as when Jesus, nearly 2,000 years before, had uttered on the cross: "Father, forgive them; for they know not what they do."

Tony Romeo, agile end for the Boston Patriots and a student at Southwestern Baptist Theological Seminary in Forth Worth, found it easy to dismiss the heckling. He recalled that he himself had traveled to Daytona Beach for spring vacation in the days before he became a "true" Christian. "Christ had hecklers," he declared. "We won't have to stand in judgment

Unrestrained fun: Students used a blanket to toss a girl high in the air. This was the mood the Christian team had to combat.

before them. We'll stand in judgment before God."

Over and over, the athletes stressed they were in Daytona Beach neither to condemn nor to "convert." Don Shinnick, bull-necked linebacker for the Baltimore Colts, surveyed the clusters of sun-seekers as the Caravan crept slowly along the beach and said, "We're not here to judge anybody, to tell them not to smoke or not to drink. We're here simply to tell them what the Christian faith means to us."

The Caravan traveled just two miles of the nine-mile beach. But it intrigued nearly everyone along this stretch, from the infrequent surf swimmer to the Negro laborer who danced to the dixieland atop an unfinished four-story motel, alone and almost unnoticed. Only a few missed the Caravan's association with Christianity.

"At least we're giving these kids an image of the church they won't soon forget," said the Rev. Mr. Peckham. "They're used to going to church and maybe having the minister tell them to forget about the problems of the world and to worship God. We're showing them that we don't want to forget the world; we want to be in the world."

For a few, a very few, the image made an immediate impact. Example: An inebriated youth in swim trunks and an old felt hat ignored the entertainment and talked for 20 minutes with linebacker Shinnick. They talked not about football, but about religion. Shinnick: "You don't like church?" Youth: "I hate it." Shinnick: "What's the problem?" Youth: "Church just doesn't reach me." His interest indicated that perhaps Shinnick did.

Example: A heckler delighted the crowd by asking gargantuan Paul Anderson to spell "Oldsmobile." Anderson, quick in his retorts from his experience in operating a home for neglected children, retorted that the youth must be too immature to drive one. The heckler, his audience lost, turned quiet. Another of Anderson's hecklers brooded over his own behavior overnight and sought out Anderson the next day to apologize.

Example: Methodist minister Peckham talked of his faith to an Iowa student. "He looked at me for the longest time," recalls the sandy-haired minister. "Then he said, 'Bill, why are you a Christian?' He held me there talking with him for an hour and five minutes."

When the Rev. Mr. Peckham speaks about Daytona Beach, his enthusiasm for youth is unconcealed. "These kids are quick to spot sham and hypocrisy in our society. One of the most common terms in their vocabulary is 'phony.' But I have a hunch we have a bunch of 'phonies' here, too. In groups they act wildly. But get to them individually—that's different."

Bill Wade spent hours with them individually, coaching them on quarterback fundamentals. "Knocky" Parker, a Ph.D. in English on the faculty of the University of South Florida, talked of jazz and how it's related to Christianity: "St. Augustine said, 'Language is too weak to speak of love.' Music can do this better. Jazz is our joy of being. It's an expression of everlasting 'yea.' "

Caravan members belonged to widely divergent Protestant denominations, from the liberal to the "Bible-belt" fundamentalist. In 1963, two of the jazz musicians in the Caravan were Roman Catholics.

The Caravan's Future

In future years, Caravan planners say, they'll make a strong effort to include Jews as well as Protestants and Catholics in the Caravan. They'll have Negroes in the Caravan, too, as what one member calls "silent witnesses" against segregation. "Notice how nice and white the beach is?" said one member of the 1964 Caravan, his sun-tanned arm sweeping toward the ocean. He wasn't looking at the color of the sand alone.

Olympian Paul Anderson. He silenced jeering students with a quick retort.

Not surprisingly, intramural disagreements arose over the particular approach the Caravan was taking. "I think we should have a beer with them now and then," acknowledged one team member as he watched a burly collegian struggling to lift some of Paul Anderson's weights. "Jesus ate with the sinners. Who knows? Perhaps there are better Christians drinking beer right here in the crowd than there are up on the truck."

As he spoke, Christian groups at other spring vacation spots were using other methods to "take the church" to festive college students. In Fort Lauderdale, Florida, scene of destructive riots in 1961, 10 staff members of the Inter-Varsity Christian Fellowship and 60 student volunteers staged discussions and revival-type "testimonies," conducted a religious survey, and handed out booklets (*Becoming a Christian, Is Christianity Credible?*) among students dozing in the mid-day sun.

In the Laguna Beach-Balboa Island-Newport area not far from Los Angeles, an Inter-Varsity team was ensnaring West Coast students more indirectly. The colder beach climate encourages indoor beer busts at night. Inter-Varsity's solution: Enlist the help of seven Christian families in the community, turn on all the lights in their houses, leave the doors open, and let the students pour in. Many came armed with six-packs of beer, and nearly as many left in wild flight when they discovered that they had wandered in on a self-labeled "party with a purpose." Those who remained stored their six-packs in the refrigerator and settled down for an evening that progressed from folk singing to Negro spirituals to serious discussion and "testimonies."

The Daytona Beach team worked closely with city officials. Daytona Beach city fathers invested $5,000 in travel expenses for the Caravan in 1964 in the belief that the Caravan's presence helps prevent the crowds from becoming disorderly. In fact, they're asking for an even larger team than the 18 there in 1963 and the 25 in 1964, to permit the Caravan to take on additional work.

One suggestion would have the Caravan station an athlete or two at the Municipal Court—"the world's largest fraternity house," in the language of Daytona Beach policemen. On the busiest day at Municipal Court, some 500 youths signed the guest register at the "fraternity house" at the request of policemen. Significantly, the police found that more than half were not attending college at all, but were college drop-outs, servicemen, or young working girls on vacation-time scouting missions.

At the beach and in their motels, thousands of other youths flirted with arrest for rowdy behavior. Endless caravans of cars loaded with merrymakers drove up and down the beach. Here and there tanned collegians played football or "four-square" with a volleyball, pausing only to ogle a coed modeling a bikini or to watch a twist session in the sand.

Where the All-American Caravan stopped, it invariably drew curious collegians. Beer bottle or Pepsi in one hand, anything from a seashell to a coed's hand in the other, they watched and listened, largely silent except to applaud.

Downtown in Daytona Beach, on the lawn of the white-frame St. Mary's Episcopal Church, stood a 10-foot cross of rugged timber. A tattered white garment with red spots floated from it in the breeze, and below the garment were propped a spear and an oversize pair of dice. At the base of the cross rested a sign: "Is it nothing to you, all you that pass by?"

On the beach three miles away, the Christian Caravan asked the same question. "Is it nothing to you, all you that pass by?" They asked it silently, implicitly. How many heard—how many cared—they'll never know. ♦

Coventry

The new Coventry Cathedral, left, rises beside the old.

A Message of Forgiveness

Crushed by World War II Bombs, a Cathedral and Its People Rise Above the Hurt to Live—And Forgive

COVENTRY, ENGLAND.

COVENTRY Cathedral was the only Church of England cathedral destroyed in World War II. Out of its destruction by German fire bombs in November 1940 has developed a ministry of Christian forgiveness and hope that continues to touch the lives of millions on every continent.

Pilgrims flock to Coventry in England's midlands to see the ruins of the old cathedral and marvel at the new cathedral consecrated in 1962. Tourists at the World's Fair in New York meditated before the Charred Cross of Coventry, two charred timbers lashed together to form a moving Twentieth Century symbol of Christian faith. Around the world, informal "response points" enlist Christians in racially torn Alabama, divided Berlin, emerging Kenya, and scores of other troubled areas in spreading the Coventry message that "the wounds of history can be healed by forgiveness and by acts of reconciliation."

Coventry sees in its history the history of Good Friday and Easter. "As I watched the cathedral burning," writes the Very Rev. R. T. Howard, former provost (dean) of Coventry Cathedral, in his book *Ruined and Rebuilt,* "it seemed to me as though I were watching the crucifixion of Jesus upon His cross." And as he entered the ruined cathedral the next morning, he recalls, "there flashed into my mind the deep certainty that as the cathedral had been crucified with Christ, so it would rise again with Him."

The current provost, the Very Rev. H. C. N. Williams, speaks of the choice Coventry faced after the German attack. "Coventry could have chosen hatred, or it could have chosen healing," he says, pouring milk into his tea in his modernistic cathedral office. "It chose healing. Christians may not hate, even though they suffer. Christians may not be unforgiving, even if they cannot forget."

The people of Coventry have never pretended they can forget. In fact, they make it a point to remember the lesson of Coventry by preserving the Charred Cross and the ruins themselves — the fire-blackened tower, the lead-splashed walls, the shattered bits of stained glass that cling to the hollow windows.

But they put the emphasis on forgiving. The words "Father Forgive" are chipped out of stone behind the altar on which the Charred Cross stands when it is at Coventry. At the altar every Friday, a raw English wind whips by the cathedral clergy as they recite a 20-line litany on the theme of forgiveness composed by the cathedral staff.

"I absolutely believe that the test of a Christian is to be able to forgive," says Provost Williams. He insists he means not simply forgiving minor faults of friends, or "forgiving" Americans because an Englishman finds some of them disagreeable—but forgiving an enemy for barbarous acts of war.

He goes further. "In a very real Christian sense, there are no enemies in war," he says. "We are separated from one another because we are separated from God, and we each follow our own national or economic gods." Thus the inscription behind the altar "doesn't say 'Father forgive you,' or 'Father forgive us.' It says simply 'Father Forgive'—forgive all of us."

To a degree, the cathedral staff believes the Coventry message filters back to British and overseas churches through its visitors; some 5,000,000 persons visited Coventry during 1962

Workmen by the dozen haul Graham Sutherland's 79-foot tapestry, boxed, into the Cathedral.

to 1964 alone. But the staff doesn't rest there.

Staff members encourage churches to recite the litany at their own altars. The litany is being said regularly at such distant places as Port Elizabeth, South Africa, and the Maseno Cathedral in Kenya.

The staff travels widely to lecture and lead religious workshops. Provost Williams, for example, goes behind the Iron Curtain about twice a year.

The cathedral silver-plates "crosses of nails"—each made of three nails driven into cathedral beams nearly 600 years ago—and showers them on churches in cities from Volgograd (Stalingrad) to Hamburg to Hong Kong that have worked with Coventry in its "ministry of reconciliation." The "cross of nails" originated a few days after the German attack when an Oxford student, now a clergyman at the cathedral, picked up three nails in the rubble and wired them together in the shape of a cross.

Perhaps most important, Coventry brings students from many countries to the cathedral each summer to live and work there for several weeks. The National Cathedral School for Girls in Washington, D.C., for example, sent work-and-study groups to Coventry in the summers of 1963 and 1964.

The summer service-and-study program originated by accident in 1962. Thirteen Episcopalian students from Alabama visited Coventry just after the consecration. Impressed, they extended their stay and worked as tour guides and

The Charred Cross of Coventry comes to the United States. The Very Rev. H.C.N. Williams speaks in dedication services at the World's Fair, New York City.

bookshop clerks.

The cathedral staff, equally impressed, invited more than 200 students from 13 nations to spend part of their vacation at Coventry the following summer. Alabama sent a second group—all white, though Negroes were eligible—that year, and a third group in 1964. Coventry, in turn, sent several of its students to Alabama in 1964 for a youth conference at Tuskegee Institute.

"Alabama needs to talk about Christian reconciliation, especially in terms of race relations," says Peggy Horn, Episcopalian youth director for Alabama. When Miss Horn travels around the state talking about Coventry, she takes a miniature cross of nails along to help dramatize Coventry's experience.

She finds that audiences are cool, even tense, when she first applies Coventry's experience to Alabama's racial problems. "But the kids are usually rather excited to discover that people have really begun to understand an enemy as hated as the Germans were." Adults, she concedes, tend to remain more detached: "They can buy the ideal, but often they can't move it into action."

Alabama's unwitting contribution to Coventry illustrates an important ingredient in Coventry's character: Because it's the newest of the Church of England's 42 cathedrals, it's more willing to try new techniques, new approaches. "We hadn't had a cathedral since 1940," says Michael Butterfield, cathedral youth officer, "so there's been no one to say, 'You can't do this.' "

The very atmosphere of modern, industrial Coventry smacks of a certain freshness and independence. A new shopping plaza, strangely out of place in old England, enhances the downtown area. Nearby, a statue of Lady Godiva, clothed only in her long hair, graces the public square.

Lady Godiva is revered here. She was patroness of an Eleventh Century church that later became Coventry's first cathedral. And, according to the legend immortalized by the poet Lord Tennyson, she once rode unclothed through the crowded market place at her husband's insistence when she appealed to him to abolish oppressive taxes. After her ride, he met his part of the bargain and abolished the taxes.

Then there is the cathedral itself, daring in its architectural design, bold in its interior art. On narrow Cuckoo Lane, just a block from the square, stands the old cathedral, a stark reminder of the hatred of the past. To the north stretches the magnificent new structure, as alive to the Twentieth Century as the Gothic cathedrals around England appear wedded to the Fifteenth. Behind its altar of stone, a 79-foot-high modernistic tapestry of "Christ in Glory" dominates the whole interior.

The Battle for Relevance

If the cathedral is modern, so is its approach. Coventry, in the phrase as fashionable in England as in the United States, is "striving to be relevant to the modern world." It bubbles with ecumenical spirit; it bustles with labor-management activity. Ministers of various denominations conduct joint worship services in its chapel of unity, in which a dramatic black cross symbolizes the disunity of Christians. Beneath the cathedral's chapel of industry, an apprentice union meets every two weeks; now and then bargainers for labor and management hassle there over contract terms.

"A Christian center has got to speak to the community as it is, not as it has for four centuries believed it to be," says Provost Williams. "We believe the way to do this is to establish a great community center that's interested in the whole life of man, not just in 'religion.' "

In its effort to be "relevant," the cathedral opened a new broadcasting studio in its basement. It's the only British Broadcasting Corp. (BBC) studio in Coventry and, Provost Williams believes, the first public broadcasting studio in a cathedral in the entire world. The cathedral operates a refectory, a dining hall that's open to anyone. A drama department stages plays in the cathedral throughout the year and, during the summer, religious "mysteries" in the ruins.

"Relevance" commands its price. Provost Williams interrupts an informal chat to answer a local reporter's telephone inquiry about his thoughts on "sex on TV." He wrinkles his nose, smiles wryly, and replies—more for the benefit of his American visitor than his English telephone caller, one suspects—that "the only programs I watch are *Wells Fargo* and *Laramie*."

To assist him in Coventry's ministry, Provost Williams has put together an outspoken, intellectual staff of 14—his "cabinet," as he calls it. Conversations among them often turn into exercises of wit; when one argued over a bowl of soup in the refectory that he preferred "a parson who knows the answers, not one who just asks questions," another retorted: "You don't belong at Coventry. You belong at Westminster Abbey."

Tired of Enthusiasm

Coventry has its critics. They resent the implication that Coventry alone is meeting the needs of the Twentieth Century. And they're beginning to tire of the staff's restless enthusiasm. "The Coventry authorities are wedded to the notion of the 'modern method' and especially of publicity in recommending the faith," noted a book reviewer in the Sunday Times. "But the pop idols might have advice for the Chapter. 'Don't push your luck.' Enough is getting to be enough."

The "Chapter" doesn't seem to be listening. "My immediate aim for the cathedral is to keep up the momentum of experiment," says Provost Williams. "While it has got this momentum, it is likely to be of some use to the Christian church as a whole."

Coventry's effectiveness derives partly from its use of new techniques. But it derives from something deeper, too—from its symbolic religious meaning as a cathedral that has endured destruction and risen again.

It is this that makes Alabama listen—and East Berlin, and Kenya. It is this that dramatizes religion in Twentieth Century terms for all the world to see. ♦

The Cross fronts the fire-blackened tower of the Cathedral that was.